Land of the Lost Souls

Land of the Lost Souls

My Life on the Streets

Cadillac Man

BLOOMSBURY

New York Berlin London

Published by Bloomsbury USA, New York

All papers used by Bloomsbury USA are natural, recyclable products made from wood grown in well-managed forests. The manufacturing processes conform to the environmental regulations of the country of origin.

LIBRARY OF CONGRESS CATALOGING-IN-PUBLICATION DATA

Cadillac Man.
  Land of the lost souls : my life on the streets / Cadillac Man.
      p. cm.
  ISBN-13: 978-1-59691-406-3 (hardcover)
  ISBN-10: 1-59691-406-8 (hardcover)
  1. Cadillac Man.   2. Homeless persons—New York (State)—New York—
Biography.   I. Title.

  HV4506.N6C33 2009
  305.5'692092—dc22
  [B]   2008041111
                    First U.S. Edition 2009

                    1 3 5 7 9 10 8 6 4 2

              Typeset by Westchester Book Group
  Printed in the United States of America by Quebecor World Fairfield

To my children

To Carol Vogel:
Never doubt my love for you

Look Who's Here
The Cadillac Man
Recycle Engineer
Have Cans Will Travel
Free Pickup Service Available

Contents

Land of the Lost Souls

Introduction

I AIN'T NO SCHOLAR.

I ain't no bum.

I have never been good in grammar, so there will be misspellings and perhaps some passages that make no sense to you.

But, hey, I'm a street person, not a Rhodes Scholar. You, the reader, will just have to bear with me. You'll see vulgar language, nudity, street jargon, romance, etc. You may laugh or cry or both. You may even say this guy is nuts and should be committed to a padded room with Demerol cocktails. And in a way you're right. You have to be crazy to live out here, but craziness is a way of survival, which I'll explain to you later.

These are my people, my friends, my enemies. I have changed their names, for some are still alive somewhere. I hope not to embarrass or shame.

Others who died (so many), I'll use their real street names to immortalize them so they can be remembered.

This is my story, their story.

Empathy!

Merry Fuckin' Christmas

Manhattan, 1994

SUN'S NOT EVEN up yet, and there's a car radio blaring: *I'm dreaming of a white Christmas, just like the ones I used to know.*

"Hey, fucko! Lower that fucking radio! It's too fuckin' early in the morning to hear that shit!" I'm wasting my time, he can't hear me. *May your days be merry and bright* . . . The car drives on, turning the corner on 54th Street, music fading away. That's it, asshole, spread your joy somewhere else.

It's near Christmas, and, no, I don't know what date it is. Winter sometime. But this much I do know: every year at this time certain radio stations play holiday music for ten days straight. Ten fucking days filled with ho-ho-hos and jingle bells. In the stores, in the diner, coming from every car radio. The military ought to use it for psychological warfare. Tie a prisoner up and have him listen to this music over and over. I guarantee you after a while he will tell you what size brassiere his mother wears! Anything you want to know and then some.

As for me, I used to enjoy it, but only in moderation. Ah, Christmas, such a joyous occasion. The gathering of family and friends. Fuck them all!

Why am I so mean and grouchy? I have every right to be. I'm homeless. For six months now, though it seems like I've been out here all my life.

. . .

Sitting up in my sleeping bag, I feel unbelievable pain. Something bad happened last night. And, damn, the sleeping bag is stained. I just got this bag, too. Last week as I was sleeping someone left it in my wagon with a note: *Hope this keeps you warm.* Prior to that my bed consisted of a garbage bag and two old army blankets.

Got up and tried to stretch and almost passed out. There's a searing pain when I try to take a deep breath. Fucking bastards! I camped last night outside of an office building by the curb, hidden by stacks of black trash bags. It seemed like the perfect hiding spot. Boy, was I ever wrong!

Come on, Cadillac Man, you'll feel better once you start walking. The first few steps were sheer torture, but I'll make it, and thankfully the coffee shop was only three blocks away. As I arrived, the owner came outside, blocking the entranceway.

"What do you want?"

"Same as yesterday, sir, four regular coffees and a buttered roll please."

"Stay here and don't move."

I don't understand it. Yesterday he was nice, we talked about the weather, the holiday, etc. Now he won't even let me in. Why?

He came back with the coffees and the roll. "Here you go."

I paid him. "Thank you, sir."

With a look of concern he said, "Better go and get yourself checked out."

"I'll be all right."

Shaking his head, he went back inside. Do I really look that bad? Went over to a parked car, and the side window reflected an ugly sight. This can't be me. It looks like a person who went twelve rounds with a prizefighter and lost big-time! Face badly swollen, right eye completely closed, and a few bottom teeth missing. I probably swallowed them. Dried blood everywhere, my shirt heavily stained.

So what happened to me?

They came in the dark while I was sleeping. Don't know how many, doesn't matter anyway. I woke up and they were kicking me all over, again and again. Trapped inside the sleeping bag, I couldn't defend myself. I can still hear their laughter. Then a miracle came: I passed out.

I came to in a pile of trash bags. The punks who attacked me probably thought I was dead and used the bags to conceal my body. The bags were heavy. Trying to push them off, I almost passed out again from the strain.

Anyway, there I am in the car window. Look at me, a fucking bloody mess! Oh, how I wish those suckers were here right now. I would cut out their hearts and send them to their parents!

Just then I heard the sound of an ambulance wailing, getting closer and finally stopping in front of me. Must have been the store owner who called them. There isn't anybody else out at this hour. I'm normally wary about medical services, but today I'm in need of assistance and wouldn't mind if they wanted to check me out.

The medic gets out and walks over to me with an alarmed look on his face.

"What happened to you, sir?"

"I slipped on a banana peel."

"Be serious, sir."

"While I was sleeping, a load of dudes decided to stomp on me."

"That I believe, sir. Want to go to the hospital?"

"Nope, no coverage."

"We'll take you to a city hospital."

"No thanks, I can't leave my wagon unattended."

"Will you at least let us check you out in the ambulance?"

"Okay." I stepped inside. Taking off my shirt, I can see there are marks everywhere, scrapes and bad bruises. He starts in with the peroxide and gauze, gives me a good going over, spending a long time around my eye where the worst of it is.

"What's your name, sir?"

"Cadillac Man."

"Cadillac Man, your eye looks bad. There may be nerve damage too. Are you feeling pain anywhere else?"

"Yeah, all over, but I can deal with it."

"Sure you don't want to see a doctor?"

"I am sure, but thanks for the cleanup."

"Okay, if you're sure." To his partner: "We're all right here. Just call it in as an RMA," which means I refused medical assistance. Back to me:

"It's very important to keep that eye clean, okay? Any sign of infection, please go to the hospital right away."

"I will and thanks for caring."

"It's our job. Be seeing you."

"Later, guys."

This is one shirt I won't be able to wear again. It's a good thing I have extras. At the church where I get my meals, they have boxes of spare clothing for us. You can take some and save a few for others because with this type of weather you need to dress in layers.

Wish I had a pair of long johns, though, because it's bitter cold. Instead, I've got my pants stuffed with newspaper. Sound crazy? It's not. Newspaper insulates the body, keeps the drafts out, and if you can't afford toilet paper, it's ideal. Others use T-shirts, socks, leaves, even a plastic shopping bag (aka dump bag).

I myself prefer to go natural when I can, but in a pinch I would use whatever I had at hand. I definitely wouldn't do what my friend Ralphie did. Stupid bastard!

It was a warm, sunny day, just this September, and a group of us decided to go down past the West Side Highway to the river, where it's cooler. Loaded up on sixes, wine coolers, and coffee, naturally! We were lucky, the pier was deserted. It's party time! Carrottop had a radio, out came the refreshments, and soon everybody was moving to the music.

The air was filled with laughter from all the bullshit stories being passed around, and that's when it happened. Ralphie got up, feeling the back of his pants, and said, "Oh, man! I gotta do me a mean dump!" Looking around and not finding a place to hide, he goes to the edge of the pier and drops his pants.

"Hey, Ralphie! Pull up your pants before someone sees you!" one of the guys yelled.

"Fuck you! Ain't nobody here but us. I ain't gonna shit in my pants!"

Then I saw it. Everybody did except Ralphie, his back was turned away. A Circle Line sightseeing boat was cruising by, jam-packed with tourists visiting our fine city for the first time, checking out our scenic views and beautiful skyline—and now this, Ralphie's big fat ass.

The tourists start to whistle, whoop, and holler. Squatting down and grunting, Ralphie's paying them no mind. Wish I had his thick skin on a cold day like today.

Anyway, cold or not, I should head over to the redeemer. I don't have much recycle to cash in, but maybe I'll get lucky and find more along the way.

It's obvious this area wasn't worked by many people. There is recycle everywhere, a virgin territory. At one location I found a big bag of cans. I must remember to come back here. At the redeemer, nobody is around. That's odd. Maybe the machines are full or not working. Nope, they're okay. I did all my recycle, cashed in my tickets, and not bad, eighteen dollars. Going to treat myself to a couple packs of smokes, no more picking up butts for a while.

My pockets are full of butts, most with a few hits left. Smokes are too expensive to pay for on a regular basis, plus they're everywhere, outside restaurants, bus and train stations, office buildings, etc. That is disgusting, you say? If you're a nonsmoker, I agree, it's a nasty habit. But save the lecture, I enjoy smoking. So if the craving for nicotine strikes, I go hunting for butts. Couldn't care less if they have lipstick, spit, or teeth marks on them. And disease? I don't worry, the streets are going to take my life before cigarettes will.

No point hanging out here, my taste buds are tingling for coffee. Swing around the corner and see my people all gathered by a Con Edison truck. Why?

Tina spots me first, waves, and heads my way. Tina isn't one of us, not homeless. She's a real fucking moocher. Beer, juice, cigarettes, food, anything. We tolerate her bullshit because she has something we all need, a place to stay in emergencies and most importantly a shower. Two bucks and you can stay overnight to sleep on the floor. Wanna shower? Five bucks and you supply the soap and towel. One last thing: no credit. Ain't got no money? Tough shit!

Tina's in her late twenties I think and perhaps was very pretty years ago but not now.

Sucked-in face with all the teeth missing, courtesy of her ex-boyfriend

Tito, a badass junkie who used her as a punching bag. He met his end a couple months back, a bad batch of dope, which Tina picked up for him. Nothing was ever proven that she had something to do with it. If you ask my opinion, no big deal, one less fucking junkie.

"Hi, Cadillac," she said, looked at my face, and stopped cold, eyes wide. She's smart enough to know, never ask questions.

"Hi, Tina, what's up?"

Trying to collect her thoughts. "Er, er, they are giving out sandwiches and sodas."

"Zaybos?" (Baloney-n-cheese sandwiches.)

"No, no, real big ones from a fancy deli! Go get one."

Sounds good. I stepped up to the truck. The guy inside was looking at me, worried. "You hungry, buddy?"

"Yes, sir!"

Reached into a cardboard box and came out with two huge heros and a can of soda. "Here you go buddy, Merry Christmas!"

"Thanks, but I only want one, save the other for someone else." He looked shocked. "There is nobody else and we're leaving now, got to get back to work."

"Okay, I'll save it for somebody else. Merry Christmas, sir."

"Wait a minute, buddy." He reached in his pocket, took out ten dollars. "Now don't use this to buy alcohol."

"I don't drink alcohol, only coffee."

"Well then, buy yourself a load of coffee," he says, laughing.

"I intend to. Take care and thank you again, sir."

Turn my back so that nobody sees me slip the ten in my pocket. It's better that way—no one can hit you up for a loan. A quarter or fifty cent, no problem, but once it goes past a dollar, try to get them to pay up.

Walking back to my wagon, I feel Tina's eyes on me—or should I say the sandwiches? Yep, I was right.

"Wow! Cadillac Man, he gave you two of them!"

"Yeah, lucky me."

"You going to hang around with us for a while?"

"No, I need to move along."

"What about a shower?"

Ah! That magic word, *shower*. It's amazing how you feel afterwards, like a new person. Something you take for granted is a luxury to us. Try going without for a week or two.

No way, you say. Okay, I'll be generous, you can use the sink in the coffee shop. That's disgusting, you say.

But it's all right for me to do it, so that makes you spoiled fucking rotten. I could see if you had a dirty job, mechanic, construction, or any other outside work, it's necessary to wash. But working in an office? What did you do, get dirty handling paper clips?

"Not right now, Tina. During the week, okay?"

"Suit yourself." Still looking at the heros.

Fine. "Here, take these," I said, handing over one sandwich and the soda.

"Oooo, thank you, Cadillac Man, I'm going to be extra-nice to you!"

"Later, Tina."

I wasn't going to eat it anyways, the hard bread would open the cuts on my gums. So for the next few days, peanut butter sandwiches. The other hero will go to someone else I'll meet up with in my travels. Always do.

'Tis the season to be jolly, the music from the truck said.

Fuck you, Christmas, I'm hurting.

Gotta do some canning, keep myself busy. I hate coming to this part of midtown, too many tourists. Can't even wheel my wagon on the sidewalk or the cops would yell at me. Walked to the deli a few blocks away for coffee and it's the same story: here's your order, now get out of here. "Thanks, Merry Christmas." I took my coffee over to St. Pat's church and sat on the front steps. The cops won't bother me here.

St. Pat's is a must-see place on your visit here, and there was a steady flow of people, mostly tourists, entering and leaving. They were staring at me too, making fun of my peanut butter sandwiches.

Finished one cup and placed it down, then something happened. I heard a clunk into the cup, then another. People in front and behind were dropping change in, paper money too! A little girl, perhaps seven or eight years old, cautiously walks towards me with a dollar in her hand, then stops. "Here, mister, Merry Christmas."

"Thank you, little girl, Merry Christmas to you too."

"I'm not little, I'm a big girl, eight years old."

Then her parents spoke, "Come on, honey, we have to go."

"Bye, mister."

"Bye-bye, big girl."

She ran to her mother. They're holding hands now. Walking away, she turned her head, looking at me and smiling. I waved back and the smile widened, revealing two front teeth missing. I had to turn my head away. I didn't want her to see my tears.

I miss my little girl, my daughter, Jessica. I fucked things up big-time, should have tried harder to be a better husband, father. Now she is going to grow up without a father, my fault, my fucking fault! It's my first holiday away from the family. It will be the last one. Oh, Jessica, please forgive me. And God help the person that fucks with me.

That night it was cold and raining, a bad time to be out. Got to find a new spot to bed down. Tina's place was nearby so I decided to go over, even if I said I wasn't going to.

She was happy to see me—or was it the two dollars in my hand? Went into the living room to find at least a dozen guys sprawled out on the floor, fast asleep. The way they were situated left me very little room to lay down, but I'm going to change that. I grabbed one little guy by the ankles and dragged him across the floor. He howled, yelled, and cursed but I didn't care. "Shut the fuck up and move the fuck over," I said to the others. In a few minutes I was down with room to spare.

Then it got quiet, but not for long. The night music started in. Not the type you hear on the radio, the FCC wouldn't allow it. No, sir, you're listening to the sounds of snoring and farting. Loud ones, long ones, short bursts, rapid-fire. Damn! Noses like a fucking marching band of trombones. I don't know how I fell asleep with all this racket, but eventually I did.

The new day came a bit colder than yesterday but the fresh air felt good on my face. Now all I needed was some coffee and some cheering up too. Gathered up my gear, went to the wagon, and noticed something is missing, the sandwich from yesterday. Somebody was here. The bag was ripped open, bits of lettuce scattered about, but what stood out was the wrapping paper leaning against the wagon. Fucking slob! The least they could have done was throw away the paper.

Looking at it, I saw chew marks. This person was really hungry. I know what it's like. In the beginning, I would eat whatever I could find from trash cans. Food so rancid, the smell would knock you down. Removing maggots to get that extra morsel of meat, wiping off slimy fruit. Old pasta, moldy vegetables—you hold your breath and take it down in one swallow. Many others like me living on the streets were doing the same exact thing. I know of some that still do, the ones that don't care anymore, the ones waiting to die.

I went over to the same deli, this time the owner let me in.

"You look a lot better than yesterday," he said. "Your eye is open a little and the swelling has gone down."

"Really?" I said, feeling my face. It's less puffy and doesn't hurt as much.

"You want the same order?"

"Yes, and thank you for today and yesterday."

"I don't understand."

"Yes, you do, for serving me and calling the ambulance."

"How did you know it was me?"

"Easy. Early morning, streets are deserted, and you're the only place open."

Outside the door, I can see customers wanting to come in. I better leave, I'm bad for business.

Something I have to check out. My eye. Stopped by a storefront looking at my reflection. The bad eye is partially open but I have this uneasy feeling. On a hunch I cover the good eye and see nothing. Did it again and again, there is no doubt, I am blind. I'm worried that it might be permanent. Lord, give me strength to fight this. Can't go to the hospital, you know why, just one more thing to deal with.

Got to keep clean, but don't want to cover up because that would make me a target. If you're disabled in any way, they will take advantage. And knowing that you got money, especially now with the holiday season and the outsiders' generosity, makes you stand out more. Let me give you an example.

Thanksgiving week was good to us, most of us had plenty of food and some cash too. On one of the days, I found a load of cans and went to the redeemer. Arriving, I saw a big dude hassling my people for money, pushing and threatening with a loud voice.

People give in, passing him dollar bills rather than receive a senseless beating. But not me, I work hard for the money and I ain't going to give it to a piece of dog shit like him.

Cashed in my tickets and went outside, counting the money in full view of everybody. What a stupid thing to do, you say. Indeed it is, but there is a reason. I'm itching for a fight and he's available.

And here he comes, so confident and sure, walking like a badass. Stops about five feet in front of me. Maybe three inches taller and thirty pounds heavier than I. Looks a little puzzled, probably wondering why I didn't move away.

"Hey, motherfucker, gimme a dollah!"

"Ain't gotta dollah."

"You lyin'! I seen you put money in your pocket!"

"Calm down, big guy, it ain't mine, you gonna have to ask her."

Looking around. "Who?"

"Your sister. I promised it to her after I reamed her ass."

Before it could sink in, bang! bang! bang! A punch in the face and two in the chest, he lost his balance and fell to the ground.

"Come on, get up!" I kicked him in the face and he turns over, lands on his back.

A voice came from behind me. "Back off, that's enough." It's the store manager. "Let him go."

If I don't do as he says, he'll close the machines early. Which the porter did anyway. You could hear the groans coming from everyone, but it's a minor setback, there are other places. The tough guy was standing, looking at me. "You motherfucker!"

Before I could answer back, the store manager said to him, "Leave right now or else I'm calling the police!" Then he turned to me. "After he leaves, you go too!"

Yes, sir.

Walking away, the tough guy yells back, "I'll see you again, mother-fucker!"

I waved bye-bye at him. Chances are we'll meet up again.

Might as well head over to the redeemer. Fuck it, so what if I'm blind, nobody is ever going to know.

Man, I don't believe it, this is usually a big recycling day and nobody is by the machines. Were they chased away? Didn't get here yet? Ah, there's Dingaling, as always sitting on a milk crate across the street. Knows everything, nosy as hell, and hardly ever does canning, mainly cashing in other people's tickets at the going rate of one dollar. Loves cheap wine and rolled-up cigarettes.

"Hey, Dingaling, what's up?"

"Hey, Cadillac Man, same old shit."

"Where is everybody?"

"Most of them went to Tina's place to wash up. Today is a big day at St. Paul's."

"What's going on?"

"A Christmas meal, turkey dinner with real food, no canned shit. They do it every year. Everybody gets a present too. Last year I got me a warm shirt and sweater. Brand-new!"

"So what are you still doing here? Go, man."

"I can't."

"Why not?"

"Look at me, man, I can't go like this."

Didn't see anything unusual, just the norm, layers of street clothes and needs a shave. Same as me.

"You look okay."

"Not to me, Cadillac Man. I stink and don't have any clean clothes."

"No big deal. I got extra clean clothes I can give you." I pick some things out of the wagon. People give me all kinds of things. Some fit, some don't. Nobody's going to come measure me before they decide which shirt to get rid of. "Here, these will fit, now go get washed up."

"I can't."

"Why not?"

"I don't have the five dollars."

Jeez, this guy. I hand him the money. "Do you need soap and razor?"

"Yeah, do you have a towel too?"

"Damn, Dingaling! What the fuck."

"Sorry, Cadillac Man, I can't seem to keep anything nowadays, somebody is swiping stuff off my wagon."

"Yeah, I know, it happens to me too. So you got everything you need, hit the road."

"Thanks, Cadillac Man, I'll pay you back next week."

"You better. And do me a favor."

"Sure, anything."

"Stop saying 'I can't,' you sound like a broken record."

"Okay, see you later at the church. Man, I'm going to pig out."

"Later, Dingaling."

I made an exception in his case by lending money, it was for a good cause, to maintain his dignity. We do hold on to certain values from our previous life, with the hope of being accepted back. But not me, I gave up. That is one reason why I won't be joining the others at the church. It would be a painful reminder. Of good times, the family gathering for a holiday dinner, singing carols, exchanging presents.

I've met a few that have been out here for years. They seem unaffected with all of this. Or are they crying on the inside? Anyway, I'm not going to last as long as they did. I don't want to.

Walking about and a generous amount of coffee made me feel better, and I wind up on the steps of St. Patrick's again. If by chance the priest appears, I'll bare my soul to him. The Boss (God) will listen and forgive me.

I see that I have company across the street. There's a homeless woman on the curb, singing to a bunch of tourists, "Have Yourself a Merry Little Christmas." She's dressed in rummage-sale rejects with a hat on the ground for, ahem, donations. Such a sweet voice.

It's Sparrow, a former music teacher. A hard-core boozer who lost everything to the bottle. Job, husband, kids, it didn't matter to her, only drinking. Midthirties I think—blond hair and real skinny now, still pretty in a way, though her skin is getting rough from being outside and she's missing a tooth or two. A nice woman, just don't touch her booze. She will cut you in a blink of an eye. Weapon of choice, a linoleum cutter, a hook-shaped blade that can do major damage. But anyways, drunk or sober, a clear, beautiful sound. "Through the years we all will be together . . ."

She's wowing the crowd and they're being very generous. Show over, she picks up her belongings and walks away. No doubt to a new location, for there is plenty of money to be made on this holiday. Might as well take advantage. When it's over, it's back to the old street hustle.

More and more people are passing by me, a few stopping to gaze or comment about my wagon, then look at me. Most of the time I get pissed off, but not with these people. They're tourists, experiencing New York City life, which I'm a part of. Perhaps this is their first and last visit here. To catch a glimpse of my people gives them something to talk about to the neighbors back home.

"Hi, Cadillac Man."

Her voice came from my blind side, took me by surprise. When I turned to greet her, she had a look of anger and concern.

"Hey, Sparrow, how are you?"

"I'm fine, want company?"

"Sure, cop a squat, only sit on my other side."

"Having difficulty seeing?"

"No, I see fine, it's just that I feel more comfortable when someone is on my right side." (Nice try.)

"Because you're left-handed."

"Yep, that I am. So what up?"

"Nothin', just resting my vocal cords, the next performance is in a few minutes."

"I heard you over here, you sing like an angel."

"Flatterer!"

"Really, you should be singing in the church behind us."

"Are you crazy? I used to, a long time ago, but I can't make any money in there. I gotta be out here singing, it's the only way I can make money.

Won't do canning, that's too much work. Panhandling, I don't have the knack, and most definitely will not sell my pussy or suck a guy off."

"Sparrow! Watch your mouth, we're in front of church."

"Sorry, God, sorry, Cadillac Man. Anyway, I do what I do best, singing for my food and alcohol. Which reminds me . . ."

She tilted her chin downward and that's when I noticed it. A straw protruding from an inside shirt pocket, its tip between her pursed lips as liquid courses through.

"Ahh! Number seven bourbon! The best!" She'd drink anything, but she loved her Jack Daniel's.

"What a clever way to stash the booze."

"Yeah, I thought so too, it would have been bad for business whipping out the bottle in front of everyone when I needed a taste. I'm hungry, do you have any food?"

"Yeah, peanut butter sandwiches, cupcakes, and Cheez Doodles."

"Mmm, sounds yummy, can I have some please?"

What she did next almost turned my stomach. Opening up the sandwich, she placed two cupcakes and a handful of Cheez Doodles in, then closed and mushed it! Munching away and sipping the booze, she looks at me. "Want some?"

"No thanks, I ate earlier."

"Mind if I make another? By the way, got any ketchup?"

"No ketchup, only soy sauce."

"Okay, I'll try it."

I gave her two packets, and son of a gun, she sprinkled them on the sandwich and ate it! I'll never eat peanut butter again!

"I better get going, my audience is waiting."

"Knock 'em dead, girl."

"Thanks, going to stick around for a while?"

"Yeah, just for a bit, gotta do some canning, don't want the legs to stiffen up from the cold."

"Thanks for the food," she said, and then kissed me on the lips. A tender kiss that warmed my insides. Backing away slightly, she smiled. "You know where I live, come see me later." She kissed me again. "And take care of that eye."

What a sight she is, twirling and dancing into the oncoming traffic. Loose and fancy-free, pausing only for liquid refreshment. This is her way of life and this is how she will die. Plops her hat down on the ground and starts singing, people stop to listen to the sweet voice of Christmas.

All those families, dressed warm for the weather and walking around the streets, happy and thinking about the warm house they're going to. Not me, not anymore. Got to go now, can't look at this anymore, can't listen to the singing. I'm so shaken that I'm a block away when I realize I forgot the wagon. What a fucking dope! Sparrow sees me coming back and waves. I feel like an idiot. Get away, faster, faster, I need to be alone, somewhere I can cry. Stopped by a deli for more coffee and a couple of cream-cheese bagels. Somehow I lost my taste for peanut butter.

After a few sips and bites, I felt a little better. Then something caught my eye off into the distance. A bridge, the 59th Street Bridge, all the way out to Queens with barely anyone on it. The perfect spot to be alone. Nobody comes here, especially this time of year, when the river breezes chill you to the bone. Doesn't bother me, I like cold weather.

I notice the entrance leading to the walkway isn't blocked off, as it usually is to deter people from taking a flying leap into eternity. There aren't any safeguards for motorists. Just stop the car and splash! It's that simple. Adventurous types take the scenic route by scaling a steel cable to the top of one tower. Incredible views all around, but do a power dive off and you might miss the water and strike a motorist stuck in the traffic you created. Or what's worse, you could hit the roadway. What a fucking splatter!

Locked up my wagon by the entrance, nobody will fuck with it here. I started walking and, when I reached the halfway point, stopped. I didn't even hear the sound of traffic behind me.

Such beauty, boats in the water, buildings of all sizes and shapes, trees blowing in the wind. So peaceful. Then I saw it, on the shore on the other side, standing tall for all to see, a big neon sign, an advertisement for Pepsi-cola. Damn that sign! My heart aches because of this place, a turning point in my life, the beginning of the end.

Right behind the sign was the bottling plant where I worked for three years. A good job, demanding and a lot of opportunities for advancement, the future looked bright. My wife and I were so happy, this career was going to make all of our dreams come true. A year and a half later one did, Jessica was born. This was the joy I had. A beautiful loving wife blessed me with a child. I was the luckiest man on this world. To my wife and child I am so sorry that I failed you. Feeling the tears roll off my face into the river down below.

The swirling of the water is talking to me. "Jump into my center and win a prize. No more pain and suffering, I give you peace."

"Hey, buddy, are you all right?" A voice of concern and authority. I turn to see a police officer about twenty feet away.

"I'm fine, officer."

Walking closer, he says, "What are you doing here?"

"Just taking in the views. I used to work for Pepsi over there," I said, pointing.

"Thinking about hurting yourself?"

"No, no way. I have no reason to." I heard a sound on my blind side and turned to see another officer standing by.

"How did you get here?" the new officer says.

"Through the entrance."

"The entrance is closed."

"Not the one I came through," I said, pointing downward.

"Show us."

One by my side, the other behind me, we walk to the entrance. Arriving, I unlock the wagon, and they seemed surprised.

"Been homeless a long time?"

"To me it has, about six months."

"You know, there are agencies that can help you. We can give you phone numbers."

"No thanks, this is something I have to deal with on my own."

"It's getting colder out, you should find shelter somewhere."

"I will. Can I go now?"

"Yes, but don't let us catch you over here again."

"I'm not coming back. Merry Christmas, officers."

"Hang in there, buddy. Merry Christmas."

I feel their eyes watching me and purposely walk straight across the street, then a few doors down to the deli. Bought more coffee. Leaving, I heard the whooping sound of a police siren and looked up to see one of the officers waving. I waved back.

Had they came a minute or two later, they wouldn't have seen me. So I should be grateful to them for saving my life, but the pain is still there and I don't know of any other way to make it go away. Have to keep busy, do some serious canning. Be strong. Walked a greater distance, more than I usually do, all the way down to the west 20s and back, and it felt good. Now it's late. Streets void of people, with only a passing car or two.

I need to talk with someone and the only person I can think of that's available at this hour is Sparrow. She's about a half hour away, in a little pocket between the East River and the highway where no one else would go after dark. Got to give her credit, it takes balls to live where she's staying. On my way there, you can feel the temperature rapidly dropping and a frosty wind slaps your face.

Luckily for some, winter hasn't reached us yet. 'Tis the season of tears and death. Lord, hear my prayer.

Arrived at last, I see her wagon and faintly can hear music. Christmas carols? Coming closer, I can hear that it is, but Sparrow is nowhere in sight. A scary thought entered my mind and I walked over to the seawall. The walkway's light illuminated the water only so far out. The rest is total darkness, the tide so strong a good swimmer would struggle.

Oh, Sparrow, did the demons of the mind and alcohol make these waters inviting? Or did you have to go somewhere? Where? There aren't any places around here that are open at this hour.

At her camp, the piss and dump bucket is unused, a few empty half-pint bourbon bottles around. Sparrow, please be all right. Of all the good hiding spots in this area, why here? In front of you the river and behind you the FDR Drive. You can reach this spot by way of the several overpasses, but with a wagon, it's a mad dash across the highway no matter what the hour is.

Where are you, Sparrow? A minute later I got my answer. There was a huge pile of blankets behind her wagon leaning against the seawall. From underneath the blankets I saw a little hand creep out and turn off the radio.

I took several steps back and said, "Yo, Sparrow! You there?" It's better to let someone know you're coming than to sneak up on them. No telling how they would react, and if you're street people, most likely it will be with a weapon of sorts. Blankets flipped over a bit, revealing her head, body turning until she was able to look at me.

"Cadillac Man! It's about time you got here. I thought you weren't going to show up."

"Sorry, Sparrow, I lost track of time."

"Apology accepted. Tie up your wagon next to mine, then get underneath the blanket with me. Or are you too shy?"

"Me shy? Fuck no!" I laughed and started walking toward her.

"Hold on!" she said, and I stopped. Maybe she had second thoughts about having company. Out came one hand holding a nasty-looking butcher's knife.

Whew! I almost did a dump in my pants!

"Relax, it's for my own protection," she says, putting it under her wagon. I must have still looked startled, because she laughed at me and said, "I know your type, not afraid of anything." She slid over. "Come join me." Lying down and overlapping the blankets.

"How is your eye, Cadillac Man?"

"What eye?"

"The eye that should have noticed when I stuck out my tongue at you! Wait a minute." She rolled over me, taking her sweet time doing it, onto my other side. "Now you can see me, right?"

"How did you know?"

"Back on the church steps, the way you were moving your head too far over, people with normal vision don't do that. When are you going to have a doctor look at it?"

"Next time I'm near a hospital."

"Can you see anything?"

"Everything is a blur, but I'm okay. Now enough with the questions."

I don't know where the bottle came from, but she got one and took a generous swig.

"Damn, Sparrow, you got a liquor store under these blankets?"

"That is my secret, Cadillac Man." She took another swig.

"Whew! It's hot under here, I'm starting to sweat."

"That's because you have too many clothes on. Why don't you take them off?"

"Are you fucking nuts? It's winter, cold as a witch's tit."

Flipping over a blanket, she said, "Do my tits look cold to you?"

"No, they look very nice. I mean . . ."

"Are my nipples hard from the cold or soft from the warmth here? Go on, touch them."

Touch them? Hell, I'm going to kiss them! Yep, they're soft.

"Now will you take off your clothes?" Okeydokey.

Just picture in your mind what happened next, trying to take off everything under the blankets. Moaning and groaning, yanking and wiggling. The boots were the worst!

Meanwhile Sparrow is laughing, finding all of this entertaining. "Oh, Cadillac Man, such an effort just to get laid. Why didn't you stand up? It would have been a lot easier."

"Now I know you're fucking nuts, Sparrow, me stripping down for the whole world to see. I can see it now on the front page of the *Daily News*. 'Homeless man shows off his hairy ass, causing major auto accidents on the FDR Drive.'" Sheesh!

She's laughing again. "All you had to do is hide yourself within a blanket and strip one piece at a time."

"Yeah, okay. I'll remember that for the next time I'm with a naked lady by a freezing river during the winter."

With nothing more to say she drew closer to me. So close that her breasts were rubbing against my chest, her hand caressing my face. Tenderly kissing her hand, I said softly, "Sorry, Sparrow, had I known this was going to happen, I would have shaved."

She smiled. "It's okay, Cadillac Man."

Touching, feeling each part of our bodies. Tasting the tears brought on by the memories of past loves. Two lost souls. It wasn't the need of sex that drew us together, it was the need of closeness, to feel wanted.

"I miss my family, Cadillac Man."

"I know you do, Sparrow, so do I."

"Daddy! Wake up!"

Leave me alone, Jessica, I'm tired.

"Wake up, Cadillac Man!"

Leave me the fuck alone, whoever you are!

Suddenly my throat is on fire, I'm awake and choking. Sparrow is furiously rubbing me all over, saying, "Thank God, thank God!"

I've got this funny warm taste. Bourbon?

"Sparrow, what the fuck is going on?"

"Oh, God, Cadillac Man, you were blue."

"Blue? What the fuck are you talking about?"

She took a swig from the bottle. "I woke up, had to take a piss, and didn't notice you at first. When I finished, I looked over and saw the blankets were off you! So blue I thought you were dead! I tossed my piss bucket into the river and ran over to you. Covered you up quickly, then I slid under, rubbing my body against you. You were so cold I was getting goose bumps. I was calling your name over and over and you were getting a little warmer, but no answer. Then I poured a little bourbon in your mouth.

"That did the trick, you coughed and opened your eyes." Bang! She whacked me hard on the chest. "You bastard, you nearly died!" She's crying now.

"Oww! I'm sorry, Sparrow," I said, then started kissing her. "Thank you for saving my life, I owe you one." She wrapped the blanket around us tightly, no chance of wiggling out. Even in the darkness I could feel her eyes on me.

"Go to sleep, Sparrow." I dozed off seconds later.

A whooping noise woke me up. I know that sound. A voice came from a loudspeaker. "Time to get up, Sparrow."

"Good morning, officers!"

"Got company?"

"Yes!"

"Only fifteen minutes, Sparrow."

"Okay, officers! Bye-bye!"

"What is that all about?"

"My wake-up call, telling me to clear out of here."

"Why hustle you?"

"They're not, just reminding me that the joggers and dog walkers will be here soon. Let's hurry up and get dressed, you're buying me breakfast."

"Am I? Why should I?"

"You got laid. I think that is an even exchange, sex for food. Don't you?"

"Hell yes! I'll even buy you lunch!" We're both laughing.

"Only breakfast, Cadillac Man. Now, shake a leg."

Took no time for Sparrow to get dressed, but I took forever, going through the same ritual as before, only letting her help with my boots. All packed and ready to go, we were out on the highway, where traffic is building up, morning rush hour approaching.

Our wagons side by side, Sparrow was looking, waiting for the right moment. "Cadillac Man, how fast can you run?"

"Just say the word, lady, and watch me haul ass."

"Run!"

It took me a split second to react. Sparrow was already several yards ahead of me, damn that girl can fly. I picked up the pace, cars roaring past on both sides. Then the unthinkable happened, I tripped, went down, and landed flat on my face. Sparrow was screaming, "Get up! Get up!" I could hear oncoming cars honking their horns. Stood up and stopped, not moving. There was no fear, only relief in sight, please let it be quick. But not today. Horns blaring, they swerved to my left and right so close I could reach out and touch them.

"Now! Now!"

The urgency in her voice made me realize that this was not the time and place. I ran to her. Hitting me with her fists, she was yelling, "You stupid bastard, you almost got killed! What were you thinking?"

"Sorry, Sparrow, I froze up." Oops, wrong choice of words.

Bang! "Damn you, Cadillac Man. Will you at least stay alive until you buy me breakfast?"

"I promise to be extra-careful and to look both ways."

And wouldn't you know it, on the way to the restaurant a delivery truck came hard around a corner and we had to jump for the sidewalk. We both stood there panting. The thing almost creamed us!

I looked at Sparrow. "Not my fault."

We placed our wagons on the opposite side of the street facing the restaurant. That way we could keep an eye on them and also wouldn't have to deal with the stares from others.

Before entering, she looked in and said, "Are you sure you want us to eat here?"

Inside, the place looked expensive, with all the waiters and waitresses in matching outfits, fresh flowers on every table.

"Cadillac Man, let's go somewhere else. This place is too high-class, look at the way they're staring at us."

"It's just your typical outsider, thinking they're better than us. We're paying customers. Come on, let's get a table by a window."

Breakfast was good, and we both needed it. The waitress was buzzing around us, trying to make us pay before the food came, but I gave her a big tip and she changed her tune. We both stopped at the bathroom on the way out—you never know when you're going to have your next chance, and a restaurant bathroom beats a bucket. The men's room had one urinal and two stalls, both with full rolls of paper, which I stuffed into my coat pockets, then emptied the paper-towel dispenser.

Leaving, I passed the cashier again. "Everything all right, sir?"

"You're all out of toilet paper."

Stare of disbelief. "I'll see to it right away, sir."

Ah, there she is, coming out of the ladies' room.

"Come on, let's get out of here!" she said.

Adios, sayonara, we lickety-split real fast. Grabbing the wagons, we burn rubber for a few blocks before stopping.

"What did you get, Cadillac Man?"

"Two rolls of paper, paper towels, and a napkin. You?"

"Two more rolls, tampons, salt and pepper shakers, three sets of utensils."

"Three sets? We only had two."

"Yeah, I took one from ours, and two from a table that was unoccupied, plus the shakers and, oh, two more napkins. I couldn't resist."

"Damn, girl, you're lucky you weren't caught!"

"They were too busy to notice me. I was careful."

"Here, take half the paper towels and the napkin."

"Want some utensils? Tampons?"

"Just give me one knife, for my peanut butter, and what the hell am I going to need tampons for?"

"Well, I guess we should part company here, Cadillac Man. Thank you for a most enjoyable evening."

A passionate kiss that stirred up the juices; she must have felt it too. "Maybe some other time."

"Be careful, Sparrow."

"Bye-bye, Cadillac Man."

I followed her for a while, not intentionally. We were headed in the same direction, and only when she stopped at a liquor store did I pass her.

I should be grateful that she saved my life, but I'm not. I deliberately tossed off the blankets, and just my luck, she happened to wake up to take a piss. Three attempts, three failures, in less than twenty-four hours. Can't I do anything right? Must mean the Boss isn't ready for me yet, and at least the sadness is gone for now.

Got a load of stuff here, might as well head to the redemption center. Cash in my cans, and still nobody, where is everybody? Over at Tina's? Nah, it's late, almost lunchtime. Probably at the church and that's where I'm headed. I feel a need to be around my people. Arriving, I see them all clustered around a van. A few see me and wave for me to come over.

"What's going on, Frankie?"

"How do I look, Cadillac Man?"

"Got yourself a new, warm coat. A wool cap too?"

"Yeah, and gloves, all of this from the people inside the van, from some charities. Go get yours."

"Why not, can always use extras."

Mostly everybody wore two coats, with the one in worse condition on the outside to prevent the good one from getting ruined. But the ones they're handing out are heavy-duty arctic, and the only thing can be worn underneath is a sweater. Some tried with another coat on and looked like the Michelin Man from TV commercials, too bulky.

Also, with layers of clothing on, they're too hot even in colder weather. Still we are grateful for the things we receive. Thank you. Now it is my turn.

"Hi there! Merry Christmas!"

"Hello, same to you."

"What is your size?"

"Extralarge or bigger is better."

"You're in luck. I got a double X, is that okay?"

"Yes, thank you."

"And to go with it, a warm cap and gloves. Merry Christmas."

"Same to you, sir."

Man, the coat was huge. I knew it would fit me, but still put it on the side for future use. The others saw me stuff the items deep within my wagon. They won't ask why and are probably thinking I'm keeping them to sell if the price is right. A pack of smokes, few bucks, or even cans and bottles, everything has a price.

Now everybody was lined up on the church steps. It's lunchtime. Blessing the food, the nuns gave out a sandwich, one piece of fruit, and one milk. I wasn't hungry and passed mine up. As I was about to leave, Tina appears.

"Hey, Cadillac Man, wanna take your shower now?"

"Maybe later. I need to make some money first."

"Suit yourself. Be careful tonight. I heard over the radio temperatures dropping into low teens. Will you be all right?"

"Yeah, got plenty of blankets and warm hiding spots."

The need for a shower was severe, but I'd rather be on the road. Stopped at the corner store, picked up coffee and smokes, and then headed to the park for a nap. With this type of weather and the outsider at work, the only company I'll have is perhaps a few senior citizens and pigeons. I feel

sorry for them. Walking or sitting on a park bench alone with their memories. Clearly forgotten by their families, they come here hoping to meet an
old friend. But loneliness creeps in and after time they will strike up a
conversation with anyone that shows any interest. Just a casual greeting,
eye contact with a smile, starts the ball rolling. A fascinating lot. They
could keep you spellbound for hours, days, telling tales.

So why are they sitting here? A chronic disease called old age. Your
children, adults now, make up excuses why they can't visit and you accept
their reasons, truthful or not. Then you wait for the day to arrive, spirits
high, feeling a little better, everything is grand up until the time when
they have to leave. The house, filled with laughter and joy a few minutes
ago, now void of life. I'm thankful in a way my end won't be that way.

Central Park was deserted, the crisp breeze probably kept everybody out.
Deep inside, near 85th Street, I found a secluded park bench and did a
perimeter of peanuts around me so that if someone was to try to sneak
up, I would hear them. I settled in for a nap, sitting, not lying down, because all I need is a few hours. I'm well insulated, don't have to worry
about going a Jack Frost like my pal Maxie's friends.

This was in Chicago, several years ago, before I was on the streets. One
bitter cold night they decided to camp out in a park. Two were hard-core
juicers, Maxie didn't drink. With a couple of sixes and bottles of cheap
juice, they partied through the night and made no attempt to keep themselves warm.

The alcohol was doing that, Maxie knew. Twice he covered them with
blankets, only to be tossed off, then cursed at. "Leave us the fuck alone,"
they said. Maxie was worried watching the bottles go back and forth, the
laughter increasing, so he stuck around, trying to stay awake. But sleep
wins you over all the time. He woke up suddenly, thinking he dozed off
for a few minutes, then, seeing the sun, realized he'd slept for hours.

It was so quiet, the only sound coming from birds chirping, nothing
from the others. Went back to sleep, thinking they're okay, they probably
ran out of juice and then bedded down. But he had an uneasy feeling that
turned into panic, causing him to flip over the blankets and leap up.

They were sitting side by side, one's head resting on the other's shoulder.

The other's head was tilted downward, his hand holding a bottle in a death grip. As scared as Maxie was, he had to be certain, so he touched one's face. Hard and cold as marble, a ball of frozen snot caked on his lips. He kept staring until he heard a voice in his head say, "Maxie, get the hell out of here, now!"

He packed up his stuff and left the park, then called the cops from a distance away. Didn't want to be there to answer questions and see his friends removed in a meat wagon. Several days later, he left town, never to return. Now he mostly sleeps by himself. He started drinking too. Go figure.

But the cold is good, it keeps people away. It's so peaceful here, as if I'm the only person left on this planet. Just a few squirrels scurrying about. Hope they don't eat too much of my alarm system. I opened my coat a little from the top, enough to tuck my face inside, and went to sleep. A dreamless state, yet restful. A short time later, a voice woke me up. "Hey, buddy!" It was two officers, a safe distance away. "Are you all right?"

"Yeah, I'm okay, just catching up on some sleep."

"Out here? It's fucking freezing! Want to go to a shelter?"

"No thank you, I want to live to see my next birthday."

"That bad, huh?"

"Worse than you know, officer."

"You know what my next question is."

"Not a drop, I don't drink, only coffee."

"I hate doing this, but we got a call, you got to leave the park."

"Not a problem. Merry Christmas, officers."

"Merry Christmas, buddy, and try to get off the streets. You don't belong."

He's wrong, I do belong. I had a good life and I screwed up, plain and simple. But if I start thinking about it now, depression will set in again. Got to keep busy, focus on working to exhaustion. Time to do some serious canning.

I worked the tourist spots, Times Square, the theater district, and near the cathedral. Pickings were good and I met a lot of nice people, mostly foreigners. A few offered money, with respect. I refused, but they were most insistent, saying it would be a personal insult if I didn't accept a token of their goodwill. Not to embarrass them, I took it and thanked them profusely. Different cultures, their methods of helping others I praise. But our country, I'm ashamed to say, is a fucking joke! This mighty nation yearly gives out billions of your dollars in foreign aid, some of which goes for food, medical supplies, and housing construction. I agree it's very humane of us, but we need to take care of our own first! Right now there are so many here lacking a proper diet. Bureaucrats say apply for food stamps. Bullshit I say. If you're lucky to meet all the requirements, the amount of stamps given won't last until the next allotment. Here we are so close to Christmas, and a lot won't be able to have the traditional dinner. Or any dinner at all.

By nighttime my right eye was throbbing. Infected? I gently probed with my fingers, sore to the touch, then covered the good eye. Still can't see anything but a gray film. Swell! I should buy a fucking eye patch then change my street name to Pirate Man! Fucking motherfucker! So filled with black anger, I kicked my wagon over onto the street. People on the sidewalk cautiously picked up the pace away from me. I don't blame them.

Trying so hard to calm down, I couldn't even light a cigarette! I stood there and took deep breaths until I was feeling better and went over to lift up my wagon. It was a struggle. I didn't realize how heavy it was.

Relaxing outside a department store, sitting on one of their water pipes. A woman approaches me. She looks vaguely familiar.

"I like your hat, here, take this please, and Merry Christmas." Handing me ten dollars.

"Thank you, ma'am, Merry Christmas."

What was so special about my hat, you ask? It was a baseball cap with a message: KIDS NEED HUGS NOT DRUGS. The woman? Took a few minutes to remember: Jackie Onassis. Or maybe someone who looked just like her. It's been a while since I watched the news.

Time for me to leave, it's getting late and I don't want to be here when they light up the decorations. A beautiful sight to behold, people stopping and staring, more picture taking, an atmosphere of joy for all except me.

I stopped by a volunteer dressed as Santa, standing next to a makeshift chimney for donations. Rapidly ringing his bell, children dragging their parents over. "Mommy, Daddy, look, it's Santa Claus!" Might have been the tenth time today seeing one, but you know how kids are. "Wow! Santa is everywhere!" The parents make another donation, surely thinking, "Hopefully no more after this, I have no change left."

We make eye contact. As I'm getting nearer, there's a look of apprehension on his face. Is he thinking I'm going to do something crazy? Walk away from my wagon and head towards the chimney, where I insert the ten dollars. "Merry Christmas, Santa!"

That cheered him up. "Ho ho ho! A merry Christmas to you too, sir."

"Daddy! Daddy!"

Jessica? Could it be?

"Daddy!"

I am so afraid to turn around, to have her see me this way.

"Daddy, pick me up pleeeeeease!"

I'm crying again. Slowly turning. It's not my Jessica, just another beautiful child being held by her daddy. She smiled and waved at me. Oh, God. I couldn't look at her again, got to leave here now.

Streets congested, more and more people, it seemed as though everyone was blocking my way out. Out of sheer desperation I launched myself and my wagon into oncoming traffic. Yelling, car horns, brakes screeching, they all swerved around me just like before. Farther up, the crowd thinned out and I managed to slip through, have to remember to leave here earlier next time. If this area wasn't good for canning, I would never come back. Will just have to wait a little while longer until the holidays are over. Lord, hear my prayers.

Walked several blocks and saw George's deli still open, stomach growling for food. Perfect timing, no customers inside.

"Hey, George, burning the midnight oil?"

"Hi, Cadillac Man, how have you been?"

"Same old shit, different day. What are you doing here?"

"I open and close the place, six days a week. Coffee?"

"Yes, please. Gee, that's a lot of hours."

"That's the price you pay as an owner. My sons want no part of it. They're grown with families now, so it's me and the missus here for another two years, then retirement in Florida."

"That's great, George."

"You hungry? And sorry about the coffee, it's several hours old."

"Taste good to me. I'm so hungry I could eat my sister's flea-bitten, stanky underwear!"

Laughing, he went over to the steam table, reached for an aluminum pan, and loaded it with cheese macaroni and meatballs. Yummy.

"Here you go. More coffee?"

"Yes and, wow, there's enough food here to feed a marching band!"

"Eat! Eat! I made extra for you."

"Why so much, George? I can't afford all of that."

"Who said anything about paying? It's on me. I can't save any of this for tomorrow, it has to be thrown out. My missus prepares the food fresh daily. The steam table was her idea, business has been great ever since."

"Thank you, George. Can I at least pay for the coffee?"

"No, I was about to drain it, it's closing time."

"Drain it? Wait a minute, I'll be right back!"

Went to my wagon, searching, ah, there you are!

"Here, George, fill 'er up please."

"A coffeepot? Amazing!"

"Yeah, I found it in the trash a while ago, still works. Then I bought a camp stove. Hot coffee whenever I want."

"You know, I can't tell you what to do, but the cold weather is coming. You should try and find a warm place to stay."

"Thanks, George, I'll be all right. If need be, have lots of warm hiding spots out here."

"You don't deserve to live a life like this."

Looked like he had to say more about the matter, then changed his mind.

"Well, better close now and head home before the missus starts to worry," he says.

"You're a lucky man, to have someone waiting at home."

"Yes, I am. Thirty-three years together."

"Want me to stick around and help you with anything?"

"No, thanks for dropping by, come in anytime."

"Okay, I will, but only on one condition."

"What is that?"

"That you let me pay for my food and coffee next time, please."

"Okay, Cadillac Man, I understand. It's a deal," he says, shaking my hand.

Secured the goodies in the wagon. I moved across the street and watched him close up.

Wish there were more like him. And I meant what I said about paying next time. By making a gesture of payment I would feel that I'm not taking advantage of him. Going back all the time to receive freebies and not doing anything for it just doesn't set right in my mind.

Brrr! Tina was right, the temperature's dropping fast. If I left now, would be at her place within an hour, but not tonight. I want to be alone, to sleep under the stars and to pray. Sometimes I pray out loud and don't want an audience, just me and the Boss, one-on-one.

To voice my concerns and innermost thoughts, even at times to vent out anger. To ask why I was put in this position and to end it as quickly as possible. Seems to me some people will only talk to the Boss when there is no other way of resolving a problem. They need a miracle. Whether to heal a loved one, a job, or a new beginning in life, he hears them all. Bet I know which ones he gets a laugh from.

After walking several blocks and not wanting to go any farther, I came across an island in the middle of the street that had a park bench. A good spot for a cookout. Set up my stove on a milk crate, then reheated some of the food. The aroma filled my nostrils and made my stomach growl, hard to believe I ate about two hours ago.

Perhaps it's the thought of what George said, home cooking. Wherever you go or whatever you see, there are reminders of the life you once had. Food always tasted better when it was made at home, right? What George gave me tastes really good. I put the coffeepot on the stove, and that was when I got company.

"Hey! What the hell you think you're doing?"

Look to my left. "Heating up some coffee, sir."

A police car pulled up, disbelief etched on the officer's face. "I don't believe it!" he said as the both of them got out. Coffee is really brewing now, steam filling the air, the bouquet touching our noses.

"I don't fucking believe it, making fucking coffee on Park Avenue! And in the fucking middle of the street too!"

His partner was trying to keep his composure but finally lost it. "Ray, we're not in the middle of the street. We're on an island."

"Yeah, yeah, I know that Manhattan is a fucking island." More laughter.

"Ray, what we're standing on is an island too." Looking down at his feet.

"No fucking shit?"

Now Ray's partner is staring at me. I'm trying so hard to contain the laughter inside.

"Coffee is ready, would you officers like some?" No thanks, said the partner. Watching me pour, they look spellbound. I guess you don't see this sort of thing every day, not in the street anyways. "Look, Bill, he has fucking cream and sugar too! You got any glazed doughnuts to go with it?"

"Sorry, sir, I ate the last one earlier."

"Bill, this fucking guy is incredible! Listen, the reason we stopped, I saw the flame and thought you were going to torch up the fucking place."

"Only reheating my food, sir."

"I see that. Look, do me a favor and put away the stove before someone driving by sees it, then thinks you're a fucking crazed arsonist and calls the fucking fire department."

"Consider it done, sir." I put the lid back on the Sterno.

"Look, Bill, he has fucking cooking mittens!"

"I don't want to burn my hands, sir."

Bill grabs his radio and talks into it. "We got a call, Ray."

"Okay." Ray looks at me. "How much longer are you going to be here?"

"Just a few minutes, to put my stuff away, then I'll leave."

"Good, because we'll be back later to make sure, it's nothing personal, it's—"

"Ray! Come on!"

"Hold on a sec! Anyway, these fucking rich people on Park Avenue complain about everything and that includes your type, get the picture?"

"Yes, I do, sir."

"Okay, then take care of yourself and a merry Christmas."

"Same to you, sir, and, sir, a quick question."

"Yes?"

"You're from Brooklyn, right?"

"Yeah, how did you know?"

"I recognized the accent." The *fucking* accent, I mean.

"Born and raised!" Then walked back to the car.

Back inside, he says, "Stay warm tonight!"

"I will. Merry fucking Christmas."

Such a big grin he had. "Okay, Bill, let's haul fucking ass!"

Flashing lights pop on and away they go.

Less traffic now, which means it's late, I stayed here too long. St. Pat's is about a mile away if I take the long way around to avoid any late-night tourists. A good plan. There's a bitter cold wind, only a few people out. Arriving by the side entrance I slowly, quietly pulled my wagon up the stairs into the churchyard.

So peaceful, my heart felt his presence. I whispered softly, "Thank you, Boss, for allowing me to bed down in your house tonight. Amen."

I'm on holy ground.

"O Heavenly Father, protect my wife, children, and family and hope that someday they will forgive me. Please, Father, take this tired soul of mine into your kingdom tonight. Amen."

Prayers done, I happened to look up at the rectory. Standing by the window was a priest, gesturing with his hand the sign of the cross. I was being blessed.

Motioned with my lips, *Thank you, Father*. He then closed the curtains. I covered myself up, sleeping bag like a shroud. "I am ready, Father."

Closed my eyes, and perhaps a minute later a shadow appeared, crossing over my closed eyelids. He is here. I smiled and whispered, "Thank you."

Someone is shaking me. The Boss?

Removing the covers from my face, I see a priest smiling and a bright glow behind him.

"The Boss sent you to get me?"

"Excuse me, my son?"

"God sent you. You came for my soul, right?"

"None of that, my son, I have come to check on you, you are very much alive. My prayers were answered."

"You prayed for me? Why?"

"Because last night was so cold."

"Last night?"

Causing me to sit up so fast. He stepped back, startled. It's early morning, and that bright glow behind him was the sun. "Shit! Dammit! Sorry, Father."

I'm crying. "It's not fair, Father, I wanted to die and he knows, yet he's keeping me here! I don't know how much more of this I'm going to deal with, Father!"

"What is your name, my son?"

"Cadillac Man."

"You have an unusual name, Cadillac Man."

"It's street, Father. All homeless have one. We don't want anyone to pry into our lives. Just leave us alone! Why did you interfere, Father?"

"Me? What did I do?"

"I wanted the Boss to take me last night. I even saw his shadow go across my eyes, and at that moment I thought I was leaving for heaven. He heard your prayers, then decided not to take me."

"Do you really believe that, Cadillac Man?"

"Yes, I do! I can't think of any other explanation why he would keep me here."

"Perhaps he has other plans for you."

"Other plans? Such as?"

"That is for you to find out, when the timing and the circumstances are right. God will be by your side to guide you. He needs people like you."

"Like me? What the hell can I do?"

"I know you're suffering, my son, but remember, Jesus suffered on the cross for our sins. Keep your faith strong, believe in the Almighty, and find comfort in prayer. He loves us all, we are his children."

"I'll try, Father. I owe you an apology."

"An apology? For what?"

"For raising my voice, using profanity, and saying that you interfered with my plans. Father, you can pray for me whenever you want to."

He smiled and placed his hand on my shoulder. "I will pray for you."

His words brought tears to my eyes. Nobody had ever said that to me. My heart felt at peace. "Thank you, Father, I will add you to my prayer list."

"Thank you, Cadillac Man, and now I must leave you, there are church affairs I need to attend to. Go in peace, my son," he said, blessing me.

"God bless you, Father."

That smile of his came back again and so did my tears. As he was entering the church, I called after him, "Hey, Father! I'll come back someday to see you!"

"I would like that very much, you are always welcome in God's house." Then he went inside.

At that moment I wanted to walk through those doors too.

After a few minutes of praying and a lot of effort I walked outside, to find several tourists taking pictures of my wagon, then posing alongside of it. They were having such a good time, I stayed back and watched. Two little Asian boys grabbed my flags and ran around with them until a woman said something and they put them back.

That was when I approached. They have fear in their eyes. I get this sort of reaction from most. Gosh, do I really look that scary? I figured out a way to put them at ease, went over to my wagon, took the flags, handed them to the boys, and said, "Welcome to America!" The boys were thrilled, the woman smiled.

More and more people arriving, my cue to get out of here. Just before I left, the boys ran over to me, said something, then bowed. I bowed back and said, "You're welcome," causing them to giggle. Waved bye-bye.

Perhaps they'll remember this part of their visit here and the flags too. I was glad to do it, besides, I have extra ones in my wagon. Why are they on my wagon? To show to everybody how much I love our country, America, land of opportunity, to walk freely regardless of your ethnic and religious background, a place to pursue all hopes and dreams.

Time to split, my stomach roaring like the MGM lion. Bypassed George's place, he's probably busy with the morning crowd, and went to a bodega I knew for a real cup of coffee, probably the best in town. So strong and good-tasting it will keep you awake for days. Primo rocket fuel.

Time to get to work. Depending on how much I make today, may decide not to work tomorrow and just hang out with friends. It's times like this you look forward to, catching up on the latest gossip. Nothing ever mentioned about local and world news because none of us reads the paper. There's no reason to. Don't ask what date it is, maybe a few would know, especially the ones that are expecting a check.

Go over and ask Old Crow who is president. He will tell you Jimmy Carter. My guess is that was true when he became homeless. It's his last Christmas too. He's dying. He knows it, we all do. For some time, he's had a real nasty cough, chucking up huge globs of blood. Is he scared? Hell no! Death is our only escape. When it happens, I will pray for his soul as I have for so many others. We'll erect a street shrine in memory, candles, cigarettes, and a bottle of cheap juice, one of his favorites. We won't talk about Old Crow in the past tense, we'll keep his memory alive, as if he still walks among us.

Will they do the same for me? I hope so. No juice please, though, only coffee.

Now that he's too weak to go canning, we feed him as much as possible, keep him well supplied with juice and smokes. It's not out of pity. The things we do he has to earn, cashing in tickets or watching our wagons, simple jobs. It's a way of preserving his dignity. So I'm headed to the redeemer to see my friend, my brother, to light up a smoke together and to listen to whatever he has to say. There is a chill in the air, but the love for my friends keeps me warm. And I know they love me too.

No, we don't use that four-letter word. It's expressed in other ways, a hug or hand gestures and street language. Still, it has the same effect. No kissing though, unless of course you're getting laid or someone is whistling on your skin flute. Or both, if you're a lucky bastard!

At the redeemer, everybody's there except Old Crow. Tina spots me and comes running, something happened. Old Crow? Damn hope not. Maybe another problem.

Stops in front of me, a steady flow of smoke puffs while trying to regain her breath.

"Yo, Tina, breathe through the nose instead and slowly. And shut your fucking mouth!"

Trying to snap her out of it.

"Better now, Tina?"

"Yeah, thanks. One of these days I have to quit smoking."

"Yeah, right, you and me and a million others. So why are your balls in an uproar?"

"Cadillac Man, do I look like I have a pair of balls?"

"Sorry, just a figure of speech. So what's wrong?"

"It's Old Crow."

"Is he—" I won't say *dead*.

"No, thank God. He's inside his house and doesn't want to come out. Cadillac Man, he hasn't eaten in days!"

"What? Where the fuck is Bobby?" Bobby takes care of him.

"Don't get mad at him. He leaves food, then comes back later and it's untouched. He tries to talk him into eating, but Old Crow tells him to get lost. Even I tried. I bought a bottle of juice to lure him out and got my ass chewed out. We got to do something."

"Maybe he is too sick to come out, Tina. I'll check him out."

"Can I come along? And what if he won't listen to you?"

"Sure. Oh, he will listen to me. I have a way of convincing people."

Cashing-in can wait, my gut is saying something isn't right. Fortunately his house isn't far, only a few blocks away. Tina looks nervous. "What are you thinking?"

"Not thinking anything. Just praying."

Approaching, I see Bobby is already there. Old Crow's guardian to the end. Over the years the two of them hoisted many a pint, so I heard, and now I feel bad for him.

"Any luck, Bobby?"

"No, Cadillac Man, he still refuses to come out. I don't know what else to do."

You could feel his pain and sorrow. "Stay here, both of you."

Walking towards his place, I realize it looks like an oversized coffin. Perhaps someday it will be. To clear up any confusion you may have, his house is an old cardboard refrigerator box. Still sturdy and big enough to accommodate someone my size or in his case quite comfortably. Thickness alone makes it weather resistant, to keep you dry and the draft out. Add a few blankets and you have a winter home. We call them box Hiltons.

Old Crow's place is located behind an apartment building and carefully concealed by a row of garbage cans. The kindhearted super lets him stay. In exchange he keeps the place clean. But now Bobby does his work. It pains me to think that a person, any person, will be found dead in this manner. Then again, it's his choice, a place to rest his body before embarking to the Land of Lost Souls, the final destination. I knock on the cardboard, causing it to wobble a bit. "Yo, Old Crow! It's Cadillac Man!"

No answer. Knocked several more times. "Yo, Old Crow!" Still no reply. Is he sleeping? Ignoring me? Or worse? The last thought frightens me and there is only one way to find out.

At the end of the box is an opening. Easy to get in by crawling, but once inside you're totally helpless and open to attack. It does happen on occasion. Had to get down on all fours to do a look-see, then it hit me, a horrible stench. Bad but familiar. Eyes burning, fighting the urge to throw up, I quickly raised my head up and sucked in deep breaths of the cool air. Pulled myself up and went over to the wagon, searched through my bags until I found what I was looking for.

Tina said, "What's wrong? Is he all right?"

"Not quite sure, I'll let you know in a few minutes."

I unscrewed the cap and poured a generous amount of aftershave lotion into my hand, then spread it onto my face. It burned like fire on my sores and scabs, but at least it would counteract the odor within the box. I'm hoping. Back down on all fours again, tilted my head inside. Now the odor is strong but bearable.

He's completely covered with blankets, in a fetal position. I see no movement. I start praying.

Then a low moan, my prayers were answered. Thank you, Lord. In a low voice I said, "Yo, Old Crow, it's Cadillac Man."

More movement, the blankets muffling his voice. "Go away, Cadillac Man, please leave me alone." Sounded so weak.

"Sorry, my friend, not today." Reached up and under the blankets and grabbed his ankle, then gently pulled him towards me. It was so easy.

Too weak to put a struggle, he was saying, "No, no, please." Blankets unraveled, he is naked. And something else, from the waist down, smeared with caked-on shit. I wanted so much to hug him and say, "Everything will be all right," but that would be a lie. Oh, man, now he is crying. I put my head out the opening. "Hey, Bobby! Come over here, I need some help!" He comes running, Tina by his side.

"No, no, please," Old Crow was saying, "don't let them see me this way."

"Don't let it worry you, you're among friends who care."

Bobby arrived first, took one look, and said, "Aw, dammit!"

Tina stopped short, a few feet behind, frozen as if in fear.

"Help me pick him up, Bobby."

As we were lifting, I looked over at Bobby. He was crying, Tina still not moving.

"Hold him while I go in for the blanket."

I reached in, pulled one out, snapped it into the air, and pieces of shit went flying. Something else too, a rat, a good-sized one. Looked at the blanket, stains everywhere. I dropped it to the ground. For anyone to live under these conditions is unthinkable, not caring what happens next.

Take a good look at Old Crow standing. Look at him! Just an empty shell, life's being and soul long gone. Down to skin and bones, body completely covered with sores, shit stains, dried and some fresh, probably even has maggots inside him. Was once part of a family and for whatever the reason wound up with us.

His end is near. We'll comfort him as much as possible. I went to my wagon to get an extra bag of clothes I keep on hand for those in need, plus several packets of diaper wipes. An unpleasant task ahead.

When I passed Tina, I asked if she was all right. She nodded uh-huh but then let loose with a spray of vomit. Guess she wasn't okay, but I had more important things to attend to.

"Bobby, tilt over the box, find his shoes, and be careful, some four-legged critters might scurry out."

Damn, I hate those things!

"Wait, go to my wagon first and get a plastic bag for all of his belongings you can salvage."

All during the conversation with Bobby, Old Crow remained silent.

"Old Crow, I need you to do me a favor. Can you stand on your own for a few minutes?"

His head down, looking at the pavement, I just barely heard him. "I don't think so."

With Bobby busy, I need an extra pair of hands and there was one person left available. "Yo, Tina! Get over here!" Slowly walked towards us, then took one look at Old Crow and threw up again. "When you're finished barfing your fucking stomach out, I need you to hold on to Old Crow. Hurry up!"

She came over.

"Hold him up. If you have to barf again, turn your head.

"All right, my friend, I'm going to clean you."

"I'm so sorry," he says.

"For what? For being a little dirty? No big deal."

"I'm dying, Cadillac Man."

I was so choked up I couldn't reply, just kept on scrubbing. Never seen so much shit in all my life. There was even some in his hair and face. I did everywhere, including the ass, balls, and pecker. Made no difference to me. Just like doing a kid.

"Cadillac Man, do you have a cigarette?"

His voice took me by surprise, a spark of life. "Sure. Anything else?"

"I'm cold. Hungry too." More life!

"Okay, let's put some clothes on you. I have a nice heavy shirt with sweater and a pair of jeans. Sorry that they're a little big on you. Hey, Bobby, find his shoes yet? Got any juice?"

"Just found them, and, yeah, I got a bottle in my back pocket."

"Get over here then. Old Crow's feet are cold and he is thirsty!" That remark brought a smile to his face and mine too. Handed him the bottle and he took a generous swig. "Hey, Old Crow, save some of that for me," Tina said, grabbing the bottle. By the time it got back to Bobby, it was almost empty and we all laughed.

"Okay, next step. Tina, bring him over to your place for a hot shower and hot meal."

"Me too?" Bobby said.

"You too."

The look on her face was priceless, one big O without the teeth.

"Relax, Tina. I got plenty of food, macaroni and cheese with meatballs bigger than my own, enough for the three of you."

Took my wagon. "Come on, guys, I'll walk with you."

So the four of us went to Tina's place. Along the way we took several breaks because Old Crow was tired. His coughing spells scared us, too much blood. Arriving, I handed over the food, extra clothes, and blankets. Tina reminded me to drop by later, and Bobby said I should spread the word around to get Old Crow a new box. Just before I left, Old Crow called me over.

Standing in front of him, waiting for a reply. His appearance was breaking my heart. Extended my arms and he walked into them, we hugged each other. Kissed his cheek to show respect and my love. As we parted, I said, "Old Crow, don't forget to wash behind your ears!" causing both of us to laugh.

"And between my toes too!" he said. More laughter.

"I'll be back later. Tina, make sure he stays awhile!"

Felt so drained, physically and mentally. I stopped by a coffee shop a short distance away, bought coffee and an egg sandwich, then headed to the redeemer. The place was empty so I did all my stuff quickly, then cashed in my tickets and left in a hurry. It's too quiet here. Went by the church and nobody is around. They're probably hiding out, taking an afternoon snooze, or back out canning. It's what you do, day after day, same boring routine, especially during the wintertime.

Less people out and that means less trouble from predators, seems like most take time off for the holidays. Merry fucking Christmas. I think in my case I was in the wrong place at the wrong time. I want payback so badly I can taste it, but the chances are slim to none of ever meeting up with them again.

Damn, I don't even know how many there were or what they looked like. I still can't see out of the one eye. Maybe there is permanent damage. Well, there's nothing I can do about it now. Another part of street life and no doubt more to come. What horrors Old Crow had to endure over the years, I cannot imagine.

In no mood to sleep, so I went canning, steering clear of the holiday-crowd area, even though the pickings are fat. I opted for a quieter residential area, row after row of brownstones with their fire escapes and windows adorned with Christmas decorations and lights. Was the true holiday spirit lurking inside, or were they just showpieces? A lot of unhappy people are alone for the holidays, waiting by the phone or hoping to receive an unexpected visitor to cheer them up, let the holiday season begin! But you know and I know that only happens in the movies. So many curse this time of year, especially when they hear of the ways others are going to celebrate. You don't want to turn on the TV or radio, more reminders, worst yet go for a walk, decorations everywhere!

Never again will I make love with my wife. Never again will I hear my children say, "I love you, Daddy." Losing this, I cease to exist. Merry fucking

Christmas. And look at the aluminum cans I just picked up, a nice picture of fucking Santa and his fucking reindeer.

A car stops and double-parks on my right side, a tree strapped on top. A young couple get out acting all excited. If I was to venture a guess, it's their first Christmas together. They both looked at me and smiled. "Merry Christmas, sir."

Yep. Probably newlyweds. "Merry Christmas to you too!"

Visions of my wife and child putting ornaments on the tree without me came pouring in, it was devastating. Yanking my hair out, trying to remove the thoughts! Jessica's mother picking her up to put a star on top. Didn't realize I was yelling out loud until I noticed people walking towards me abruptly crossed to the other side. One of them said, "Shaddup and get a fucking life!" Usually that sort of remark, the guy would win a free trip to the emergency room. But not this time. Lucky for him, it's the holidays. Plus, he is right.

A few blocks away I found a neighborhood joint, a place that basically caters to the working stiffs and people who just want to get a cup of coffee and hang out for a while. Hassle free. I feel better, right at home here. So what if the cook has a cigarette in his mouth. Ashes won't kill you. The smells are overwhelming. Fried eggs, hamburgers, cigarettes, ah, paradise! Looking at the menu, I see one of my favorites, meat loaf, mashed potatoes, peas. I give my order to the waitress, who then yells to the cook.

"Yo, Pete! Gimme a dead dog in a green blanket!" Don't you just love restaurant lingo? This lady has class!

When the food arrived, my eyes bugged out, such generous portions! And the coffee? The best! Good and strong, probably never washed out the urn, doesn't matter to me! She came back asking if I wanted a second serving of anything. Sure, I said, of everything. It's not every day I get to eat like this.

Paid the bill and was all set to go when I noticed the waitress waving at me to wait. What happened? She was holding a brown paper bag. "Here, sweetie, in case you get hungry later. Merry Christmas."

Took a whiff, more meat loaf. "Thank you, ma'am, Merry Christmas."

I bet if I walked in with no money saying I was hungry, they would have given me something. Unlike the yuppie restaurant that will chase you away, then afterwards any leftover food is dumped in the garbage. One day right in front of me and some of my people, an employee at one of those places deliberately dumped bleach over all the food in the dumpster, pouring slowly and watching our reaction. I wanted to bash that fucking smirk off his face, but that would have created problems for everyone so I did the next best thing. I started hanging out in front of the place. Picking my nose or scratching my balls in plain view of the customers, and others did the same.

On my way back to Tina's I stopped for a cigarette break and noticed I had company a distance away. A dog. I tried eluding him by going different directions, but it was useless, he had my scent. Maybe he smelled the food too.

Not your typical lost dog. Looked like a junkyard mutt, weird-looking and very big. I've seen this type before in my travels, usually in packs, extremely skittish, avoiding human contact. Never try to get friendly with them, they say. I heard stories that they get scared and then turn mean with no warning.

His size tells me to keep my bayonet within reach, just in case. I can't outrun him, I'd have to stand my ground if he attacked. Just as an experiment, I turned the wagon around and started walking towards him. He took off in the opposite direction.

I went back to canning, filled up most of a bag. But an hour later on another break, there he was again and this time even closer. I'm sitting on a stoop and he's slowly creeping up to me. I didn't make any sudden moves. My bayonet was out of reach. Still coming. Then he stopped and sat down in front of me, barely a foot away, just staring now. I did the same back, and he started to growl. Low and tough, like he means it. My only course of action would be a kick to his face, but I doubt I could hurt him from a sitting position. Growling got louder, teeth flashing, and inched closer. I kept staring, not wanting to move. As strange as it sounds, I felt calm. The growling stopped and now he was sniffing my hand. A confused look on his face, starts to lick my fingers. Slowly, with my other hand, I reach out and pet his forehead.

I never in my life had a pet. My parents were against it. Most in my neighborhood were. Just another mouth to feed. We had a few strays by the river, and I'm sorry to say as kids we used to abuse them, throwing bottles and other things at them. A sick way of having fun, even the grown-ups did it. I always wanted a dog, though. Especially now, a companion to keep company with on those lonely nights.

"We're both homeless, fella, let's be friends. First you need a name, bet you never had one before."

It came to me right away: Recycle. Seems right, doesn't it? He was found on the streets. Said the name several times out loud, and he turned his head a little each time I said it. All of a sudden, he stopped licking and started backing away, growling, then he turned and ran off. I guess he didn't like the name. I waited a half hour, but he wasn't coming back.

Oh, well, guess it wasn't meant to be, and out here you never get your hopes up. For a brief moment I had a new friend. Nice to have one, felt good to pet him, feel that warmth. I got up, grabbed my wagon, and got moving. A few times I turned to look, but nope, no sight of him.

When I arrived at Tina's place, I put my wagon in the backyard and tapped three times on her first-floor apartment window. It's everybody's sign to let her know we're coming in, and there she is with a big, tooth-less grin peeking out from the window shade. Took the bag with the meat loaf, Old Crow is going to enjoy this. Or else! Greeted me at the door with such a kiss, it felt like she sucked the lips right off my face! Damn!

She laughed a little. "Sorry, Cadillac Man, I'm so happy to see you. I was worried thinking you weren't going to show up. Come on in." The place was nicely furnished and orderly, smells so clean you would think you were going into a hospital ward.

Anyone staying overnight would have to sleep on the floor, covered with a thin plastic sheet, because some of the guys do have accidents. But one thing that really drives me fucking crazy, there are cats everywhere!

Not living, breathing ones, but pictures, posters, blankets, a huge fucking carpet with two big-eyed, smiling kittens!

I can't even take a dump because the seat cover has decals of dancing kittens. All of this stuff and the funniest thing is, she's allergic to cat hair! Makes her sneeze and break out with hives all over. Go figure. Behind her back the guys call the place Cathouse or House of Pussy.

"Tina, where are Bobby and Old Crow?"

"They left about an hour ago to get something to eat, then Old Crow wanted to go back to his box. I told them they could stay here for the night and some of my food, free of charge. But no dice."

"How was he feeling?"

"Sounded better. When he came out of the shower, I hardly recognized him, he looked like a new man. Bobby too.

"That reminds me," she said, reaching for a garbage bag. "You know the drill, Cadillac Man."

"Indeed I do, and you might as well take this." I handed her the paper bag.

"What's this?"

"I wanted Old Crow to have it. Being that he's not here, I hope you like the meat loaf and side dishes."

"Meat loaf? That's one of my favorites. Thank you."

One of Tina's rules is clean body, clean clothes. Makes sense. So while you're in the shower, your clothes are being washed, and anything that drops out or is found in the pockets is hers. Finders keepers, losers weepers, she likes to say. I'll play the game, a few crumpled-up dollars and all of my loose change to keep her happy, but my big money is in a plastic bag tucked inside my shoe.

Ah! A shower. I get goose bumps every time I think about having one. Entering the bathroom, I see something new, the shower curtain. Unfuckingbelieveable!

"Yo, Tina!"

"What's the matter, Cadillac Man?!"

"When the fuck did you get this shower curtain?"

"Do you like it? I think it's cute."

"Cute? A bunch of fucking cats prancing around playing fiddles. That's fucking cute?"

"Yes, now take your shower!

"Cadillac Man! Want anything to drink?"

"Yeah! Coffee if you have it!"

I swear, if there are cats on the coffee cup, I'll run out of here screaming, clothes or not. Word is bond. She came in with a serving tray with two large cups of coffee and, hooray, no cats on them.

"Someone is tapping on the window, listen," she said.

Sounded urgent. Tina left and came back with my clothes, clean and hot.

Opening the door, I was greeted by late-night winter's chill. It's rare that I spend much time in a warm place, so it took me a few seconds to readjust to the temperature. Turning the corner, I saw a familiar face.

"Yo, Bobby! Quit the tapping, you're waking up the whole fucking neighborhood!"

Looked startled at first, then relieved. "Sorry, but it's important!"

Just then Tina joined us. "What is it, Bobby?"

"Old Crow is sick again, really sick. His cough's worse than before, I don't think he's going to make it too much longer."

"Don't say it like that, Bobby!" She's crying.

"Sorry, Tina, we have to face up to the fact he's a goner."

Better get over there, a friend needs me. Wouldn't you do the same? Said good-bye to Tina, took my wagon, and hauled ass, hoping and praying we get there in time.

"Damn, this shortcut is taking forever, Bobby!"

"Trust me, the usual way, we would have to travel another thirty minutes, but by cutting through these alleys we'll be there in five, tops."

Word is bond, we arrived in the amount of time he said. It really pays to know the streets, every nook and cranny. Don't waste your time trying to remember street names or numbers, use the landmarks instead. Shape and/or color of building, sometimes a park, signs that stand out from the rest. If you ask me where Tina lives, I can honestly say I don't know the address, yet through the twists and turns with my wagon and shortcuts, I'll get you there. Forget about using a car, I would get the both of us lost.

Then I heard it, a sweet sound of sorts, a hacking cough that sounds horrible but means that he's still alive. Thank you, Lord.

"Bobby, I can't believe he wanted to go back in that stinking box!"

"It's a little better now. I brought some cleaning supplies and scrubbed it out."

Even through the thickness of the box, his cough was much worse than earlier. Stooping down and leaning inside, I said, "Yo, Old Crow, it's Cadillac Man. I've come to see how you're feeling and if you need anything."

Between coughs, he said, "I feel like shit. Where's Bobby?"

"He's here, a few feet away from me."

"Ask him if I have any juice left. I could use a taste right now."

Bobby reached in his back pocket and came out with a pint and handed it to me.

"Yeah, he got some, slide down a little, I'll pass it to you."

Reaches down and takes a swig, passes the bottle back.

"Take a taste with me, Cadillac Man, please."

Everybody out here knows I don't drink anymore. But to eat and drink with someone who is dying is a sign of respect, a toast to the hereafter. Took a big swig and almost choked. "Damn, Old Crow, what's in this shit, antifreeze?"

He started laughing weakly. "Better than that—Old Crow piss." Then had a coughing fit. I looked at Bobby, the sound scared the hell out of us.

It made me take another swig. I passed it back to Bobby, who took a huge taste, leaving just enough in case Old Crow wanted more.

"Bobby, go to your house and get some sleep. I'll stay with him."

"No, man, I'm staying. Old Crow and I have been friends for a long time." Without saying another word he walked over to the box, then crawled in. Inside I heard him say, "I'm here for you, buddy, go to sleep."

Now he was praying out loud and I joined in. Lord, hear our prayers. Made my bed next to the box, then lay down looking up at the stars, thinking, "Will there be one more taken tonight?" Leaned my back against the box to let them know I was there. Sleep came seconds later.

"Rise and shine, Cadillac Man!" It was Bobby's voice, sounding cheerful. Flipped the blanket off my face, morning sun was bright and blinding. I made out two figures standing above me.

The one good eye focused in. Finally I see Bobby and next to him with a big grin, Old Crow! Thank you, Lord! Tried to hide my joy by pretending to be grouchy.

"One of you better have some coffee!"

"And if we do?"

"I'll kiss your ass and say whoopee!"

"Word is bond, Cadillac Man?"

The way he said it, I got this uneasy feeling. "Word is bond, Bobby." Then I noticed both of them had one hand exposed, the other behind their back.

Bobby looked at Old Crow. "You want to go first?"

"Nah, let's do it together. Ready? One, two, three!"

The other hand came from behind, each holding a container of coffee. I was stunned! "You know what this means. Pucker up, Cadillac Man!"

"Guys can I have coffee first?"

Bobby said, "Yeah, but hurry up, it's cold out here and I don't want my ass to freeze up."

Both of them clowning, unbuckling their pants and showing me their asses. We all started laughing, they helped me up, and I hugged Old Crow. "How are you feeling today?"

"A lot better, thanks to you guys." But his eyes were saying, *I want to go home.* Where we all want to be, a place that will accept us for what we are, our home in the Land of Lost Souls.

"What are you guys going to do today?"

"Taking Old Crow to the diner and fatten him up. Then we'll go to the subway station and hustle up a few dollars. What about you? Going back to Tina's for a morning piece of ass?"

"Fuck no, I don't want to see any more asses this morning, male or female. I got a load of shit here to cash in at the redeemer. After that it's back to work picking up again. It keeps me busy."

"That's too much work for me," Bobby said. "I'll stick to panhandling."

"We hustle any way we can, Bobby, you're a panhandler and I'm a can handler. And a poet too." We were all laughing. Went over to Old Crow and gave him another hug. "Take care of yourself. Bobby, if you need me for anything, put a plastic bottle on the spiked fence by the church. I'll find you." He knows what I'd need him for, for when Old Crow comes to the end. With a heart full of sorrow I left. But Bobby will watch over Old Crow. He's a good friend to have, and I hope when my time is up, there will be someone like him by my side. Lord, hear my prayer.

Got to the redeemer and only the can and the plastic machine were working. This is not going to be a good day. I have a load of glass, and I can't go around town with a rattling wagon, too noisy and conspicuous.

Stopped in a diner for a quick breakfast, four coffees and two egg sandwiches plus two containers of coffee to go. If I'm lucky and make good time, I'll be able to catch up with everyone at the church for lunch.

I'm up near the edge of Harlem, north of 120th Street. Very depressing going through a neighborhood like this, most of its residents have double or triple locks on their doors. Playgrounds barren and lifeless, no children here, only remnants of the concrete jungle, needles and empty crack vials.

Saw a homemade memorial on the sidewalk, someone has died from a stray bullet and there will be more.

The redeemer is coming up. I'll have company, not my people, the gang-bangers and wannabe gangbangers. By the machines, five of them goofing around, but they could turn serious in a heartbeat.

Damn these fucking rattling bottles. Yep, I just got spotted. Oh, please, just let me do the bottles and I'm out of here. Don't want any trouble from these guys, got to play it cool. Avoid eye contact, and should they say anything to me, just ignore it.

Now they're huddled together, then separating to take positions by the machines. I still have time to turn and walk away, but that would make matters worse for me. I'd look like a chump, a coward, and therefore easy prey.

I moved forward.

Got to the glass machine and saw it was working, so far so good. I'm fortunate that they're on the side where I have full vision, although it will be hard to focus on them and the glass slot at the same time. Started feeding the machine rapidly, pretending not to notice them, any sudden move I could easily bash in the face of the closest one with a forty bottle. Faster I go, the glass grinder greedily gulping down each one, making an unnerving sound. Still no movement, what are they waiting for? Finished, I don't believe it! Was tallying up the slips when I heard, "Hey, old man, how much money did you make?" Wonder how much he makes, just sitting here in front of the store all day, taking five or ten bucks off everyone who comes. It's a short, stocky kid, maybe my weight and six inches shorter. Time for me to split, and quick. Avoiding eye contact, I cashed in my tickets and left without looking at them or crossing in front of them.

It took a while to reach familiar streets, to let my guard down a bit and to relax the aching legs from too much speed walking. I sat down on my milk crate and lit a cigarette. Feeling much better already. Looked at my watch and, dammit, I missed the church lunch by an hour. Even if I was to leave right now, by the time I get there everybody will be long gone, to their sleeping spots, maybe the local library. It's a good location to get out of the cold, just grab a large-size book, put your head down, and snooze. The staff won't bother you.

It gave me an idea, why not take an afternoon siesta? Lots of empty park benches across the street, it's perfect. Ah, I love weather like this, cool and crisp. I found a nice comfy park bench to rest on. Want to give it a try? Forget I asked, I already know what you would say.

The blind eye was beginning to throb. Reached into my pocket for some aspirins and popped a few. Stretched out, then covered my face with a blanket to prevent any outsiders from staring at me. Not to mention that sometimes accidents happen from above, meaning bird shit from the sky. Their accuracy is uncanny. And it doesn't taste good either!

Damn, this eye is hurting!

"Daddy! Please come home. Santa Claus is coming!"

"I wish I could, Jessica, perhaps someday."

"I love you, Daddy."

"I love you too, my darling, be a good girl for Mommy."

Sucks big-time, waking up crying. Not the sort of dream you want to think about for the rest of the day. Toss the blanket off, I have company.

It's a dog. Looks half-dead, scratched up and beaten. It's Recycle!

He's lying down by my side still sleeping, but for how long? Been in a fight for his life, looks like, chunks of missing hair, some fresh bite marks, and dried blood too. Growling now, perhaps dreaming about the last encounter, then the growling turns to whimpers.

Rather than scare him by petting him, I talk softly first. "Hi, Recycle."

His head jerked up suddenly, teeth flashing, and growling just like the first time we met.

Snout covered with gashes, must have been attacked from all sides to get these type of wounds. And still he prevailed! He knows I'm not afraid and slowly inches towards my swollen hands, sniffing and then finally licking them.

"Welcome back, Recycle. Good to see you again." Petting him. "Did you miss me? Well, I missed you!"

Then I made a big mistake. I slowly started to get up. He stepped back, barking at me. "Yo, chill out, I'm not going to hurt you. Be nice." Then he ran away. A few outsiders saw him coming and jumped out of the way, but he paid them no mind and kept going.

What am I doing that is so wrong that I can't make friends with a junkyard dog? And how did he know I was here? Now I'm worried that something else might happen to him. I never prayed for a dog before, but he needs it right now. "Lord, watch over Recycle and bring him back to me. Amen."

Might as well head over to the church. If nobody is there, I can go inside and light a few candles for my people and my children. One for Recycle too. Along the way I stopped in a grocery store and picked up a supply of canned dog food and biscuits.

The church was deserted, the kitchen closed until tomorrow, and everyone's probably seeking other places for an evening meal. A hot meal before bedtime keeps the body warm and sleep comes more quickly. (At least with us it does.) A good feeling, a reminder of the life we once had. But there's good news. I look to the spiked fence and there's no plastic bottle, meaning that Old Crow is still with us! One more night of good sleep and Bobby and Tina watching over him, maybe he'll be all right. At least he's all right for now, so my friend will be with me on Christmas. Time to give thanks to the Boss. I go inside.

Words couldn't describe the sheer joy and beauty, the essence of holiness. Lighting the candles, I felt him by my side. I prayed for my children, for their safety and well-being, and that someday they will forgive me. Old Crow for his suffering to end soon, for Sparrow. For my people's struggles and for our family in the Land of Lost Souls. And for Recycle to come back to me.

It was time for me to go, I had had my say with the Boss. I felt like I was leaving home. But this home I will always return to and be forgiven.

Going down the steps I am warmly greeted by churchgoers, reminding me about the holiday-eve midnight mass coming up. "I'll be here, looking forward to it. Merry Christmas, everyone!"

And maybe I can get Old Crow, Bobby, Tina, and others to join me. Nobody should be alone on Christmas. Reaching for my wagon, I noticed dollars stuffed within. I gathered them up, went back inside, then placed them in the poor box. There are people who need this more than I.

Out on the street the snow is coming down, a perfect Christmas scene. I retrieve my wagon and find a park bench to sit on and watch as the snow turns the city white. As I sit, people are clearing out of the sidewalks, going into shops to buy last-minute gifts and get out of the weather.

I'm there for a while before I realize I have company, looking at me from the corner. Through the snow, I can see the shape of a dog. Recycle! Not coming too close, but looking at me, as I'm looking at him. Moving very slowly, I reach into my wagon and take out the box of biscuits, open it up, and take one out for him. He's still just standing there, giving me that dopey look, but he's not running off this time. Merry Christmas, Recycle. Merry Christmas.

How I Got Here 1

I WAS FORTY-FOUR when I came out on the streets. Before then, I had a whole life, maybe a lot like yours. Childhood, growing up, some time in the army. Jobs (sometimes). And three beautiful kids, one way too early, when I was fourteen, and the others from my two marriages.

I was married for the first time in 1974. Laurie Havens, a lovely girl from the neighborhood whose father had mob ties. I was in the auxiliary police at that time, and she came in to sign up. She was seventeen years old. Back then you could join that organization at that age. I took her out on patrol with me several times and we just hit it off. The following year we got married, and the year after that we had our daughter, Christie. She's twenty-eight years old now. And then we had problems. Laurie started going out with my best friend, who happened to be the captain of the auxiliary police. So he made all kinds of accusations and got me demoted. After we got divorced, in 1981, she married him, and six months later he died. She went out to Jersey and inherited his business, his co-op. I didn't see my daughter until years later. The last time I was in touch with her she was living in Howard Beach. She told me she had gotten engaged and was getting married. That was 2000, New Year's Day.

My second wife, Kathy, I met through the police department too, at Midtown North in Manhattan. This was in '81. She was being interviewed for a position there, and I took one look at her and I said wow, she's the one for me. She was five foot nine, about 130 pounds, flaming-red hair, lots of freckles, green eyes, very, very pretty.

She wanted to be a volunteer cop, and I was there in the same capacity. There was something about her—even when I found out later she was a Jersey girl. At that time, she was living about a block from the precinct. She was working at the Blount Center and I was still working days at the meat market. This was Washington Beef, right on 9th Avenue and 42nd Street. I was in charge of shipping and receiving.

At that time I was a sergeant with the volunteer police, so I supervised the officers who would come in on any given night, who went on patrols and what have you. I wasn't really too happy with the way Kathy patrolled. Once I had to get after her about her appearance, the way she kept her uniform. A cop can't go out there with a hat on sideways, you know, your hat is supposed to be on straight. But other than that, when I got to know her, I started to like her.

There were times when we would team up together, and then there were other times when I would have her inside doing clerical work. I liked it more when she was inside, because back in the seventies and early eighties, New York was a real cesspool. We called it fun city, as a joke, but it was a zoo. I couldn't see her out there.

We started hanging out at the end of the tour, the way you do on any job. I saw something in her and then I took her out on a couple of dates. I really liked her. I fell in love with her.

We dated for six years, and then we got married. This was twenty years ago, so I was thirty-seven. She was seven years younger. After we were married, everything changed. She said, you want to marry me, we're going to have to go to New Jersey. She was a Jersey girl and she wanted to go back home. She had brothers, friends, the whole nine yards. And her parents, living out in Princeton.

Love is blind. We moved to Jersey. But I still had my job in New York so I could tolerate it. I said to myself, I only have to sleep in New Jersey, I don't have to really live there. We moved to Bergen County, a town called Rutherford. We rented a garden apartment. And in 1989, we had a child, Jessica. She just turned eighteen last month.

Jessica was born on Super Bowl Sunday and everything was working fine. I was commuting from Jersey, coming into the meat market. Then I left the meat market in 1986 because I was having some problems with the bosses. From there I went to work in a liquor store several blocks farther north on 46th and 9th Avenue, Piemonte Wines and Liquors. At the store, I clerked, stocked shelves—I did everything in the place, even managed it on occasion.

I worked there a little over a year, till '87, when the manager/owner Steve got cancer, they closed down the store. So I was out of a job and went through the papers to look for work. I sent out resumes and Pepsi happened to call me back. The warehouse was located in Long Island City, so I went over there for one interview, then they sent me to Brooklyn for a second one. A couple of days later I heard from Long Island City, this guy named Marty. I'll never forget his name as long as I live. He called me up on August 1, '87. He called me up and said, I want to welcome you to Pepsi.

I started off as what's called the checker. Basically, when the trucks come in at the end of the day, you've got to count all of the product on them. The drivers submit their paperwork and it has to correspond with what they left with, so you figure out how many cases were sold, how many were coming back. I was there for about three months, in this one section called Queens Garage, and then I got promoted to go over to the Manhattan Garage on the other side of the complex, doing basically the same job.

My superiors saw what I was doing and they said, we're going to offer you a position in warehouse management; would you like the job? Why not, nice promotion. It was two thousand more a year. At the meat market I was like a boss. I was supervising all the workers to make sure that all the trucks were loaded on time and out of there on time, and plus at the liquor store I used to order some things. But this was different. I loved this job. I saw a great future in it. The job itself was so challenging to me. I was the warehouse manager. On any given day I might be in charge of the whole operation of the plant in Long Island City. If I worked on the overnight shift, the eleven-to-seven tour, I would have roughly forty men who answered to me. When I worked the earlier shifts, the two-to-eleven shift or the six-to-two shift, we're talking at least a hundred men. I loved it. Whenever there was a problem, I always made the right decision. I was getting letters of praise from my superiors for the work I was doing. And basically I taught myself. I had other people walk with me at first, but they would only give you about a week with another manager, then after that you're on your own.

I felt this job was my destiny. I felt very comfortable being there, and that each position would lead to a bigger and better position for me. With some jobs you only could learn so much and then that's it, you stop. With Pepsi there were so many different job descriptions I could have fallen into. So that was the beauty behind it. When I told people I worked at Pepsi, you know, they were impressed. People would actually listen to me, especially when they would see me with a suit on or my Pepsi uniform on.

I was just so happy. I said well, now, I have a child, I'm making more money, so I could just see bigger and better things for my family. My wife was in seventh heaven. She used to say my husband works for Pepsi, so proud. When I was working at the meat market and the liquor store, she was working too, for the *Bergen Record*. When I worked at Pepsi, she was at home. The plan was, when Jessica was born, Kathy would stay home for the first five years. I was making enough money. It was the American dream right there.

But then the bottom fell out.

One night, I saw one of my superiors doing something that he shouldn't have been doing. He was coming in drunk and then he was bringing company with him. Another woman. Now, this guy, O'Neill, was married, two kids and everything, and he was my immediate supervisor. He was a good boss, but he was feared by everyone. If you got on his bad side, forget it, he would make your life a living hell. I mean, he was really tough. He used to fire people like giving out candy.

He was coming in drunk during my shift, late at night when nobody else was around. He would be there to supervise, to make spot checks. On three occasions he brought a woman in, taking her towards his office. Not a looker, but then again, when you're drunk, anybody looks good. No big deal, I thought, but don't come into the job, right?

Once in a while he would come over to me and talk big in front of his girl, saying, keep up the good work. Maybe he thought I would tell other superiors that he came in with this girl and he was drunk. It was no secret. You could smell it off him, and he'd be slurring his words and everything. But quite frankly I didn't care. I didn't see anything wrong with it.

After a few months there, he gave me a very bad evaluation, saying I wasn't doing my job properly. I didn't understand. Everything was running smoothly, everything. Nobody stole any merchandise. The trucks were on time. I evaluated myself over and over again. What did I do wrong? If anything, I was being too nice to people. I wrote up some discrepancy reports, wrote several people up for screwing up, and he was happy about that. But the next evaluation came around three months later, and it was even worse.

I had plenty of time to think about it, trying to figure out what I did wrong. When he was giving me these evaluations, I was saying to myself, wait a minute, he's wrong, he's wrong, he's wrong. But he was my boss. And what happens when you fight with the boss? They'll tell you to take a walk, so I just bit my lip thinking about my wife and daughter.

The call came about two weeks before Thanksgiving in 1990. It had been a few months since the last evaluation, and it was nearly time for the next one. I had just come into the building past security and went upstairs. I was talking with a friend of mine in the inventory-control section. They had gotten a phone call asking if I was there and saying I was to go down to O'Neill's office. So I went. His secretary brought me into the room, asked me if I wanted coffee, I said no. I was standing and he was behind the desk, looking down, not too pleased. When you give bad news, it's hard to look another person in the eye. And he just told me, Tom, I'm not too happy with your job performance. You're out of here. Just like that.

I did something I never did before. I begged. I begged. I said, my gosh, couldn't you wait until after the holidays. Please, can't you wait till after Christmas, then I'll leave. He said no, I want you to leave now.

I was shocked. I just couldn't believe that it was actually happening. I didn't do anything wrong. I heard someone say, come with me, Tom. I turned around and it was the head of security. We went upstairs to my locker, took my stuff out, went downstairs, and gave them my ID card, and they escorted me off the premises.

I'm thinking to myself, what am I going to tell my wife and kid? What am I going to tell Kathy? It was November '90. I'll never forget that date. That's when my life ended.

Those three years were probably the best it had ever been. At that time our rent was about seven hundred a month. With the Pepsi job, I could cover that easily. Plus Kathy had money for maternity leave from her job. We probably had seven or eight thousand in savings, so we were okay.

I got home that night and I did something I swore I would never do: I lied to Kathy. I told her I got laid off and that I would get my job back soon. I couldn't tell her the truth. I should have talked to her more about it. I don't think she knew how humiliated and hurt I was. She was having problems of her own, having a tough time accepting Jessica. I think she was more concerned about what we were going to do now.

Fortunately, though, after I lost Pepsi I just happened to be going past the meat market—talk about a blessing in disguise. I was talking to one of my former employers and he told me, "Boy, I wish you could come back to work here." I said, "You want me to come back here? Why?" He said the guy that replaced me had died. That was kind of spooky, but never mind, I needed work. I said, "Okay, we'll talk about it," and he bought me lunch. I told him, well, if you want me to come back here, this is the amount of money that I want, and he said, well, I'm going to have to talk to my father about it. His father was a little reluctant, but his uncle, who was the president of the company, said, yeah, I want him back, and they hired me. I was content being at the meat market. Not truly happy, but the bills were being paid.

We changed. The marriage changed. Kathy was disappointed with me. She threw me out of the bed that we were sleeping in. She wanted her old captain's bed that her father made her and I slept on the couch.

Pepsi was something to talk about. Now I had to go back to a job that really wasn't much to talk about, with no real future and no name to it—Washington Beef, what is that? Pepsi, that's a job. So it was a status thing with her. She just had high hopes. With Pepsi, we were going to get a house. I was pulling in twenty-five to thirty thousand, which was pretty damn good back then, back in '90. I couldn't figure getting a house with the meat market. I couldn't see that. The meat market was about the same money, and I was fortunate to be getting it, but it was always going to be just the same amount of money. I was never going to go any further.

And then in '92 the boss decided to close the place down. The butchers' union, Local 174, they wanted a new contract. My boss told them, hey, business isn't so good right now; stay for a year and then I'll work something out with you guys. But the union, they said, no, no, we want a contract right now. And he says, I'm going to put this right on the table, either you wait a year or I'm going to close the place. They didn't believe it. But one day he told them, I'm closing and retiring, that's it. I don't need this aggravation.

When I heard the news, I said, what, again? I'm going to lose my job again. But I didn't line up another job because—well, I was confident that I would get another job within the meat industry. Right down on 14th Street Market there they always need somebody as a lugger or what have you. They go through those people like no tomorrow, so I said, all right, I lost this here, I can go down to 14th Street. Plus, I was loyal to the boss. When they closed the place, they kept me on a little bit longer to liquidate the stock. I was the only one that they kept, and being that I wasn't in the union it was no big deal.

For a week after the meat market closed, I didn't tell Kathy. I guess I was blaming her for other things. I felt like a failure, to lose one job after the other. I was depressed and I figured, well, she's not going to listen to me. She never asked me about work; never asked, how was your day at the job? At the meat market, what's to talk about? Sides of beef, boxes of chicken? But I should have told her about it. Would she have treated me differently? Perhaps. Would she have been more supportive, encouraged me more? Perhaps. Maybe she would have given me a hug and said, that's all right, honey, things will work out.

She found a job just like that. She went back to working with the *Bergen Record*. So in two years everything flipped over completely. I went from being the breadwinner to being at home with Jessie, and I resented it. I resented it. I wasn't fulfilling my obligations as a husband and a father. The stay-at-home dad is just a recent thing; it was nonexistent back then. Then the bills started piling up more. I was out of work almost a year.

So she got a security job too. She was like a zombie, pulling two jobs. And then I said, all right, I'll get a job. Being that she did security, I said I can get a job as a security guard. With my background, I thought I shouldn't have a problem. So I got this one job. I can't remember the name of the outfit, but they assigned me a position in West Caldwell, New Jersey, and she had to get up every morning at five to drive me there. She wasn't too happy about that.

She quit her security job, but she still was working at the *Record*. Her hours were flexible enough that I could do the security work, and once I got off work, she could go to her job and I'd be home with the baby. But after a couple weeks, they canned me.

Another job lost.

They found out I had a record. But here's the thing: I already told them about it. You know how you fill out the application and they ask, have you ever been arrested or convicted? I wrote down, yes, I was arrested for shoplifting a few months before. Which I was. This is what happened: It was in September of '93, when I wasn't working. It was on a weekend, so Kathy was at home during the day. I told her that I was going to go out for a little while and I didn't tell her where. At that point she didn't really care what I was doing. So I went over to the little storage hut that we had around the house, and I went in there and I got my pint and decided to have a few drinks. I was still on an emotional roller coaster after losing the job at Pepsi, and I did a little bit of drinking behind Kathy's back. Jack Daniel's. I always had a pint on me. I was smoking again too, and she wouldn't let me smoke around her. But nobody could see me in there.

I don't know if I finished the pint, but I know I was feeling good. I just happened to be going past ShopRite, and I said to myself, well, while I'm here, I might as well do some shopping. So I went in there and I don't know what came over me. I just loaded up the cart, I mean loaded it, and next thing I know I'm out in the street. This girl jumps right in front of me and she said, did you pay for that? Then I came to my senses and said, I'm sorry, I don't know what I was thinking. Went back in and said, I'll pay for this stuff. I even showed them the money. I couldn't stop apologizing. But the cops came and slapped the cuffs on me. I couldn't believe it. I'd done it to other people, but when you actually have it done to yourself, it's awfully strange to feel that steel against your flesh. It sobered me up a little bit. So they brought me over to the police department in Lyndhurst. They kept me in a little holding cell and I'm saying to myself, oh, boy, how am I going to explain this to Kathy. I had visions that they were going to call her up and say, hey, your husband's in jail. But they took me out, printed me, asked me the obvious information, then they put me back in the cell. Well, they said, you got to stay here while ShopRite figures out how much stuff you stole. I said, wait a minute, I didn't steal it. I went out of the store with it. I don't know what was going through my head. About two hours later they said, all right, we're releasing you now. I went back where the detectives were, and they gave me a piece of paper telling me what date to appear in court. When I got out, I just didn't tell her.

But I did tell the security company, and since it was right there on the application, I figured it was all right. Then one day I get a phone call from them telling me don't bother coming in, you're fired, turn in your uniforms.

This time I told her. I told her for the simple reason that I couldn't lie to her. The next day, it was like, oh, you know, you don't have to drive me up to West Caldwell because, well, because I don't have a job. She was devastated. She was crying and saying, what are we going to do now? I'm at my wit's end.

So I was going through the papers, looking for work, and I noticed that under security they had this position called fire-safety director. They're the ones that monitor the security systems within hotels, motels, highrises, what have you. They had a course at John Jay to get the license, so I said, all right, let me try it. We took $250 out of savings and I applied at John Jay and took the course, got certified in hotel/motel as a fire-safety director.

Basically the job is to monitor the fire systems, make sure everything is running properly, the standpipes and the sprinklers and what have you. Starting pay was fifteen dollars an hour, not bad. So I went to this place called Mandel Security on 42nd and I saw a sign right outside saying that they were hiring fire-safety directors. I said, hey, this is great. I went in there, showed them my certificate. I didn't tell them about the shoplifting thing, I didn't think it would matter. The first thing out of their mouths was, we only hire people with experience. I just graduated, I said. Well, sorry. Tough luck. I went to Burns, I went to Pinkerton, and the same thing: they only hired people with experience, not just out of school. So that two-fifty went down the toilet.

I gave it one last try. Several months later I got a bright idea about asbestos, which paid big money. The school cost five hundred dollars, so I called up Kathy's folks and asked them if I could borrow off them. They were more than happy to do it. The school said that they had excellent job placement, excellent. After I graduated, I would go back there every day, and they would say that this job site needs X amount of people, or sometimes they'd just go down the line picking people out, you, you, you, you. Never got picked. I tried to apply at a couple other places. They asked me the same thing: what kind of experience do you have? I said, my gosh, nothing.

A few months after I was fired by the security company, Kathy got the mail one day, and there was a reminder to appear in court. She said, what's this about? And then I told her. She said, why didn't you tell me sooner? I just felt it was my business, not hers.

I pled guilty because I was told to. If I had pled not guilty, I would have had to hire a lawyer and the whole nine yards. They will still hire you as a police officer if you have a misdemeanor arrest. But this was a violation. I could never get another security job.

After that I just gave up. Just to get away from Kathy I would say, well, I'm going to go into Manhattan and look for a job. She knew damn well I couldn't look in Jersey because we needed transportation. I was dead weight. I'd go into the city, walk around, walk around, that's all. If I saw a friend, I'd tell him my situation, and sometimes they'd feel sorry for me and give me a few dollars. Lies were building up like you wouldn't believe. I was looking for work but in the wrong way. Growing up in Hell's Kitchen, you didn't really need an education. If you knew somebody who worked on the docks, they would get you in there or get you into one of the unions in the area. I thought one of these guys would come through for me for all the things that I'd done years ago. So rather than actually go to a place of employment, I would see someone I knew, maybe a friend from the meat industry, and go, hey, man, how are you doing, do you know of any work around here, got any jobs? The answer was always, no, we're not hiring right now.

I was coasting day to day. If I could get some money, I would say to myself, well, do we have enough food in the house? If the answer was yes, then I'd get a bottle. If not, it would be coffee. But after a while I was out of people to ask for money. That's when depression really sank in.

It was around April '94 when I first decided to not go home. It was towards the weekend. I hung out at a friend's house. Wilfred, a guy from the neighborhood. He said, of all things, well, where's your wife? I said, oh, she went to her folks' house for the weekend. I wasn't wasted. Wilfred wasn't a big drinker and I didn't have that much money to spend on a bottle. I just cried myself to sleep that night.

The following day I called her and I just poured out my heart and soul. She was really angry at me, which I don't blame her for. I was just at some corner crying my eyes out, feeling sorry for myself, not thinking about my wife and child. She had called the VA hospital, every hospital in the tristate area to ask about me. Then she got Jessica on the phone and Jessie told me to come home.

Jessie was five. I consider myself a lot different from most parents. Whenever I took Jessie out to play, I really *played* with her. We'd roll around in the dirt together, things that most parents wouldn't even think about doing. By the house there was a park. We would go there every day. At home, she would love to draw, and there were some games that we'd play. Candy Land. Those little things I remember. I know she cheated a couple of times, but, you know. We always had fun. So I got home and she ran over to me and told me that she missed me, jumping up in my arms, and I told her I missed her too. Kathy was saying, well, the least you could have done was tell me. And I said, yeah, you're right, I apologize. She didn't make another issue over it.

Things calmed down somewhat after that. She was just happy that I was home, and I was so apologetic for what I did. She suggested that I should seek some help for my depression, and I went to check out the clinic in Lyndhurst. They set me up to see a psychiatrist. But you know something? I never went. Talking to a total stranger about what I was going through, nuh-uh. I wanted a friend.

Kathy let it go, figured it was just one more thing that I didn't follow through with. Then the depression really, really hit me hard. They had this thing in the papers, a suicide hotline. And I got this lovely girl on the phone and we were talking and she says how do you feel right now and I told her. She said, why are you feeling that way? And then it dawned on me: what really got me depressed was that Jessica wanted a Playskool dollhouse and I couldn't afford it. I couldn't afford it. The girl said, don't hang up on me now. Don't hang up on me. Do you feel like you're going to hurt yourself? I said no, no. I kept on talking about the Playskool dollhouse, and she said, I'll get you one. I gave her the address, and within a couple of days there was a knock on the door. There was this girl with a friend of hers with a Playskool dollhouse. I freaked out. I couldn't believe it, and I told Kathy about it—that I spoke to these people and that I felt better for some reason. Her tone of voice, it sounded like she really cared. That was a big surprise. But then I lost interest in it. I was like, all right, I got past that, I didn't need that anymore.

I spoke to my pastor a couple of times about the situation, and what it all boiled down to was, the whole situation would improve greatly if I did find work, and she said that she would try to find work for me, but she wasn't able to. After a while I just moved away from everybody. I just wanted to be alone.

With Kathy, there would always be a point where she would stop the conversation and say, when are you going to find a job? I knew she was right, but just the way she said it, I found so aggravating. It got to the point where, God forgive me, I couldn't stand being with her. When we went out as a family, we'd put on false faces to make it look like we were happy. But it just wasn't going good.

I should have been a better husband. I should have done the right thing and taken any job—but I wanted something that would pay well, as opposed to working in Burger King or McDonald's. She would never tolerate that. That would be a big embarrassment to her. Some wives love to brag to others what their husbands are doing for a living, and if she had to tell anyone, "Well, my husband works at Burger King," forget about it.

So then two months later I did it again. I walked out, same MO. This time a friend came over to see me, Tony Speranza. He came in and said, how are you doing? I'm doing fine. And he says, how's your wife doing? He was the best man at my wedding. I said, okay. Then he said outright, I got a call from your wife. She said that you haven't been home. He says, go ahead, go home, give her a call. So I called her and she told me to come on home and she sat me down. She was nice and quiet and she said, I just can't deal with your lies and your comings and goings. She said, I want you to leave and never come back. The conversation was only a few minutes. I'll never forget her words as long as I live: and now I want you to go. I heard it in my mind over and over and over again over the years, that voice. I got up, and as I got to the door, I saw a picture of her and Jessie that was in the local newspaper. And then I walked out the door and never came back, never, never came back.

It didn't really sink in until I got to the bus stop. I felt like, okay, if she wants me to go, I'll go. We had the 190 bus from Rutherford, and I took it into Manhattan. I just kept walking, and then I looked at this one spot on 50th Street right near Park Avenue and said, this is where I'm staying tonight.

It was summertime. I didn't have anything with me. Just a long-sleeved shirt—I never did like short-sleeved shirts—and pants, that's it. I barely had any money. I had spent my last cash on the bus going in.

I could have stayed with Kathy. But I gave up. I put her through so much hell; I lost her trust. You know, if I said that I would change, I don't think she would have believed me. And I know me; I probably would have done it again, really. If by chance somebody had come over to me miraculously and said, hey, I got a job for you, then I might've called her and said, I got a job; maybe she would have taken me back. Maybe if I had something to offer, then I would have called her.

I stayed that first night in a very rich area, right around the corner from the Waldorf-Astoria, as a matter of fact. I don't know why I picked that spot. I guess I was just so tired that I decided to plop down on the sidewalk, right opposite St. Bartholomew's. No bushes, I was in full view. Right across the street there was a pile of cardboard they were throwing out, so I just put it flat there and went right to sleep. Nothing to cover myself, nothing. I didn't feel the cold.

I could've called a friend, but I was just embarrassed. I took the attitude that whatever happens, happens. I guess I wanted to punish myself. For being a failure. For not trying hard enough to keep my family together. I didn't care. I wanted something to happen to me, something where I would get hurt or killed during the night. I was hoping somebody would be dumb enough to pick on me. Maybe then I would feel better about it, let all my anger and frustration out on somebody. But of all places, I chose the East Side—not my hood, where there's more crime. Go figure. So, in the early morning security came and woke me up and chased me away. I couldn't have slept more than four, five hours.

I didn't think I was going to stay out there that long. I was sober. I had two dollars on me and I was hungry. I realized, that's it. I'm homeless. After a couple of days I just didn't care.

Irish

Manhattan, 1995

HIS NAME WAS IRISH. Ask anyone and they would say, that's old Irish. I met him on a rainy day, coming from the recycle center, down to eight bucks in my pocket. There he was, right on 52nd off 11th Avenue, lying facedown on the ground. Shit man, this guy looks dead, I thought. I don't see any blood, maybe the old guy had a heart attack. But what the hell is he doing down here? Looks like he was sitting on a milk crate and fell off. Well, let's look and see.

I don't see any cuts, bumps, or bullet holes, but, hey—he's breathing! Son of a bitch, his eyes popped open. My heart was doing the cha-cha-cha. He looked up at me and said, "Come on, help me up."

No problem there, he's five foot six, about 140 pounds. Probably late sixties or early seventies with snowy white hair and blue eyes. Up we go. Damn, his breath was bad, reeking from cheap wine. (Hey, EPA! Do I have a job for you.)

He stretched, moaned, and groaned. "Thanks, you're mighty kind to help me."

"Name's Cadillac Man. What happened, old-timer?"

"Everybody calls me Irish."

"What happened, Irish?"

"Well, Irish—"

"Name's Cadillac Man." Why's he calling me Irish? Haven't had red hair since I was a kid.

"Well, Irish, I—"

"Cadillac Man, Cadillac Man, Cadillac Man." Sheesh!

"Okay, Okay, you don't have to yell.

"Well, Irish, I"—oh, forget it—"was sitting in my chair having a taste of my pint and I got sleepy."

"Sleepy, hell. If you're tired, you should go to bed and not be kissing the ground."

"Come on, Irish, let's go inside out of the rain, and besides, I need another pint."

"Inside where?"

"Inside here." He pointed to what looked like a garage, just off the street. It's unusual for someone to invite you into their home the first time he meets you, but this guy seemed all right. Plus he was half my size; no danger there, especially now that my bad eye was healed up. He took out a bunch of keys, chose one, and in we went. He flicked on the lights—lights? Oh, wow. I saw an office off to the left and even a bathroom. It had the usual smells of a garage: tires, motor oil, and exhaust fumes still in the air.

"I worked here over twenty years," he told me, "and my cab was the star of the fleet. Every day I would get here early to wash and wax her. She was mine, number 366, and I put in long hours so that nobody else would use her. Old man Jake, the owner, didn't mind. Even when I was sick or on vacation, nobody touched my 366."

Man, this guy's a talker.

"Worked here for years, as I said, then one day I nearly killed a kid. Some woman screamed and I hit the brakes just in time. My vision was blurred. I thought I was just tired. But each day it got worse, and finally my Mary dragged me to the doctors. They gave me all sorts of tests and told me my driving days were over.

"My Mary was thrilled—not with my condition but that I had to retire, which meant more time together. In the beginning it was hard. You work so many years, then stop. But Mary had other ideas, keeping me busy doing this and that, driving me crazy. One day she decided that while we still had time, we had to take a vacation to the homeland. Oh, she was so happy, doing all the planning and stuff. I couldn't do anything, she was in charge. I would tease her, saluting, clicking my heels and saying, 'Yes, sir!' and she would throw little things at me, giggling like a girl."

He was deep in the story, like I wasn't even there.

"The night before we were going to leave, I planned to get up early and surprise her by making breakfast. Tea with toast, no butter, and orange marmalade. My Kitten—my pet name for her—ate the same thing every day, and if we went out to a restaurant and they didn't have orange marmalade, she would want to leave and find a place that did.

"Oh, we were so happy. We made love and fell asleep in each other's arms. And in the morning my Mary was dead—died in her sleep. You see, Irish, my Mary was sick, and I knew and she knew there wasn't much time left, yet she never complained."

Man, the tears were rolling down my face.

"The funeral was small, just a few friends, we didn't have any living relatives except our sons. Two boys, twins, and on their twenty-first birthday they decided to see the world. Left twenty years ago and we never heard from them again. Mary and I were heartbroken and hoped that someday they could come back married with children. They didn't come back for the funeral.

"I gave the undertaker Mary's wedding dress. My God, he did some job, she was beautiful. He even put a wedding bouquet in her hands. I looked at her, thinking back to our wedding. We were so young, eighteen years old. What fun we had!"

This was hard to take, yet I couldn't stop him, and I didn't want to.

"Do you know what the worst thing is about losing someone?" Irish asked.

Hard question. I had lost Recycle just a few weeks back. Hit by a car. The ASPCA came, and I had to lie and tell them I was taking Recycle to my brother's house. When they left, I took him to Central Park and dug a grave with my bayonet. I put him in with some dog biscuits and a can of his favorite ravioli and stayed with him all night before I covered him over. Since then, I'd been alone again.

"Companionship, I guess."

"The worst is going home and no one is there. So I went home and packed up my Mary's clothes and gave them to charity. The photos, everything, I stored in the closet. But the place still had a smell of her, and when I went to bed, our bed, I would imagine hearing those little snore sounds she made. I knew then I had to spend less time there."

He stopped for a moment to collect himself. "Want to hear something crazy? After the funeral, I went to every grocery store I could find and bought up every jar of orange marmalade. They must have thought the old geezer lost his mind. So I put them in two plastic bags and tossed them in the river. Makes sense to you?"

"Irish, I understand. If your Mary couldn't have it anymore, nobody should have it."

"With nothing to do and being lonely, I started to hang around the garage. Old Jake didn't mind, and seeing old friends helped. But my friends retired or died and I started drinking a little more. Old Jake had to hire new kids. 'Empty cabs, empty pockets,' he would say, but I could see the sadness in his eyes, wishing for the old days. They were driving him crazy, not showing up, playing loud music, having accidents. Some guy even wiped out my 366.

"One day while I was there, Old Jake wasn't feeling well all day, and just before closing time he collapsed. He had a bad stroke and I knew he would never come back here. He didn't have any more family, just his son, Gary. He was a snot-nose kid, used to come in always needing money, money, money. Old Jake would tell me the excuses his son gave. We both looked at each other, our eyes saying, *Bullshit*. But then Old Jake would shrug and say, 'Irish, he's my only son,' and I understood. Now Gary's a big snot-nose lawyer. So the next day the big snot-nose came in and gave a speech and we were the jurors. Blah blah my father's health blah blah temporarily closed blah blah you'll be notified when to come back blah blah blah thank you. In other words, this company is mine and I don't need you or want you.

"As everyone was leaving, he waved me over. 'Irish, how are you? I'm sorry about your wife and that I couldn't make the funeral. I was working on an important case.'

"Bullshit.

" 'Irish, I need a favor and I'll pay you. Since you're retired and have some time to spare, could you watch the garage and answer the phone? Anyone that calls or drops by, tell them we're temporarily closed, that's all you know. Okay? Hey, remember when I was a kid, I wanted to be a cabdriver and you and Dad gave me a cigar box with change in it? Ah! What memories, ha ha! Wow, look at the time. I've got a meeting with a client. Remember, Irish, we're temporarily closed. See you soon.'

"Bullshit and bullshit. Closed for good was more like it. At first I didn't mind, the longer away from the apartment with its memories, the better. But the ghosts of the past are here too.

"I hear them, Irish, and, no, I'm not crazy, and, no, it's not the wine talking.

"I went there for several days, but nobody dropped by or called. So I decided to call Gary, but the phone was dead. I walked up the block to the pay phone and dialed the garage number first. A recording came on saying, 'The number you have dialed has been disconnected.' No wonder I didn't get any phone calls. That cheap bastard would do anything to save a cent. About a month later I was sitting outside getting stewed to the gills when he pulled up in his Cadillac.

"He was not alone, there was another guy, looked like a big snot too. You know the type—well educated, I'm-better-than-you-and-my-shit-doesn't-stink attitude."

"Plus, those fake smiles," I said. "And they're so cheap their shoes squeak!"

It was good to see Irish laughing.

" 'Irish, how are you?' the big snot said. 'You look great.'

"Bullshit.

" 'I want you to meet my associate,' Mr. I don't remember his name. We shook hands and it was like touching a baby's butt, so soft and dainty.

" 'Irish, did you get any messages?'

" 'No, I'm having problems with the phone lately. Like there's no dial tone.'

" 'Really? Don't you worry, Irish, I'll have the telephone company send someone over tomorrow.'

"Bullshit.

"I asked him how his father was.

" 'Not good. He may have to go into a nursing home. His medical coverage is limited to another month.'

"You cheap bastard, I thought.

" 'Irish,' he told me, 'I'll come to the point as to why I'm here.'

"Here it comes! I thought. Hear ye! Hear ye!

" 'My associate and I came to the same conclusion. We're moving the cabs out of here to a bigger location where they can be leased out. Everything else will go too—the spare parts, tools, everything.'

"Bullshit, I thought. You sold everything and your father can't stop it.

" 'The movers and drivers will be here in a few days. One of them will have my business card. Double-check it, okay? We don't want any unauthorized persons taking them away, right?'

"He slapped me on the back.

" 'I didn't forget you, Irish,' he said. 'When I get back to the office, I'll draw up a check with a bonus and have my secretary mail it out right away.'

"Bulllllshitttt!

" 'We better get going, my associate and I have had a busy day with clients. See you soon, Irish, and guard the fort.' He laughed.

"So there they went in the shiny Cadillac, grinning like they'd both gotten blow jobs off a two-dollar hooker. A week went by and guess what? No check, no phone company. Just as well, my heart would have stopped if the bastard would have come through. The following week came and there they were waiting for me. I was coming from Sam's Liquor Store with a case. Better to buy by the case—it saves money, and I don't have to walk as much. Anyway, five guys and a rent-a-truck, and these guys look like escapees from jail or a nuthouse. The big, ugly one came towards me with something in his hand. 'You Irish?'

" 'Yes?'

"He said, 'I have a message for you from your boss,' and handed me an envelope.

"A check? No such luck, just big snot's business card and a note on the back saying, 'This is Frank and his crew to take everything.' And that they did, you name it, they took it, even the toilet paper and phones. Why was I not surprised?

"While they were working, I heard some banging coming from the front door. I walked over and, son of a gun, there it was: a For Sale or Rent sign with a phone number I didn't recognize. They were done in four hours. Old Jake's life's work gone like it never existed! I was mad as hell and there was nothing I could do.

"Everyone was gone except Frank, who said to me, 'Okay, Irish, get your gear and let's get outta here.'

"I went to the office to get my case and few belongings. Amazing—they left behind a desk, a chair, and a couch. I guess they weren't worth taking.

"'Okay, Irish,' said Frank, 'lock up and give me the key.'

"I locked up, handed over the key, and he tested the doorknob, twisting, turning, yanking, until he was finally satisfied the door was locked.

"'Well, Irish that's it.' And then he left.

"I heard laughter as he drove off. That's right, asshole, laugh, I thought. True, I gave you the key, but guess what, asshole, not *the* key. While you were picking your nose, I did the old switcheroo. Come back later and find out it doesn't work. You'll need a sledgehammer to break down the steel door because big snot is too cheap to hire a locksmith."

"All right, Irish, way to go, man!" The old man was deep in his story, and so was I.

"There's not much of a chance big snot or anybody else will come this way again. There's nothing here but a few chop shops, and their entrance is around the corner. I'll sit outside all day and maybe see a truck or two, that's it, not a single person."

"So it's a good thing by chance I was walking this way when I saw you kissing the ground, Irish."

"I'll tell you, I do get sleepy in the afternoons, it happened before and it'll happen again."

"If you're gonna take a nap, just go inside, man."

"You worried about me?"

"Yeah, but don't tell anybody. They'll think Cadillac Man is going soft."

"Thank you, Cadillac, that's mighty kind of you."

I made to get up and take a leak, but apparently there was still more to Irish's story. He said, "I kept looking at the sign and got an idea. I went to the hardware store and got some spray paint. Came back, sprayed it on, and good-bye to the sign. I let it dry for a whole day, then I rubbed in some dirt with water. I did this over and over until it looked weather-worn. Now nobody would know.

"Then there was one more thing I had to do. I had to go and see Old Jake one last time to say good-bye.

"Old Jake's hospital was in Long Island, and I wouldn't have cared if it was on the moon! I wanted to see my friend. I hate hospitals, lily-white and clean. And that smell. No matter how hard they try to make it cheery, it is still depressing. So just as I'm about to enter Jake's room, a doctor comes out.

" 'Are you a family member?' he asked.

" 'I wish. He's my friend for over thirty years.'

" 'Hospital policy dictates immediate family only. Since he's had no visitors in two months, I'll make an exception. Mr. . . .'

" 'Call me Irish.'

" 'Dr. Simon.'

" 'How is he doing, doctor?'

" 'I'm sorry, Irish, he's on life support.'

" 'Does he stand a chance of recovery?'

" 'No, he had a secondary stroke, causing severe brain damage. He's—I'm sorry to say this. He's clinically dead. His son will be here shortly to—'

" 'Please, doctor, don't say it.'

" 'It's his son's wish.'

" 'Can I please see him to say good-bye to my friend?'

"I went into the room. My God, was this my friend? Old Jake had tubes inside of him everywhere, a breathing pipe taped on his mouth, wires on his chest. Machines were making swooshing and beeping sounds. Please, God, I prayed, I never want to be like this.

"I reached out and held his hand.

" 'Hello, Old Jake, it's Irish. I'm sorry I couldn't see you sooner. I was busy clearing up some unfinished business of Mary's,' I lied. 'My friend, you'll be leaving soon. To a place where there's no pain, only peace. Do not be afraid, you're not alone. Elizabeth is waiting to hold you again. Together, forever in heaven. These tears are for you, my friend. I'll miss you. I'll never forget you. And I'll tell you a secret, I loved you like a brother.'

"Dr. Simon came in, told me it was time to go, Jake's son would be there in a few minutes.

" 'You hear that, Old Jake, it's time for me to go. Good-bye, my friend, till we meet again. Say hello to my Mary and say, 'I'll see you soon.'

"I kissed his hands and forehead. I knew in my heart that he had heard me.

"I thanked the doctor for his kindness. Then I left. I didn't want to see big snot.

"I started spending time here. Couldn't bear to be in our old home. I started drinking a bit more too, truth be told. Quite a bit, sometimes." Irish sighed. "Well, I talked too much. Let's go to the office. I need a taste. My throat is dry."

"Irish, you can talk as much as you want, I don't mind," I said.

"Thanks, it's good to have a friendly soul to talk with. Sorry that I don't have anything for you to drink."

In his office, there were bottles everywhere and not a few—dozens, no hundreds, a winos' convention site. It was so bad you couldn't see the floor. I wished there was a deposit on them, I wouldn't have had to can for at least six months.

"Gee, Irish, are you planning to build a glass house?"

"No, I'm just plain lazy. But if you stick around for a while and help an old man clean up . . ."

"Ha! Old man, my ass. I wouldn't want to mess with you, and if that is an invitation to stay, I accept."

When you're living out in the street, you should always plan ahead. Cold weather was drawing near, and when a situation like this comes along, you grab it. This was different, though. I truly liked the guy.

But, man, what a fucking job it was cleaning Irish's place. There were bottles everywhere, even in the bathroom and the utility room. It was going to take a while. I cased up the bottles neatly and put them with his garbage. I also did errands to earn my keep. I'd go to Sam's Liquor Store, south of the Clinton Towers near the park, and pick up Irish's pints of cheap wine. At first Sam was leery of me; after all, I'm street people and very capable of ripping you off. But I told Sam not to worry, that wasn't my style.

Want to know who's a good judge of character? A liquor-store owner. He can tell by the way you make a purchase how you're doing in life, what you need, and how bad you need it and maybe even why.

So Sam said, "What's going on with Irish? He's acting different. It's not the booze. He hasn't changed his brand in years." I can't believe it. That stuff would peel paint. But Sam tells me, "You know, years ago, it was fashionable to drink that stuff."

Amazing! The old-timers probably wined and dined the ladies and probably got laid with it too. I was starting to like Sam. He too was worried about Irish and his drinking.

There were days when I would take the bottle away from and force-feed him if necessary. Other times he ate like a pig. I got him to wash, change clothes, and pay the bills. I stopped him from carrying too much cash and went to the bank with him.

The garage was drafty in the winter, so we stayed in the office, warmed by space heaters. We spent our nights playing cards—rummy mostly—and bullshitting. As I had found out during our first encounter, Irish was one hell of a storyteller, and on many occasions I nearly pissed in my pants from laughing.

What to hear a few? You be the judge.

One night Irish started in, "I just drop a fare off at Grand Central when another enters. Without looking I said, 'Where to?'

" 'Uh, City Hall please.'

" 'No problem, sir. First time in New York?'

" 'Uh, yes.'

"Not much of a talker. I get a glimpse of him in my mirror—sweet Jesus, I don't believe it, Elvis Presley is in my cab. They said he died years ago and is still being seen all over the country. And here he is in my cab—Elvis Presley holding a shopping bag on his lap.

"'Are you . . . ?' My mouth is dry.

"'Uh, yes.'

"Think, man, I tell myself, think what to do. What to say!

"'Sir, it's an honor. I'm a fan.' The only thing I know is a song about dogs. 'Doing a benefit at City Hall?'

"'Uh, no, getting a marriage license.'

"'Congratulations, sir, my best wishes to you and—'

"'*Baah.*'

"Baah?

"'*Baah baah.*'

"I look in the rearview mirror, and there is a sheep in the back with Elvis Presley.

"'Uh, I had to hide her, uh, my fans might get the wrong idea.'

"What the hell, a fare is a fare. We arrive at City Hall, he leaves a good tip and walks away singing—not sure I got this right, but if my ears weren't mistaken, it was 'Love Me Tenderloin.' "

Right, sure, Irish.

Wait! Don't get the hook yet! Here's another:

"I don't like rainy days, even though it's good for business. Cats and dogs they call it. One afternoon, I was going to put on my Off Duty light and get a bite to eat when I saw them. Through the rain, he was waving madly and propping up a woman. It looked like an emergency. So I pull up and help the woman inside.

"'Thank you for stopping for us,' the fella says, 'nobody else would.'

"'No problem,' I say. 'Hospital, right?'

"'Yes, please hurry, my wife's water broke.'

"'Water broke? You mean she's—'

"'Pregnant, yes. The baby is coming.'

"'Hold on to your wife, mister. I'll make this cab fly.'

"I knew that the hospital was far away, but I had to try. Breaking every traffic law, going through lights, driving against traffic and on the sidewalk. Horns honking, people yelling, I didn't care.

"Then suddenly I hear a siren and see flashing red lights in my mirror. Police, thank God. I pull over and this big black policeman comes over.

"'What the hell is the matter with you?' he says. 'Are you on drugs or something?'

"'No—baby.'

"'Listen smart-ass, I—'

"'No, *baby*, the woman in back is having a baby.'

"She screamed.

"'Holy cripes!' the cop says. 'Hey, Charlie, call for an ambulance. Move over, gentlemen, give me breathing room. Relax, lady, help is on its way. I helped deliver five of my own and three on patrol. You're in good hands.'

"We stood by helpless, then we heard two beautiful sounds, a baby crying and the arrival of the ambulance.

"'Make that number nine. It's a boy!' the cop says. We were laughing, crying, hugging each other.

"The father and I went over and thanked the policeman.

"'Hey, cabbie!' he says.

"'Yes, officer?'

"'Drive safely, no more stunt driving.'

"'Yes, sir, slow and easy.'"

That story I might actually believe. Anyway, I want to.

After a couple months, Irish started getting moody, and every time I asked what was wrong, he said, "Nothing." He didn't want to eat and I could only do so much. Sometimes he took a swing at me and I put a bear hug on him. I just didn't know. Finally one night while we were playing cards, he stopped and looked at me and said, "It's time for you to leave."

"What? Why?"

"It's almost summer. I want you to go. I'll give you some money."

"Irish, I told you before I don't want your fucking money." I was mad now.

"Why not?"

"Because you're my friend, dammit!"

"Calm down. I'm sick, I haven't been myself lately."

"No big deal, we'll go to your doctor and—"

"No doctor."

"No doctor, why? And it better be a good reason, because if I have to, I'll carry you . . ."

"I'm dying."

"What are you talking about? You look fine."

"I'm old and tired and I miss my Mary."

"Don't do this, Irish, you have plenty of years ahead."

"To do what? Play cards, drink, eat, and sleep? Irish, I'm running out of time and you'll know the same feeling someday. So please, please, my good friend, leave. Don't watch me die. You'll understand."

As much as I hate to say this, I did. To see anyone you care for dying before your eyes is painful. Death is a two-way street, everyone suffers. Irish was right, sooner or later I would have told him that I had to leave too.

"Okay, Irish, I'll be leaving in the morning."

"I'm sorry—"

"Don't say it, let's finish the game."

It was late evening when I left. I picked up my friend like so many times before and put him on the couch. Cigarettes, clean ashtray, and a bottle on a chair close by.

Taking a quote from Irish, I said softly, "Good-bye, my dear friend."

It was weird. I first met Irish on a rainy day with eight bucks in my pockets, and now it was raining and I still had the same eight bucks.

Lucky for me the summer went by quickly. I stayed on the street mostly, around the neighborhood, a few nights in cemeteries here and there. I had a few fights not worth mentioning, and best of all there were no deaths to report. The last major street festival took place in September, and that meant serious canning time, nickels from heaven. What I made that day would last for at least a week. And guess what? Within walking distance of the canning zone was Irish's garage. I had been thinking a lot about him lately, and here was my chance to drop by and see if he was all right and . . . I would stop by with my shopping cart loaded and tell Irish that the redeemer closed early and I didn't have anything else to do. If he got mad, I'd leave, this time for good.

I was a little scared of what the outcome might be.

Outside the garage, everything was the same. Everything but the milk crate that Irish sat on when he took his showers. The milk crate! Holy shit, what the fuck was it doing in the middle of the street? I panicked and ran to the door and began to pound it with my fists, yelling, "Irish, Irish." I don't know for how long.

I couldn't call five-O because it would reveal Irish's hideout. It was a last resort. But first I went to see Sam at the liquor store. He would know. When I got to Sam's, he was busy with customers, but we made eye contact briefly. Something was wrong, I could feel it. Out here we call it street vibes, the feeling you have when something is going to happen or you're about to get bad news.

Sam was in there with customers behind a counter full of bottles. I couldn't stand it any longer.

"Sam, where is Irish?"

"Can't you see I'm busy?"

"Sam!"

"Get out of here, I told you."

I wanted to trash the place, but I respected Sam and so I went back out onto the street. Sam would tell me in time. I felt weak and sat down on the curb. I made a promise to myself after my brother died that I would never, never become attached to anyone like that again. It had been eighteen years since then.

"Cadillac Man." It was Sam. "Mind if I sit down?"

"Sure, Sam. Who's watching the store?"

"It's lunchtime, I close for an hour."

"Sorry, Sam, I acted like an asshole." I paused. "Sam?"

"Yes?"

"Did Irish . . . ?"

"Yes."

I could hardly speak. "When, where, how?"

Sam had teared up.

"Everything, Sam. I need to know."

It seemed like forever, but finally he said, "One day a few months ago he came to the store very quiet like, which meant something was wrong. I asked him, 'Hey, Irish, how are you today?' I was trying to act cheerful.

"And Irish said, 'He's gone, Sam.'

"'Who?' I asked him.

"'Irish.'

"'You mean Cadillac Man?'

"'Yes, he left.'

"'What happened? Did he do something?'

"'No. I told him to leave.'

"'Why?'

"'We were getting too close, not only as friends, but looking at him, I started thinking of my sons.'

"'I'm sorry, Irish. Did you ever hear from him?'

"'No, Sam, it's been months. All the things he did, running to the stores, cooking and doing the laundry and, damn, he even folded my shorts. Every time he came from the store with change, I told him to keep it, he said, "What do I need it for?" One time he got really mad at me when I offered to get him off the streets and to find a place to live that I would pay for. Sam, I thought he would bite my head off. I'm pissed off that I told him to leave.'

"'Why?'

"'I'm tired, Sam, so tired. I want to be with my Mary. Don't worry, I'm not going to do anything stupid, you know what I mean?'

"'Yes.'

"'He was a friend and a son to me, and I didn't want him there to see me die. Sam, I envy you.'

"'Me? Why?'

"'You have a wonderful wife, children, and grandchildren. Me, all I have is the memories of my Mary, my sons, my sons who I know I'll never see again.'

"'You have friends, Irish.'

"'Yes, friends, but nobody likes to go home to an empty house, Sam. Sure, you can keep yourself busy, but the loneliness creeps in when you're not. Ah, never mind, Sam. I'll take three of my usual.'

"'Irish,' I told him, 'do me a favor. Are you still at the garage?'

"'Yes.'

" 'Please be careful, and if you need anything, call.'

" 'Don't worry, down there I'm lucky if I see a pigeon or two. Take it easy, Sam, and don't run out of my favorite vintage!'

"He then turned and left. It was all downhill after that. Every time he came in to pick up his usual, he looked terrible, like a skid-row bum, un-shaven, piss-stained pants, the whole nine yards. At times he would ask if I seen you or Mary."

"He asked for me by name?" I asked.

"He still called you Irish."

"Sam, the condition he was in, you could have refused to sell to him."

"Yeah, but then he would go to the other liquor store up the block. This way I could keep an eye on him, sometimes get him some food at lunchtime.

"I'd tell him, 'Hey Irish, I have some food, let's eat.' Sometimes I would grab the bottle and threaten to break it if he didn't eat. He was losing weight fast, and for a man his age that's scary. He was dying. He knew, he just didn't care.

"Eventually, I couldn't let him in the store anymore. I had to bring his wine outside. He would take it and without looking at me say, 'Thanks, Sam,' and walk away. I prayed over and over, 'Please, God, end his suffer-ing and take him soon.' Imagine praying to God to take someone's life, especially a friend's.

"Anyway, my helper, Juan, was out sick for a few days and, boy, was I busy, makes me appreciate good workers like Juan. I was doing double work, no time for lunch, and staying late after hours to clean up and re-stock. When he came back, I was just happy to have everything back to normal. That night as we were closing Juan said, 'How come I no see Irish today? He is sick?'

"My God, he was right, I was so busy that I didn't notice Irish hasn't been in for three days! I locked up and told Juan to come along. My heart was pounding, I was pissed for not noticing!

"We went over and pounded on the door, but nothing. I pushed, and the door wasn't locked. Then I saw him and I knew it was all over. He was lying in the fetal position, bottle in one hand and Mary's picture in the other. As bad as his body looked, his face was different. Totally at peace. I swear he had a smile. Juan and I said a prayer, then I called the police on my cell phone.

"The police were empathetic and asked a lot of questions, mostly about why he was down there. I told them that he had worked at the garage for many years. I didn't say he lived there. I said he went there to drink. He wasn't robbed, still had money, and the coroner said death by natural causes.

"I lied to them when I said Irish hadn't any relatives, just lots of friends who will take care of him the proper way. We gave him a good send-off. Obituary notices, contacted the taxi union, had a kid put up notices all over the neighborhood.

"He looked great at the funeral—years younger, decked out in his favorite blue suit, and the picture and mass card of Mary between the hands.

"I'm sorry we couldn't contact you," Sam said.

"It's all right, Sam. I bounce around a lot."

"Irish left some impression on people."

"To know him is to love him." I put my hand on his shoulder and said, "You're a good man, Sam."

"Oh, man, look at the time, time to open up again for the after-lunch crowd. So, I guess you'll be going, Cadillac Man."

"Yeah."

"Do you need anything?"

"The only thing I need is for you to be my friend."

"Always, Cadillac Man."

Leaving is hard. Perhaps someday I would settle down in one spot and wait for the man upstairs to come calling.

Oh, well, it was early, still time to go to the redeemer.

"Hey, Cadillac Man!" It was Sam and he was carrying an envelope.

"I told you I didn't want anything!"

"Take it easy, Cadillac Man, it's a letter from Irish. About two weeks ago, maybe three, he came in halfway sober and handed me this envelope. He said, 'If you ever see Irish again, make sure he gets this.' Then he picked up his order and left. I almost forgot, then I noticed it taped on the side of the register."

"Stay here, Sam, I'll read it to you."

"No, I gotta get to the store, I left the door open. Tell me the next time you come around."

"I promise."

"Be careful, big guy."

"Slow and easy, Sam."

Hmm, the letter was a little heavy. Let's see. A key, but for what?

Irish wrote, *Dear Cadillac Man*—hey, he said it!—*I gave this letter to Sam hoping that it will reach you someday. As you read this I am with my Mary at last. Do not weep. I couldn't go on without her. Thank you for spending time listening to me and playing cards even though you cheated. (Only kidding.) I hope and pray that someday God will smile on you. In the meantime, the key is an extra I made for the garage. Feel free to use the place. I'm willing to bet the electric is still on. I'm going to miss you my dear friend. Remember me.*

Irish

P.S. If you get in, sorry for the mess, my Mary once said I was a born slob, but a cute one.

The redeemer could wait. There was something more important to do. I hoped the store up the block would have what I needed.

Ah, yes, here it was! It was easy to conceal my shopping cart on this block. Several abandoned buildings had deep, dark entrances to hide it in. Must not forget the package and milk crate. I held the milk crate tightly in my arms and visualized Irish sitting with his wine and cigarette, laughing and telling stories.

Amazingly, the door still looked the same, and I saw that Irish had scattered broken bottles and newspapers about. The key turned and I was inside.

Before I reached for the light switch, I stopped and inhaled deeply, then slowly exhaled. Same garage smells but I sensed Irish was here. I had a crazy thought that when I flicked the lights on, he'd be standing there and say BOO and I'd clock him down the stairs. I kept one hand in my pocket just in case.

Ready, set, and no Irish, yet I still had this feeling, and the lights were working.

Good, there was work to be done. Holy shit! Let me rephrase that. There was a lotta work to be done. The office looked like the first time I saw it. Bottles, bottles, everywhere. "Irish, can you hear me?" I said. "You're a slob." A slob who I miss.

No time to go to Sam's for boxes, so I bagged the bottles carefully and carried them into the corner of the garage to be dumped later.

"Irish, did you have holes in your pants?" There was loose change under the couch, under the desk, in the bathroom, and I even found a few bills, over thirty dollars all in all. Done! "Irish, can I do my work now? Thank you."

This place was ideal for use as a "house," but first it had to be booby-trapped against predators while I was gone. That took most of the night. There was one more thing I had to do, but I was tired. It would have to wait until tomorrow.

Did you ever wake up and think, where am I? Then it takes a few seconds to realize where you are. I felt the recent months were just a dream and that I was still in the garage with Irish.

Then an imaginary alarm clock in my head went off and said, wake up, Cadillac Man, Irish is dead.

Please let me sleep.

Then I heard Irish's voice. "Irish, there's something you must do. Remember me, remember me please."

I was awake now. I will, Irish!

I pulled the desk to the center of the garage. Let's see what's next. Ah, yes, I found a full bottle of wine and the cigarettes, matches, and ashtray. Then the milk crate and four prayer candles. I set them up and lit them. "Irish, I know you're here. I can feel your presence. You asked to be remembered, and so here is this street shrine in remembrance. 'Why the four candles?' you ask. One is for you and the other three are for the people you spoke of. I wish that I met them in person, but the loving way you told me about them, I felt that they should be included in the shrine. Mary, Old Jake, and Elizabeth, I dedicate this shrine to you too. I'm leaving now, but I'll be back someday. Irish, I'll never forget you. You're part of my life now that cannot be taken away. And, Irish, while you're 'up there,' look in on my brother Hoppy. Tell him I miss him and I'm still mad, he will know what I mean.

"Irish, Mary, Old Jake, Elizabeth, be at peace. Gone but not forgotten. Farewell, my dear friends."

One last glance and I locked the door behind me.

It was windy out there and suddenly something blew into my face. An advertisement for a taxi service called Taj Mahal, and that was it! I always gave names to my houses, and son of a gun, Irish, I bet this was your idea, it's perfect. I read once that an Indian prince spent his entire fortune to build the Taj Mahal as a memorial to his young bride who died.

So this is my Taj Mahal, and no, I didn't spend millions on it. It cost me more than riches—I lost my friend.

Chocolate Milk and the Ladies of the Evening

Bronx, 1994

IT WAS JUST your average night in Hunts Point, and the Rubber Man was in the neighborhood. "Good evening, ladies! What will it be for tonight? I got long ones and short ones, dry or wet. Colors and different flavors are my specialty. For the adventurous I also have ribbed and studded for that special night you are alone with your main man. Or your number-one customer?"

"Sorry, Rubber Man, business is slow. Five-O has been chasing us all night and I needs to turn four more tricks before I can go home."

That was Amber, one of the girls I was getting to know there. Then Lucy said, "None for me either. I am so desperate I'm about to go half-price."

Then Sweetheart, the one I couldn't help looking at, the one who came to talk to me the most, said, "I'll take a dozen, Rubber Man, but on one condition."

"Damn, Sweetheart!" said Lucy. She was short, pretty, with shoulder-length dark hair. "Is there a convention in town I don't know about?"

"No, I'm meeting the Shoemaker and his friends later." I knew enough to know that the Shoemaker was a good trick—he'd pay a hundred dollars to lick your shoes while you were jerking him off.

"But what about the others?" Lucy asked.

"Okay, see that guy with the wagon across the street?" Sweetheart pointed at me. She was giggling, up to something.

"Yeah, I know him. Cadillac Man."

"All you have to do is bring him over to me, then you and I will do business."

"Oh, the things I do to keep my customers happy. Be right back, ladies."

"Hey, Cadillac Man!" The Rubber Man was waving his arm at me.

Shit, the first chance I had tonight to sit down with a cup of coffee and a stick, and here he comes. Rubber Man! I could spot that hat of his in a crowd. We crossed paths a few weeks ago when a couple of wannabe gangbangers were pushing him around as I was coming out of a store. No respect for their elders. Punks. We scuffled, then I heard five-O sirens coming our way. The wannabes ran like roaches, and I grabbed Rubber Man from the sidewalk.

"Let's get outta here!" I yelled. "Five-O is coming and I don't like to be around to answer any questions."

"My freeth! My rat!"

"We'll talk later! Shake a leg!" Had to put my arm under his to pick up the pace.

"My freeth! My rat!"

"Sorry, old man, I don't understand a word you are saying."

He then pointed to my hat, then opened his mouth, revealing nothing but gums.

"My freeth! My rat!" Pointing over to the curb.

Then it dawned on me. "Your teeth and hat are over there?"

He nodded. "Yes, my freeth, my rat!"

"You are fucking crazy, old man, five-O is going to be here any second."

"Fleas, fleas!"

Fleas, fleas? Oh, I got it: Please, please.

I didn't believe what I was about to do.

"Okay, old man, uppers and lowers?"

He nodded yes.

"Stay here and don't fuckin' move!"

I had to be brain-dead.

Five-O pulled up by the curb. Keeping a safe distance, I spotted the teeth some twenty feet behind the officers. I snatched up the teeth. Fucking disgusting! Then I spotted the hat behind the rear tire of the squad car. Too close for comfort. I couldn't risk it.

Then just like that, five-O got back in their car and drove away. Go figure. The wannabes were gone too! I got the hat.

"Here you go, old man, your teeth and hat."

Went over to my wagon to get some Handi Wipes to clean my hands. Those dentures were nasty, stained from food and who knows what else.

"Thank you, young man."

Turning around. "You're wel—shit!"

It wasn't the toothy smile that stopped me in midsentence. It was his hat! I didn't notice it before, just picked it up and handed it over without looking. A hat is a hat, right? No, not this time! In big block letters, FUCK YOU! And on the bill was a small rubber hand with the middle finger sticking out. Talk about drawing attention to yourself. No wonder the wannabes were on him.

"Are you fucking nuts, old man, wearing a hat like that?"

"In my line of work, I have to advertise my product, and this is the best way I know."

"It's a good way to get knocked on your ass over and over. What is it that you're selling? Is it worth the risk?"

"Allow me to introduce myself. I am the Rubber Man and I promote safe sex by selling condoms."

"Damn! You gotta be kidding me, to drugstores?"

"No stores, strictly one-on-one. And with this hat the customers come to me. They ask, 'What's with the hat?' I tell them what I sell, then they laugh and buy some. My best customers are the ladies of the evening who want to keep a low profile. But enough about me. What is your name, young man?"

"Cadillac Man."

"Let me guess, you owned or used to sell Cadillacs?"

"No, my wagon is my Cadillac." That's not the whole story, but it would do. The whole story is that one time I got hit by a Cadillac. I've been clipped by cars lots of times, but this one hit me so hard the logo left an imprint. When I got back to the hood and showed my friends, everyone started calling me Cadillac Man, and the name just stuck.

"You're homeless?"

"Yep."

"I'm sorry."

"Don't be—it's not your fault."

"Anything I can do for you?"

"Yeah, stop with the questions. I gotta get going to make some money if I want to eat tonight."

"Wait, Cadillac Man. Before you leave, have some of these." He gave me a string of condoms. "You never know when it will happen, so be ready."

I hadn't seen him since then, but he recognized me, and there he came dodging through traffic in the big stupid hat.

"What up, Rubber Man?"

Wheezing, he said, "Cadillac Man, I—"

"Take it easy, you wanna have a fuckin' coronary? Sit down a minute."

"I need you to do me a favor."

"No, I won't pose nude with one of your condoms on."

"Huh?"

"Never mind, what do you need?"

"I have a customer across the street who will buy a dozen with one condition—that I bring you over to talk to her."

I looked over at the three working girls. All three were wearing hot pants that revealed their ass cheeks and very little coverage over their tits. They liked to mess with me, waving, teasing, winking, and it brought back that familiar pain in my groin.

A car pulled up. One of the girls looked in, then approached slowly. They spoke briefly, then she said, "Get lost! You fuckin' sicko!" He drove off. I noticed his license plate—an "outer," an out of towner.

Sonna bitch! He came around again and this time stopped the car, got out, grabbed his crotch, did a little dance, and started to sing, "Heyyy, babeee, please doooo meee, please dooo meee!" The girls were all cursing at him, he was blocking traffic, car horns were blaring, then finally the show was over and he took off. A typical outer asshole who wouldn't dare try this kind of stunt in his hometown.

The girls were pissed and looked at me. I was nodding in agreement. Coffee break over, it was time to hit the streets again and do some serious canning. Said good-bye to Rubber Man, then called across the street, "Have a good night, ladies, and be careful!"

Grabbed my wagon, and as I turned the corner, two blocks from the market, I had to leap for my life, the sonna bitch almost ran me down. Thank you, reflexes! I came down hard on my side. I was yelling at him as I got up, and it took a minute to realize my arm was all scraped up.

I went to my wagon and dug out the medical supplies. The scrape had a lot of dirt and gravel embedded in it. If I didn't treat it fast, infection would set in, then I would be screwed. Infection and illness are two major concerns out here. Some of us can't wash or bathe every day, and that's when you get sick. I got out gauze, peroxide, antibacterial cream, and I was all set.

"Hey, Sweetheart! Come here please!" She'd help me out.

She came across the street. "Oooo, your arm looks bad, maybe a doctor should look at it."

"Waste six hours in an ER? No thank you, I got everything to do the job right here."

"Here, let me do that for you."

"Okay, start from the top, then slowly work your way down and don't put too much peroxide on the gauze pad."

She wiped the cut carefully with the gauze pad.

"There is a piece of glass inside," I told her. "Go in my bag. I have a pair of tweezers. Pour a little peroxide on them."

I pinched the area. "Get real close, Sweetheart, and if you can't see it, get the flashlight hanging on my wagon."

She did. "I see it sticking out, it's green."

A beer bottle. "Okay, now take it out gently."

Felt it come out with little pain. "Now pat the area with peroxide."

Now *that* hurt. But even with my head throbbing from the pain, the first thing I noticed were Sweetheart's breasts.

"You like what you see?" she asked.

"What?"

"You're staring at my boobs."

"Sorry. Doctoring comes first."

I made a fist and the blood oozed out, flowing down my arm. I had to make sure there weren't any glass particles left inside. Meanwhile Sweetheart was looking all fascinated, staring at the wound and the bleeding.

"Okay, Sweetheart, it is time to go back to work."

"Gonna look at my boobs again?"

"Don't tempt me." I laughed.

She had done a great job, tweezing out the glass, applying the antibacterial ointment, and finally placing an extralarge Band-Aid over the cut.

Saddle up, I told myself, time to go back to work.

I had a good night canning, saw just a few street people, who kept to themselves. I'm a NKOB to them, a new kid on the block, and this was their turf, I had to respect it. If I stayed here long enough, they'd approach me at the redeemer and inform me who was running the show out here. The street boss was someone everybody looked up to. He was respected and feared as judge, jury, and executioner. In most cases when a major rule was broken, the guilty party had his or her ass kicked big-time and was told to find a new canning zone.

At the end of the night, I was too tired to go to my usual sleeping spot and wound up in a park. I found a secluded section behind some benches. It was very dark, and if by chance someone walked past, all they would see would be an abandoned wagon with a lot of recycle on it. They wouldn't think to look down where I was, well concealed, covered in dark blankets. I hoped that I didn't get any creepy crawlers in my mouth or nostrils. Funny, they never feasted on the crack of my ass. I wonder why? Wrong cuisine? Ha ha ha. Time for the Cadillac Man to go to sleep.

The next few days were uneventful. I made good money canning and from outsiders' generosity. Street people were still avoiding me even at the redeemer, but I didn't care, I was feeling good and getting plenty of rest. But after a while I got bored, needed fun and excitement, so I went to the

Strip, up near Van Cortlandt Avenue. The Strip came alive at night, with enough action to make Hunts Point look dull. What is the Strip? you ask. Come on, you know. There's one in every town, yours included, though maybe the area is referred to by a different name. The residents complain, five-O make clean sweeps, but everyone always comes back; there is too much money at stake. To the few who don't have a clue as to what I am talking about, the Strip is a flesh market where all your sexual fantasies become reality, provided you got the cash. If you want to get a blow job, hand job, or a straight fuck before going home to your loving wife, not a problem. There are even a few "he-shes," who conceal their cock and balls with heavy padding or a fake pussy they bought on the Deuce (42nd Street). The he-shes try hard to disguise their voices, but then their makeup doesn't disguise the fact that maybe they didn't shave close enough. The "No straight sex today, I have my period" excuse is another giveaway.

Yes, indeed, all sizes and shapes. Big tits, small tits, no tits, fat asses, little asses, and some you have to inflate in order to find them. Just steer clear of the crackheads, they are too cheap to buy condoms. They tell you "I love swallowing cum" or "It's okay to cum inside me." If you believe that shit, you are a fucking moron. Be wise, wear a bag! Your wife or girl-friend will thank you for believing in safe sex—after they beat the living shit out of you.

So pull up a chair or be like me and sit on a stoop with a large coffee and plenty of cigarettes. The main characters are slowly coming into view. Some came by cab, others are dropped off by their boyfriends. And a few seem to materialize out of the nearby buildings. Gone are the days of the pimpmobile, those flashy cars that stood out from the rest, which led to their demise and that of their owners too. As if on cue they position themselves at various spots on the street, waving and yelling to each other in recognition.

Acting like sisters, they talk about the johns or tricks, their clothes, their dream of someday getting out of the profession. In reality most won't, they just disappear. The lucky ones move on to another location, the unlucky you read about in the newspaper. The world's oldest profession is also one of the world's deadliest. The leading causes of death are pimps/boyfriends, johns, and in some instances other working girls. And suicide, the final act of desperation, which allows a girl to get out of this profession quickly.

It was early evening and already the motorists were whistling, screaming, "Hey, baby! Come here, I got something for you!"

One of the girls yelled back, "Wait right there! I'll go get your mother, she is working on the next corner." That started all the girls howling! Me too. Bet they never saw that guy again.

"Hey, Can Man! Wanna date tonight?"

"Name's Cadillac Man! Sorry, no money, only cans!"

"That's okay! I'll take whatever you got! Name your pleasure!"

The girls howled. One thing was for sure, the girls had a sense of humor. Working these streets you need a way to release that nervous energy. You are scared like everybody else is and try not to show it.

Five-O made a sudden appearance and over their PA system said, "Let's move along, ladies." One of the girls yelled, "Hey, officer, did your wife have the baby yet?!"

"Yes, a girl, eight pounds two ounces."

The girls clapped and cheered.

"Thank you, ladies. Now move on please before my sergeant comes around and makes my night hell. And you know what that means." So the girls disappeared for a half hour. Then they slowly crept back, now more cautious, more alert. One of their biggest fears was of being locked up.

Five-O would go around picking up the girls in vans and off to jail they went. Known as the Pussy Posse vans, once they came into view, all the girls scattered. Nobody wanted to be stuck in a holding cell overnight, then visit with a judge the next day. If the judge was in a good mood, you just got time served and paid the fine.

Girls who had been busted many times probably got some jail time. Then they endured the dreaded trip home to face the pimp/boyfriend. I heard stories of severe beatings, even disfigurement, yet they still went back to their main man. A few girls told me, "I didn't earn enough money. I got this because I deserved it." Go figure.

Tonight everybody was back, and so were the johns. The parked cars were bobbing up and down. I even saw the Rubber Man, surrounded by the girls. He saw me, waved, stuck out his tongue, then leaned over to the closest girl and licked her boobs. Bang! What a fucking shot she gave him, his hat went flying off, yet he still stood. Served him right. He just started laughing and moved on to the next group.

A little later they got visitors, their pimps/boyfriends. Fancy cars, designer clothes, a few looked like walking Fort Knox with all the gold jewelry, and trying to act cool and serious. The girls were eating it up and discreetly handing over the money they made, but if you have street eyes it was very noticeable. I would rather see these girls work freelance and keep the money for themselves, but the risks are high and they do need some sort of protection.

But look now, the girls are having a good time, laughing, flashing and strutting their stuff to the drive-bys. A few stop, then it's a mad dash to see who gets there first.

Time for me to go.

Farewell, my ladies of the evening.

As I was leaving, one of them called out, "Hey, Cadillac Man! Where are you going?"

I made a hand gesture as if holding a cup to my mouth.

"Coffee, huh? Well, hurry up back!"

I nodded and waved.

The next day I got to the redeemer and once again it was all eyes on the new kid. One guy using the can machine saw me waiting, stopped what he was doing even though he had one more bag to do, and walked away. A few others had cans and I gestured to the machine, but nobody moved. So I did my cans and cashed in tickets, forty-six dollars exactly. Hooray! When I came out, they hadn't moved one inch! They were waiting for me to leave! Now I was really pissed!

"What the fuck is the matter with you people? I'm street, just like you! Name's Cadillac Man!"

I would have gotten a better response if I spoke to a fucking brick wall. I stopped at the corner and turned back to see the mad dash to the can machine. What was going on with these guys?

Stomach growling, thermos empty—it was time to get some chow. Evening was approaching, and in order to stay up all night, the belly needs a good hearty breakfast. Unlike the outsiders, who need three meals a day, we can get by with one, provided there is enough food. Our bodies have adjusted to feast or famine. I could get by on saltine crackers with peanut butter or on packets of ketchup and mustard that I "garnered" from restaurants. I only eat when I am *really* hungry, and I don't care what the time is.

So I went to the diner, placed my order, and they didn't blink an eye. A customer is a customer. I ate my chow in peace, had my thermos filled, paid the bill, walked out, and—shit! What the fuck was going on?! On my wagon there were another three bags of cans and a bag with four cups of coffee. Someone was definitely watching me. So I wheeled my cart to the redeemer on the street.

There was nobody by the machines so I deposited everything quickly and went inside to cash my tickets. I was now entering the twilight zone! Soft elevator music filled the air, interrupted only by a young, sweet voice describing what was on sale. "Have a super-nice day!" the voice said. Super? But what scared me the most was that everybody there was grinning widely. Store manager, stock boys, cashiers, even some of the customers. Whatever was causing it, I had to get the hell out of there before I became like one of them.

Cautiously, I handed over my tickets to the cashier. "Welcome to Super Finest," she said as she counted them with a big grin. "You have forty-six dollars, sir," she said, still smiling.

"What? Again?"

"Excuse me, sir?" She was still smiling.

"Nothing, I was just thinking about my childhood. Thank you, I will come back later to do some shopping."

"And, sir, don't forget your Super Finest discount card. Bye-bye, sir."

I made a beeline to the exit, dogged by the crazy thought that a group of smiling zombies were going to sneak-attack me from behind. So the next time you go food shopping and see a smiling face, ask yourself, "Is it real?"

I was relieved to see that nothing else was added to my wagon this time.

I headed back over to the Strip. Sweetheart got out of a car, saw me, and waved. I waved back just as she jumped into another one. Lucky guy.

As for me, I'm back to my place on the stoop, watching the goings-on. Then a voice: "Cadillac Man!"

"Amber!" I leapt off the stoop, picked her up in my arms, and twirled us around, laughing at each spin.

"Cadillac Man! Please stop, I'm getting dizzy!" she said, laughing.

"Amber, it is so good to see you! How are you feeling?"

"I'm okay, thanks to you."

I kept an eye out for Amber on the street, and she appreciated it. Once I'd scared away several guys who'd been bothering her, and she'd never forgotten it.

Then a voice boomed out of the night, "Hey, youse! Put her down! Now!"

"Damn, what the fuck was that?" I said, looking at Amber.

"Are you deaf? Put her down!" the voice came again.

It felt like the wax in my ears had melted and the sidewalk was shaking. What a loudspeaker! I thought. But to my horror it wasn't!

Over by the curb was the biggest black man I had ever seen. It had to be Chocolate Milk. People talked about him sometimes, a street enforcer in this neighborhood. I'd never met him, but there was no mistaking a guy who looked like that. He was so fucking massive that if a grizzly bear saw him, it would go into early hibernation. At least six feet eight inches, three hundred plus pounds, and all solid muscle. His face would make you piss in your pants.

I put Amber down. "Get behind me and get ready to run like the wind. I will try to stop him," she said.

Yeah, right, how? I thought. Hit this guy head-on with a freight train and he would use the cars as toys for under a Christmas tree! My wagon was too far away, and anyway the weapons I had hidden there wouldn't scare him. It was times like this I wished I'd had life insurance to pass on to my kids. He stopped about six feet away, just standing there eyeballing me. He was trying to psyche me out, but I wouldn't budge. My adrenaline was in overdrive, my muscles waiting to react at the slightest movement.

Then finally he spoke. "Are you Cadillac Man?"

"No, I am your father! Don't you see the family resemblance?"

He stared at me for a moment longer, then he began to laugh, and hard. He smacked a car hood, setting off the alarm, which caused me to laugh too. Amber started giggling too and ran to his side.

What the hell was going on?

"Hey, baby brother, Cadillac Man isn't afraid of you," Amber said, still giggling.

Baby brother? Really? Her and *him*? I don't believe it. I extended my hand and said, "I am Cadillac Man."

He reached over and pulled me towards him. In the next instant I was off the ground, trapped in an unbreakable bear hug.

"Youse watched over my little sister, thank youse," he said. While he was still holding me, he felt the pocket where my wallet was and ripped it off. Then released me. I was furious that he ripped my pants. I got in a stance ready to hit him when I saw Amber waving, shaking her head no.

He opened my wallet wide, turned it upside down, then, shaking his head, he said, "Look, Amber, nothing but a dollah. Don't youse white boys carry any money?"

"Nope, we spent it on your women and soul food, both lip-smacking good!"

"Youse a crazy white boy."

He took the dollar, put it in his pocket, pulled out a wad of cash, then stuffed my wallet full. "This is for watching my sistah. Thank youse," he said.

"I don't want it, big man."

Amber looked shocked. Chocolate Milk looked confused.

"Hear me out, Chocolate Milk. When I helped your sister, I wasn't thinking that maybe someday I would get a reward. You wanna give me a reward, find those bastards who messed with her and give them to me. I want them to feel real pain!"

"Youse don't have to do anything. They had a bad accident."

I didn't ask anything further. His ungodly smile sent a chill down my spine. Things happen out here, we call it street justice.

He extended his hand again, and I took my wallet.

"Mind if I spend some of it on your woman? Oops, sorry, Amber."

They both started laughing. "Youse can't date black women, youse too ugly! And . . . Amber, youse turn around!" Chocolate Milk commanded. She did. And before I could say anything, he dropped his pants!

"Do youse have one of these?"

"Damn! Hell no, not that size! Can I borrow half of it for tonight?"

"No, this is for all my women, every inch."

"You mean every foot! Damn, man, what did your mama feed you? I want her to adopt me!" Now we are all laughing.

He pulled up his pants. "Youse can turn around now, Amber."

"Did I miss anything, Cadillac Man?"

"You sure did. But never mind.

"You guys want any coffee?" I asked. They shook their heads no. I went over to the wagon for a fast cup. Then Chocolate Milk let out a laugh that almost made me drop the coffee. Amber started in too, and so did the girls nearby. What the fuck was going on?

He made a gesture for me to turn around. I did.

"Damn, white boy, youse ass shines like the moon!"

"Cadillac Man, where is your underwear?" Amber said.

"I don't like wearing them." I felt the rear of my pants and realized one whole side was torn off.

"That ain't it, youse too cheap to buy them. Ha ha ha."

"Now if you will excuse me, I have to find some place dark enough to change my pants before I catch cold or get arrested. Chocolate Milk, thank you for being so generous, and can I call you my friend?"

"Youse can," he said, grabbing me again in a bear hug.

I wheeled my wagon into an opening between two closed stores that was dark enough for me to change my pants unseen by anybody passing. Oh, and in case you were wondering why Chocolate Milk only found a dollar in my wallet, I never carry a lot of cash. It was well hidden, in the wagon for now. You do not flash the cash out here.

No sooner did I come out with fresh pants on than one of the girls nearby, Cherry, spotted me and walked over. "Hey, Cadillac Man, what were you doing in there?"

"Changing my pants and taking a piss, why?"

"Is it safe, no rats?"

"No, nothing."

"Good, do me a favor and block the entrance with your wagon. I gotta take a mad wee wee."

"A mad wee wee?"

"A wicked piss, Cadillac Man."

"Oh! Yeah, sure, go ahead, I will watch—I mean . . . You know what I mean."

Back to the Strip we went. And what a sight we were, a homeless man pushing his wagon surrounded by lovely ladies having a time of it. Naturally we stopped at the diner. I had to fill up my thermos. Got back to the stoop and waved thanks to the girls. Nothing had changed in my absence, an endless stream of johns awaited.

I wondered where Chocolate Milk was now. I was sure we would meet up again. And maybe one of my questions would be answered too: Who was Chocolate Milk? A pimp, a boyfriend? Or really her brother? I'd have to wait to see what developed.

Out of nowhere a kid appeared and started talking to some of the girls. He was wearing a basketball jersey and carrying a boom box so big I could probably live in it. Good thing this area was commercial, not residential, otherwise five-O would be here in a heartbeat.

The kid started getting down to the music, gyrating and twisting. If I was to try to do the same thing, I would be in the hospital for a month! Everybody joined in so it looked and sounded like a block party, then one of the girls yelled to me, "Hey, Cadillac Man, do you boogie?!" She said something to the kid, who then slipped in another cassette. As tired as I was, the song was familiar and the beat brought me out and I decided to join the fun. You too! Put the book down and stretch those legs. Damn! Even some of the johns and other motorists, we were all having a good time and fuck the rest of the world!

When the music was over, the girls gave the kid a few dollars, he left, then it was back to business as usual. I went back to the stoop and collapsed.

Then a car pulled up to the far corner—trouble!

Even from a distance I could hear their angry voices.

"Dirty bitches!"

"Rotten cunts!"

The girls huddled close together. Two guys stepped out first, and I could smell their ninety-nine-cent cologne, even sewers have a better scent. One guy opened the rear door and out popped three of the ugliest, most disease-ridden women I have ever seen in my entire life! Any john that picked up one of these women was either going blind or had a death wish.

A vicious verbal barrage began between the pimps and their women.

I wasn't about to interfere, it was way too dangerous. I'd probably get my eyes scratched out and balls kicked in. Nosiree, I need those for future use. And besides, so far I didn't see any blood, just a few wigs on the ground.

As the fight went on, the neighborhood girls were laughing and yelling trash at the crackheads and their pimps.

Suddenly one of the pimps ran over and started swinging at my friends! Just as I was about to intervene, a car stopped in front of me, and guess who got out? Yep, Chocolate Milk!

He grabbed the guy from behind by the collar, pulled him up, and tossed him away like a rag doll. Holy crap in a hat! I noticed another guy starting to get out of the first car, so I decided to pay him a visit. He was halfway out when I kicked the door with all of my might. He let out a scream. Poor baby! I was hoping to hear a snap, you know, the sound of bone breaking, no such luck. Must be losing my touch.

I looked over to see that Chocolate Milk was really putting a hurt to his guy. The girls were screaming at him to stop. Other people, motorists too, were gathering, but he took no notice. Damn, he flattened the guy's nose! Like a fucking pancake! Talk about major reconstruction! I snuck up on him. The girls watched me as I took a deep breath and then, with all my might, bang! bang! Two shots to the kidneys. Then I turned to my new pal. "That's enough, Chocolate Milk!" There are too many eyewitnesses.

He relaxed and, his voice lower, he said, "Youse right. Youse ladies get in my car now!" To me: "Youse know what youse got to do."

"Yeah, I do, later."

I walked away, he raced off.

The johns in the car picked up their man and put him into the back-seat. When they were all back in the car, one of them screamed out the window, "We'll be back, motherfuckers!"

I waited until they were out of sight before I returned to my wagon.

What did Chocolate Milk's message mean? Disappear for a while. I did.

For a faster getaway, I abandoned my wagon and hopped on the iron horse to my old neighborhood in Hell's Kitchen. I stayed for a week, hanging around spots where I knew I wouldn't be seen by old friends or my family. To play it safe I got a haircut, had my beard shaved off, then paid for a long, hot shower. I must admit I looked like an outsider again, and it scared me. A reminder of my past life.

I worried about Chocolate Milk and the girls. Was there any sort of payback? Did he get busted by five-O? Were the girls okay?

It was time for me to go back—that was where I belonged now. I couldn't believe my luck—I found my wagon in the same spot I left it, like it was waiting for me to return. Welcome home! I fixed her up as good as new, then onward to the Strip!

There they were! Most of them, anyway. Chocolate Milk was missing from the scene, but maybe he was busy elsewhere. I hoped.

I sat down on the stoop and noticed the girls were eyeballing me. Why? Then Lucy decided to walk up to me. She was looking at me as though she didn't recognize me! A face like mine you don't easily forget. Then it hit me. They had never seen me clean-shaven, wearing my reading glasses! "Relax, girls," I said, "I'm Cadillac Man!"

She got closer. "Cadillac Man?"

"In living color. How do you like my new face?"

"It *is* you! Hey, girls! Cadillac Man!"

A sea of big smiles and tits headed my way. I wanted to embrace them all at once. I missed my friends. Would they notice my tears? Indeed they did, showering me with hugs and kisses.

"Where have you been, Cadillac Man? We were worried."

"Hiding. Is it safe to come back?"

"Yes, now it is, but the day after you and Chocolate Milk split, we had guys asking us if we seen the both of you."

The girls told me that the guys had offered them money, but the girls had told them they didn't know us. Then the guys got nasty and made threats and stopped the girls from doing any business. The girls got scared and told the Pussy Posse cops, who actually did something about it.

A few nights before the cops had come out in undercover cars and were posing as johns when the guys showed up and started hassling the girls, making the same threats. One of them was dumb enough to threaten a DT (undercover detective). At that point the cops all jumped out and identified themselves. Those guys must have shit green seeing all the guns pointed at them. The girls certainly did.

The cops had the men on the ground with their legs spread. "Guess what they found," Cherry said to me.

"Guns?"

"Right, on all three! They found more guns in their car!"

"I am sorry, girls," I said. "Maybe Chocolate Milk and I should have stuck around to protect you."

"You crazy, Cadillac Man? Both of you would be dead by now."

"Is Chocolate Milk back yet?"

"I don't know, maybe."

"You girls better get back to work. Looks like the johns are getting restless."

Across the street, cars were slowing down—the usual approach of the johns.

"Ha ha ha," said Lucy. "Come on, girls, we got a bunch of horny bastards to take care of."

I was at the diner, where I had just ordered a huge slice of chocolate cake with coffee, and was sitting at a booth, totally relaxed and lost in thought, when a pair of hands touched the top of my shoulders from behind. "Hey, lover boy, expecting any company?" I turned my head slightly and got kissed on the cheek.

I jumped up out of the booth. "Hey, girl, where have you been?!"

"Did you miss me, Cadillac Man?" It was Sweetheart, acting innocent and shy.

I picked her up by the waist and lifted her into the air, good thing this place had a high ceiling. "You bet your pretty brown eyes I missed you!" Everybody in the diner was looking now.

"Put me down, you beast!" she said, laughing.

"Going down, please watch the closing door. Basement, women's underwear, new and used, please watch your step and have a good day!"

Looking at her, I felt like a kid on a first date.

"Well, aren't you going to say something?" she asked. "Earth to Cadillac Man, are you there?"

My loins were on fire. "Can I buy you a cup of coffee?"

"Sure, lover boy, last of the big spenders."

"All right, all right, I will throw in a piece of chocolate cake too."

"Wow! Now you're talking," she said, still laughing.

"So what's going on?" I asked, returning with her cake.

"Stacy got busted and is doing a little jail time so I had to stand in for her at the club where we all work. We perform in a circular room surrounded by shaded windows. The customers that want to see us put a dollar into the slot and the shade rolls up for one minute. There is a small opening to the side so if you want extra attention from me, slide a nice tip through. After the show I get paid, plus with tips I do okay. It sure beats working the streets, and it's a lot safer. A private taxi brings us home. On busy nights the manager hires Chocolate Milk to walk the floor and escort the sickos out the back door." She took a bite of cake. "Hey, I just thought of something, the manager needs another bouncer. I will tell him about you, and you will be hired on the spot and you'll get to watch all of my shows. Okay?"

"No thanks."

"What do you mean no thanks?"

"I don't want to work for anybody."

"Why?"

"Sweetheart, I couldn't work there seeing those perverts drooling and jerking off every time you moved into a different position. I would want to beat the shit out of all of them, and that is bad for business."

"But, Cadillac Man, I am a performer. I don't do anything else."

"I know. It doesn't bother me too much talking about it here, but to see you in person exposed to others, that would bother me big-time!"

"Sounds to me like you are jealous, Cadillac Man."

"Indeed I am."

Just then Candy came running in.

"What's wrong?" I asked her.

"The posse sneaked up on us!"

"Damn! I should have been there!" I said.

"There were two vans."

"Two vans?"

"Yeah, they got everybody, some of the johns too. I was lucky, my trick was bringing me back when I saw them and told him to drop me off here. Sweetheart, I need a big favor, there is nobody else I can ask."

"What do you need, Candy?" she said.

"It's just for tonight. Could I stay with you?"

Sweetheart grabbed Candy and they went outside and waved down a taxicab, then they disappeared into the night. Sweetheart flashed me a devilish grin as they left.

I filled up my thermos before I went back over to the Strip. It was like a ghost town, no signs of life.

I didn't see him at first. I was eyeing the streets in all directions watching out for five-O.

"Hey, Cadillac Man!" he said, waving a cane.

I never expected to see him again, a sight for sore eyes, a good omen.

"Hey, Rubber Man, get your dusty old ass over here!"

"Mind your manners and respect your elders, young man!"

"I do and I heard you are so old that when Marc Antony wanted to fuck Cleopatra, he bought condoms off you."

"Damn! Do I look that old, Cadillac Man?"

"Nah, older! Come here!" I said, giving him a big hug. "I'm anxious to see the girls again."

"Me too, Cadillac Man. I got two new condoms to show them. They are a big hit with the girls and even some of the guys in lower Manhattan."

"You sell to gays too?"

"Why not? It doesn't matter to me, a customer is a customer. What-

ever your sexual preference is, try using one of my condoms. It tells me
you have a working brain."

The girls didn't show up the next day or even the following. Marked and
unmarked five-O cars were cruising the area looking for them. Where did
they go? Indoors? I was debating whether or not I should find the club
where Sweetheart was working. It wouldn't be hard, just ask around,
everybody knew where all the flesh joints were. Yet if you were to ask
anyone around here where Central Park was, they'd say, "Gee, I don't
know." I decided against it. Seeing Sweetheart perform in front of those
sickos, I would have flipped out. To each his own, I just didn't like those
places.

Years ago I was offered a job in one of them as a porter. The manager
told me my only duties were to mop the floors and keep the video stalls
clean. I needed the job.

A customer would enter the stalls and latch the door for privacy. The
rooms were no bigger than a closet, and each had a video screen with a
coin slot and a seat bolted to the wall. You make a selection, insert the
coins, then the lights go out and you enjoy the show. What do you do
next? You drop your pants and start jerking off rapidly before the film
ends. All done, cum all over the floor, it is time to get out of there fast!
Open the door slowly, take a peek, good, the coast is clear. Walk out
quickly, head down, thus avoiding all eye contact.

Then I came along with a mop and bucket filled with pine-scented,
scalding-hot water to clean up your mess. A few left behind snot rags, tis-
sue paper, newspapers and magazines—you know what they were used
for. I was glad that nobody ever asked what I did for a living. This was
not the type of job you put on a resume. Imagine doing this eight hours a
day, six days a week.

At least the money was good, they had to pay you well because good
help was hard to find and only a nut would do this. Then one day it came
(no pun) to an end for me.

Usual thing happened: a customer made a fast exit from the stall. I
wheeled over the mop and bucket, opened the door a bit, then the odor

hit me like a blast from a furnace. I lost yesterday's three meals. More mess than a week of jerk-offs. Manager went ballistic yelling at me. And that was the end of that.

A week has passed. I was getting restless. The girls had disappeared.

I had gotten up in the middle of the night to stretch when a taxicab pulled up on the other side of the street and several women got out.

They were back! The girls had come back! I ran to them. It was like a family reunion with all the hugs and kisses when another car pulled up and more girls jumped out.

"Boy, did I miss you guys!" I said.

Candy spoke up. "We missed you too, Cadillac Man."

"May I ask, where were you guys?"

"After everybody got out of jail, we all decided it was safer to work in Manhattan for a while. Then we got chased away by the posse and came back here."

"The posse goes to Manhattan too?"

"They're everywhere. Most of them are pretty cool and just tell us to move on. But the pricks lock us up."

"I was hoping I would see you again. Is Sweetheart still working the club?"

"No, Stacy got out of jail and went back to the club. They made an offer to Sweetheart to stay and she turned them down. She was crazy not to take it. I would have jumped at it, and I told her so," Candy said.

"So why don't you apply for it?"

"I wish! Look at me. I have little tits. The manager wants girls with tits the size of bowling balls. My man and I are saving our money. By next year we should have enough for me to get implants. My friend Lois might do it too. The bigger the tits, the bigger the tips." The girls laughed.

"Anyway," Candy went on, "Sweetheart and Lucy are working for an escort service in Manhattan and don't know when they will be back."

Amber, sitting on the stoop, saw me and started waving.

"Hey, girl, lookin' good, want some company?"

"Get over here, big man, Amber needs a hug! Did you miss me, Cadillac Man?"

"You bet your sweet and delicious brown body I did!"

"Why, Cadillac Man, you are sweet-talking me? Are you trying to get into my pants?"

"No."

"No? Why not?"

"They wouldn't fit me. Ha ha ha. Of course, if you had them off already, that would be a different story."

"You a pervert. I'm going to tell my baby brother on you!"

I laughed.

"You don't have to tell me, but did Sweetheart finally hook up?" Amber asked.

"It came close, but no cigar and better luck next time."

"One way or another I am going to get you two together."

"I appreciate that, Amber, but it may not happen. She's working in Manhattan for who knows how long."

"So I heard. An escort service, right?"

"Right, anyway, let's change the subject. What's up with your brother?"

"He's doing okay. He's right behind you."

"Huh?" I turned and jumped to the side, looking. "Where, I don't see him."

"He is looking right at you, just wave your hand."

So I did, and from a nearby parked car I saw this huge hand waving at me. No doubt about it, it was Chocolate Milk.

"I guess he's waiting for someone?"

"Yes, he's waiting for a customer."

"Customer?"

"Come on, I'll show you. Chocolate Milk's about to get nasty."

This was going to be good. She took my hand and we went across the avenue to a dead-end street. Situated between two stores, it was dark and very narrow, with just enough space to allow a truck to back in for deliveries.

Then Amber spotted something and made us move away.

"Okay, what do you see?"

"The only thing I see is a car going into the dead-end street and he is turning off the lights."

She was laughing, bouncing up and down.

I was totally confused. What the hell was going on?

She looked across the street. "Watch!" she said, pointing.

Another car started up and made a U-turn right into the dead-end street with the headlights on! The driver beeped his horn loud and jumped out, going down toward the dead end. A big dude.

Another of the girls came running up, saw us, and gave a little wave and a big smile. Then we heard Chocolate Milk's booming voice. Whatever that guy in the car did to make him mad, I sure hoped his life insurance was paid in full. Chocolate Milk was tapping on the guy's window.

"Youse rolls down the window now or I break it!" he shouted, showing his massive fist.

I couldn't see the guy's face, but no doubt he was scared. Trapped, with no way out! The window opened suddenly. Chocolate Milk looked down at the man.

"Youse in my parkin' spot, pay me!"

The guy reached in his pocket, took out some cash, and handed it over. Chocolate Milk started counting, then amazingly gave some back.

"Now! Youse get out of my parkin' spot!"

Chocolate Milk backed the car out far enough for the other guy to leave, and, boy, did he ever! He screeched his tires in reverse into the avenue, then blew the light.

"Ha ha ha. My brother makes everybody pay for using his space," Amber said.

I must have still looked confused.

"All the girls know when you bring someone here, it means extra money. If a girl has her trick drive in here, my brother will give her a piece of the action."

"Sort of like being paid twice for the one service."

"Right, and he won't take all the guy's money, that is bad for business. The john considers himself lucky that my brother was so nice."

"Nice?"

"He could have taken everything—car, money—and left the guy naked with a quarter. Know what I mean?"

"I don't want to know any more, Amber."

"Good, because that's all I'm going to say, and now it's time for me to go to work." She kissed my cheek. "Watch out for us, Cadillac Man."

"You know I will. Word."

She ran across the street, then over to her brother, said something, then left, and seconds later was picked up. What a strange relationship they had. I went back to the stoop. Amber eventually joined her brother and they passed me, honking and waving. I was alone now and merchants were opening their businesses. Did they know what went on here at night?

Recently I overheard a conversation between two working girls. One of them said, pointing between her legs, "We got the power and know when and how to use it."

I rest my case. And speaking of rest, my bed was ready. See ya.

When it started to rain, I found a nearby tunnel to bed down in. It was big and dark enough to hide in, but most importantly it would keep me dry. I shined my flashlight inside and hollered, "Is anybody in here?!" and got no response. I didn't want to trespass on somebody else's turf.

I didn't want to fight for my bed tonight, either. Scoped the ground inside. A lot of rubbers, broken bottles and hypos, a perfect spot out of sight to get high or get fucked. I cleaned up an area big enough to put my bed down next to the wagon, then made a debris field as an alarm system. If anybody tried to sneak up on me, they would step on broken glass and make a crunching noise. It would wake me up instantly. I covered my face and hands with a blanket in case there were creepy crawlers or critters roaming about in the darkness. Now for a good night's sleep, er, an early-morning sleep.

Their laughter woke me up a few hours later. I saw them by the entrance—two silhouettes, a man and a woman.

"Come, babe, let's go inside."

"I don't know, Frankie, it looks spooky and somebody might be in there."

"Spooky? Who do you think is in there? Count Dracula? Ghosts? Your mother? *Aaooooooo.*"

"What is so scary and funny about my mother, Frankie?"

"Nothing, babe, I'm sorry, I was only kidding. Your mother is tops in my book. Come on, I'll protect you."

They came inside giggling and blended into the darkness. I couldn't see them but boy oh boy could I hear them. Talk about heavy kissing. I had to chew on my blanket to keep from laughing.

"Oh, Frankie, I'm all wet, fuck me now!" A pause. "Frankie, what are you waiting for?!"

"I can't find the rubber."

"Frankie! How could you be so stupid! Forget it now! Take me home!"

"Come on, babe, we can do it, I will pull out when I feel myself about to cum."

"Oh, no, you don't, I am not going to have ten thousand little men marching up my twat!"

Huh! I had never heard that one before.

"Please, babe, I'm hurting!"

"No, this will teach you a lesson not to forget the next time, if there is a next time. Now take me home!"

I saw them now by the entrance, poor guy, head down, he was proba-bly feeling sad, and I bet his balls were screaming with pain! I don't know why I did it, but I called out, "Better fuck next time, Frankie!"

What a fucking scream she let out. "You bastard! You said nobody was in here!"

He grabbed her hand and they ran off.

"Hey, Frankie! Next time go to a motel! You cheap bastard!"

I couldn't stop laughing and it was a good thing my piss bottle was nearby, otherwise I would have pissed in my pants!

I woke up later feeling refreshed. I guess the laughter had helped to relax my body. It appeared to be a beautiful day, and my watch told me I could get coffee before heading to the redeemer. On my way, I noticed the sun reflecting off a square, silvery object on the ground. Probably a gum wrapper, I thought, but when I got closer and saw what it was, I started to laugh uncontrollably. I picked it up and yelled, "Hey, Frankie! I found your rubber!"

When I got to the Strip that day, I had company. Sitting on the stoop were Amber, Chocolate Milk, and a few other working girls. It looked like the aftermath of an inspection—which reminded me of the legend of how Chocolate Milk got his street name. Cherry had told me once about how a trick had dropped her off by an alleyway. As she walked past, she heard moaning like a girl doing a trick, followed by an unusual slurping noise. She peeked down the alley, and there was Chocolate Milk, sucking on a big-titted girl. Turned out he liked to do that to all the girls with big tits, so much so that he was even said to leave black-and-blue marks on all the girls' breasts.

"Poor Peggy," Cherry told me, "she's his favorite. Three times this week, he tries to suck the milk right out of her!"

Anyway, the girls sure looked sore as I walked up, but who knows? I had other business to attend to.

"Girls, listen up very carefully. Do you know who is leaving bags of cans on my wagon?"

"What bags of cans?"

"Two big black plastic bags of cans. You don't know who left them?"

Just then Amber called, "Hey, Cadillac Man!"

I turned to see her waving. "Gotta go, girls," I said. "Talk to you later, and be careful."

"You too, Cadillac Man."

I grabbed my wagon and headed towards Amber and Chocolate Milk.

"Hey, Cadillac Man," Amber said. "What happened? Why did you leave?"

"Sorry, Amber, I know it was bad timing but I needed some coffee."

"I saw that the girls kept you company."

"Yeah, they were telling me about some of their weird customers, and I asked them if they knew who was leaving bags of cans on my wagon. By any chance would you guys know?"

They both looked at each other, then at me, and said no, a deadpan expression on their faces, but I knew deep inside they were pissed off. Too fucking bad!

"Whoever is doing it waits until I am sleeping, and, oh, I almost forgot, several times he or she has left four cups of coffee too!"

Slight facial movement. I'm getting to them.

"I would like to thank them personally and ask why," I said.

I better stop, they are really getting annoyed, time to change the subject, but what to?

"Chocolate Milk, I got a question for you too."

"What?"

"If I drink milk the way you do, will I get as big as you someday?"

Both were laughing. "Youse crazy, Cadillac Man."

"Amber, it's late, we have to go!" said Chocolate Milk.

"Okay, baby brother. Sorry, Cadillac Man, we have to go run a few errands, we will see you later," she said, giving me a kiss on the cheek.

"Later, guys, I will watch out for the girls, they will be in good hands."

Back at the tunnel that night I shined the flashlight on my sleeping bag. There was a lot of movement inside. Tunnel bunnies. Grabbing it by the bottom, I snapped it up and shook it vigorously. "Sorry, guys, I don't want any company tonight." They will be back. Why? For several reasons. One is the odor of food, so wash your hands and face. Keep the mouth closed too, bad breath attracts them. Had one wake me up trying to get into my mouth. Luckily he didn't bite. That night I was pissed off but not afraid. They are part of my lifestyle, the children of the nighttime, and like me are hungry too.

Then you have the snugglers. It's only a matter of time that while you are sleeping, they will creep back, seeking body heat. It's a basic instinct of survival, to keep warm, we all need it, animals included. Snuggle up to you, just don't move and after a while they'll leave.

Now nice and comfy, then whoa! I got company! One of them had decided to stick around and was crawling up the inside of my pants. "You son of a bitch, you bite my balls, I'll have you for dinner tomorrow," I whispered. I thought about my ice pick, then dismissed it. Even if I was lucky enough to use it, I would only have one chance. What if I missed? Forget it. I had no other course of action. Just wait and see—no, change that to wait and feel. He stopped suddenly, then turned around and ran down my leg and out of my pants! I got up quickly, grabbed the flashlight, and dropped my pants. Just a few scratches, but, whew, what a fucking stink! No wonder he left, I would have left too! I was surprised I wasn't growing mushrooms somewhere. First thing on the agenda tomorrow was to take a bird bath. It would mean giving the park attendant a fiver to open the comfort station an hour earlier. That's what I paid him the last time for total privacy. It was worth it, I came out smelling like a rose, and, yes, I washed behind my ears.

I shook my sleeping bag one last time and went to sleep, dreaming of Sweetheart.

The park attendant was pissing and bitching. What a fucking crybaby! "If my supervisor sees you, I'm in big trouble." I forked over another fiver just to shut him up. Once inside I attached a bungee cord from the door handle up to the steel mesh of the window. If someone were to try to get in, the door would only open an inch. Looking in the mirror, I saw a person I hardly recognized. So many wrinkles in the short time I've been out here. I must have aged at least ten years.

Ah! Hot water! The best!

Then someone tried to open the door. The bungee cord worked. In a loud voice I said, "Occupied!" It happened again. "Are you fucking deaf?! Fucking occupied!"

Word is bond, when I got out of there, I was going to put my foot up the park attendant's ass.

I waited a minute or two and heard nothing.

Whoever it was is gone. Probably to the women's around the back. Worked up a good lather, I was completely covered with soap and rinsing myself off. Heaven.

Sitting here on the stoop that night, I saw one of the schoolgirls waving at me. This one was the ultimate jailbait, wearing a ponytail, looking like she was in grade school. Little girl, do your parents know that you are out this hour selling your pussy?

"What's wrong, Toni?" I asked her.

"I have a problem. I'm so horny."

She had an older voice, but she was still underage.

"That's a problem? Just give your next trick some extra time and enjoy yourself."

"No, I'd rather enjoy myself with you, Cadillac Man. Take me somewhere and I will suck and fuck your balls off."

She was just looking for business. But at that very moment I wished I had a bar of soap. I would have shoved it down her throat and put my foot up her ass.

"Sorry, Toni, I am flattered, but no thanks, maybe some other time." Yes, like in ten years! "Now, turn around. There is a trick who is flashing his lights on and off. I think he wants to talk to you."

There she went, and, oh, how I wished he was an undercover cop bringing her straight to juvie. Perhaps someday it would happen, the sooner the better for her sake. These girls are so full of life, but look past the joking and the makeup and you'll see a dark underside. They live in fear of future beatings and worse, knowing if they try to leave their pimp, he will hunt them down. "Forget about the police," he says, "I'll kill you, bitch!"

They even have to be careful what they say about their pimp. They never use that term, instead they say, "He's my man." And what's also weird, some actually fall in love with their tormentor, will do anything to please him, even rat out another girl. "Better that she gets the beating than me. I did the right thing." Do they really believe that?

So many girls have told me so. But here is my favorite: "He loves me."

Yeah, right. Once I overheard a pimp say to another, "That pussy of hers is a fucking machine. My fucking ATM machine." Both were laughing. Yeah, he loves you. He loves the way you make money for him. Keep it coming.

Should something happen to her, would he care? Fuck no! Would he go to the police if she was missing or to a hospital if she got hurt? Fuck no again. He wouldn't risk his neck for anybody. He only comes around if he needs money or to check out the fresh meat.

Unless she's a big earner, losing a girl is no more than a minor annoyance. Sad but true, there are plenty more where she came from. They are everywhere—runaways, girls trying to make it as models, dancers, or actresses. The pimps wine them, dine them, then rape and beat them until they agree to work out of fear of dying. By then all hope for anything else is lost. Some get hooked on drugs and grow even more dependent.

There are pimps who have a number of girls and are willing to sell one if the price is right. She has no say in the matter, and once the transaction is a done deal, she belongs to someone else. Like a piece of property, bought and sold. They never grow old, they simply vanish. No retirement home either, just a dark hole in the ground.

Looking at all those young girls, I wondered what was in store for them. I didn't want to see any of them hurt, and if I stayed in this area, I knew I would. It was time to leave. I would have to make up a good excuse.

Times like this I still wanted a drink to numb the senses, but that was a lousy excuse to start up again. I guess I would have to settle for a large coffee. Not a bad idea, it was late and all the girls were working, not a soul or car in the street. I wouldn't be missed.

I got to the diner and the fucking place was packed! Everybody was there. Chocolate Milk, Amber, the girls, a few he-shes off to the side, looked like a damned convention. I sat at the counter enjoying my coffee when they came in. A mother and two children, a boy and a girl probably between ten to twelve years old. What were they doing here at this ungodly hour? They were clean but the clothes were obviously hand-me-downs, about two sizes too big.

All the laughter, screams, and curses ceased to exist, replaced with low voices as all eyes were focused on the mother and her kids. She ordered and went back to the table with one small order of french fries. The boy tried to grab one but she slapped his hand. They folded their hands and prayed.

Chocolate Milk walked over to the cook, spoke a minute, and pointed to her table. Within a few minutes two waitresses brought over an assortment of breakfast foods.

The mother shook her head in disbelief, probably thinking it was a mistake, and the waitress told her no, it wasn't. Looking around at our faces trying to no avail to find who it was, she started crying. I don't think there was a dry eye in the place. Even the he-shes were upset. Hell, they were human too!

One of the girls spoke to Chocolate Milk and he went back to the cook, who sent the waitresses out with more food. Chocolate Milk got up and walked towards them. They saw him and stopped eating. Wouldn't you? A giant of a man headed right your way. Looking down, not saying a word, the youngest kid started to giggle. The other joined in, and a minute later the mother started too. So much laughter. Then the kids were making funny faces, and that was when Chocolate Milk lost it. He let out a laugh that was so loud it startled a waitress, nearly causing her to drop an order in a customer's lap! I almost spilled my coffee.

Then everybody was laughing. The whole place was going nuts!

With all this going on, Chocolate Milk reached in his pocket, pulled out a wad of cash, placed it in front of her, and walked away. The whole atmosphere did an about-face, it got so quiet you could hear a pin drop, it only lasted for a minute. Chair legs were being scraped along the floor, people were getting up and headed her way.

A line formed, cooks, waitresses, the girls, he-shes, other customers, and all had money in their hands. I had something extra too. I joined in, and when I got to the front, it looked like she was a bank teller, money neatly stacked everywhere!

Chocolate Milk came over again and the mother said something to the kids and they got up, ran to him, and each started hugging his legs. What a sight! Chocolate Milk walking around with a kid on each leg holding on for life. The kids were screeching with joy. Chocolate Milk was roaring with laughter and we were holding on to anything to keep from falling over. While everybody else was preoccupied, I snuck a peek outside. Parked in front of the diner was the sorriest-looking station wagon I had ever seen. The back was crammed with personal belongings, and sitting up front was a teenage girl eating and a toddler drinking from a milk bottle. More family. Hopefully in transit to a new life where mother and children could live and grow up decently. Lord, hear my prayers. The door behind me opened and here came everybody, a few girls went to the car to look at the toddler. Boy, if the Pussy Posse had showed up right then, it would have been a clean sweep.

Time to leave, the kids climbed in, and before the mother did, she gave a long look around the room, couldn't find the words. Went over to a few girls and gave them hugs and kisses, then she focused her attention on Chocolate Milk.

They just stood there staring at each other until suddenly he extended his arms and she walked into them. They let go and he kissed her cheek. She got into the car, and while the kids were waving to us, she turned the key and the car backfired, pow! Some of us jumped back, a few screamed, the rest were laughing.

One more backfire then the car started up, making clunking sounds and spewing a lot of smoke from the tailpipe. We watched their trail of smoke as they pulled away from the curb. With all their hardships, they still held together as a family.

It was getting lighter out, meaning the breakfast crowd would be here soon, time for us to split, a few minutes later everybody was gone.

I felt so alone; my heart was empty. I looked down at my makeshift bed. Under the covers I was having flashbacks of my wife and children, wishing I could tell them how very sorry I was for messing up their lives. *Home* is a four-letter word that's always on our minds, hoping that some-day someone will come for us. Someone will say, "All is forgiven, come home."

Better face it, Cadillac Man, this is life. Nobody is going to come and rescue you, now go to sleep. I did. Can't say I slept very well.

Eddie and the Wizard

Brooklyn, 1998

"HEY, CADILLAC MAN! HEY, CADILLAC MAN!"

"Eddie, shut the fuck up! I ain't deaf." I was sitting on a bench in Prospect Park, just finishing a cigarette.

"Look! Look!" he said, waving a check. Among Eddie's habits was saying everything twice. I snatched it out of his hand. I was tempted to tear it up but looked first, a check made to him, eight thousand dollars and change.

"Very good, Eddie, cash it and hide it somewhere in your mom's place."

"Yeah, yeah, okay, come by the park, I'll buy you coffee."

"My man! I'll be there."

Eddie was an okay guy, loved his juice and didn't have to be homeless. He chose to live out here. "I want to be with my friends," he said, causing his mother a lot of heartache.

On bad-weather days she would come around with hot food and clean clothes. "Cadillac Man," she'd say, "have you seen my Edward?" I couldn't lie to her and would bring her over to the park.

Most of the time, Eddie was sitting there, bottle in one hand, reeking of alcohol, piss, and shit. But that didn't bother her. She would take away the bottle and spoon-feed him, talking softly, stroking his hair.

Other times she found him under the park bench covered with a tarp. She would plead for him to come out. When he didn't answer, she would look at me with those *please help me* eyes. It pissed me off, but I bit my lip, reached under, grabbed the ankles, and dragged his ass out, then sat him down hard on the bench. That would rattle anybody's teeth and sobered him up momentarily.

Eddie wasn't much good at canning and panhandling; I have seen his mother slip him money though. He used it to buy the cheapest, rottenest beer or booze, that way he didn't have to share with anyone.

Contrary to outsiders' belief that we will drink anything, most of us have certain tastes.

I myself stopped drinking liquor once I got out in the streets. The only time I do is with street ceremonies, memorials for the dead. I had a reason to drink and that was to forget, and once I was out there, I just totally stopped. I still like my wine, but nothing else.

Eddie on the other hand would drink anything, and he got to be a pain in the ass, always mooching. "Spare a quarter? Spare a quarter?" You gave him one just to get rid of him.

Yessiree, he hit up everybody until the day he met the Wizard.

The Wizard had been around these parts a lot longer than the couple of months I had. Word on the street was that he had mystical powers and performed miracles. When I was told this by others, I couldn't stop laughing. Go figure.

Then I heard something that I could believe: If you wanted welfare or SSI benefits, the Wizard was the man to see. Got cut off? No problem for the Wizard—he would get you on in a flash! I'll explain more later.

One day I saw the Wizard talking with a bunch of guys. He stopped and we made eye contact. Confident smile with steel blue eyes trying to stare me down while the others watched. Fat chance, suckers, I can play your game. It didn't take too long, the smile wavered, then his eyes switched to someone else.

You lose, sucker, I thought, but he did steal one last glance.

So who was the Wizard?

A truly unique character. About my height, thirtyish with long brown hair and a wide white streak in the middle down to his shoulders. Wore a dark blue coat with gold stars and crescent moons, then on his feet, white patent leather shoes! But what I liked the most, the crooked wooden cane with a big crystal on top. Actually, it looked more like a clear-plastic doorknob. Mystical powers, my ass. Yet my people flocked to him for advice and he embraced them all—for a price!

Ladies and gentlemen, ain't nothing for nothing out here.

The more the Wizard talked, the more he charged you. On check day you would find him by the bank or check-cashing place collecting from clients. People felt indebted to him for helping them get their benefits. The Wizard knew what to do or say in front of social workers and doctors. He coached you all the way, helping you with the paperwork or going to the intake center or the hospital if need be. If anybody asked who he was, he answered back, "A friend."

He knew exactly how long it would take to receive your first check from SSI or unemployment or whatever, and he would be waiting for you at the check-cashing place when the next check arrived. Mystical powers.

Which leads us back to Eddie.

He was in such a rush to cash the eight-thousand-dollar check that he raced off to see the Wizard. How much the Wizard was going to get from Eddie was anybody's guess. What was certain was that after Eddie got his money, it was party time. Word would spread like wildfire that he was carrying a lot of cash, and every piece-of-shit predator would try to mooch from him. And they did! I just hoped he had the common sense to drop off the bulk of it at his mother's place.

I'd been to her place a few weeks before. A group of gangbangers had stomped Eddie and I saw him staggering about in the park. Face like a crushed tomato, clothes torn and pockets turned inside out, he refused to go to the hospital and told me his mother's address. He couldn't walk so I picked him up and laid him into my war wagon and took him over to his mother's house, just a few blocks from the park on Sterling Place.

On my way, I got stopped by five-O asking what happened to him and I told them that Eddie fell off a park bench and I was bringing him home. Carried him up one flight of stairs, and when his mother came out, I thought at first she was going to have a heart attack. Laid him down on the couch, and he almost instantly fell asleep. She thanked me and offered a cup of coffee, so I stayed.

She told me about their lives together after Eddie's father died, the ups and downs with Eddie being on the street. I wasn't really listening until the Wizard's name came up. Lady, you now have my undivided attention.

"One day he came in all excited asking for his birth papers," his mother said. "When I asked why, he said he had a friend downstairs waiting and he needed the papers to help process his application for disability benefits. Cadillac Man, my son might not be the brightest person, but there is nothing physically wrong with him aside from the drinking. I tried to talk him out of it and he yelled at me, saying, 'Wizard said everybody out in the streets is doing it so I might as well too.' He grabbed the papers and was gone. I went to the window, looked down, and saw Eddie talking to this strange man with white hair in the middle, a funny-looking coat and stick. Wish I could have seen his face.

"A few days later while I was doing some chores, I heard police cars in front of the house and a lot of footsteps heading up to the roof. Outside there was a huge crowd across the street looking up at the rooftop. I looked up and there standing on the ledge ready to jump was my Edward! I screamed, I was so frightened I must have fainted.

"When I came to, I was lying on a stretcher in an ambulance. I asked about my son. They said he was okay, they managed to grab him and he will spend the next few days in the hospital for observation.

"After he was released, I tried talking to him. It was useless. 'Ma, I had to do it, it is the only way,' he told me. Then one night I get a phone call from the police saying that he was back in the hospital. He tried to commit suicide by slashing his wrists with a broken bottle, and this time they kept him for a month. And who do you think was there when he got out?"

"The Wizard?"

"Right. I was going to pick Eddie up and saw both of them talking. Then Mr. Wizard spotted me, said one more thing to my son, and left. Eddie stayed with me for a while, kept all his appointments, but then he started drinking again and not coming home. He would forget to take his medicine along, and when I looked at the pill bottles, some were unopened!

I can't prove it but I feel strongly that the Wizard is the cause of my son's problems." She was crying, overcome with frustration. "Please, Cadillac Man, whenever you can, please watch over him."

I told her I would try. Leaving, I felt bad that I couldn't tell her what I knew about the Wizard. Why upset her more? He used Eddie and jeopardized his life for his own personal gain. Now that Eddie had an eight-thousand-dollar check, the Wizard would be putting Eddie's life in jeopardy again. I had to find him. It wouldn't surprise me if the Wizard spread the word around that Eddie had a pocket full of cash. I hoped it wasn't too late.

I went by the bank and two check-cashing places and didn't see them. Only spot left to check out was the park. There was Eddie, and not alone. It looked like a fucking block party. Eddie was already shit-faced and everyone else appeared to be also. I had an uneasy feeling they would try to rip Eddie off. I had to get him away, but how?

"Heeeey, Caddie Man. How ya doing?"

"Hey, Eddie—and it's Cadillac Man."

"Ooops." Laughing. "Hey, Billyyyyy, come here!"

Eddie reached in his pocket, pulled a wad of bills, and peeled off a twenty. That moment every eye in the park zeroed in on Eddie's cash. It became so very quiet. "What do you want, Eddie?" Billy asked. Billy was like a walking corpse—skinny, with long black hair and this backwards Mets cap that looked like it got chewed by a dog.

Handing him the money, Eddie said, "Billyyyyy, I want you to get the biggest coffee in the world for my friend Caddie Man here, and one for you too!"

Billy is a juicer, hard-core, yet I noticed that his bottle was three-quarters full, and he was taking baby sips. Very strange.

"Billy, make sure it is fresh with milk and sugar," I said.

"Okay, Cadillac Man."

"And one more thing, Billy."

"Yes?"

"Come back today, and real soon, okay?"

He knew what I meant: if you fuck Eddie out of money, it's the same as dissing me.

"I get the message."

"Good. Now get going. I'm thirsty."

He slipped his booze into a bag and off he went. Would he come back? You better believe it!

Eddie called over another guy and gave him a twenty to buy more sixes. Another "friend" stepped in to talk to Eddie for a minute and walked away with money. I had to stop this before it got out of hand.

"Eddie!" That caught everybody's attention, including his.

"Whaaat?"

"Put your fucking money away before you fucking lose it!"

All eyes were on me, and that was good, maybe now they would have second thoughts. Surprise, surprise: Billy came back with a large coffee. Preoccupied with drinking and bullshitting, Eddie was unaware of his return. Billy said nothing and sat right back down in the same spot as if he never left. Eddie was so shit-faced he deserved to be ripped off. It happens to everybody. You expect it, and when roles are reversed, you do it too. It is the street way. But I made a promise to watch over him, and that is what I was going to do.

"Hey, Billy, come here!" I called. I wanted us to talk alone rather than to dis him in front of others.

"What's wrong, Cadillac Man?"

"You know what."

"No, I don't, and I saw them take the coffee from a fresh pot."

"The coffee is fine, but you forgot the change."

"Change?"

"Don't play stupid with me, Billy, the change from the twenty. Give it back to Eddie."

"Oh, that," he said, laughing. "That was my tip for going." As a rule you generally get one dollar for running the errand or else share whatever you bought.

"Billy, Eddie is my friend. You fuck with him and that means you fuck me. You deserve a tip for going, but you better give back to Eddie at least fifteen dollars right now or I'm going to shove this in your fucking heart!"

His eyes widened as I gave him a brief glimpse of my ice pick.

"Okay, put it away. I'll give it to him."

He was scared and probably pissed. Nobody out here likes losing money, no matter how it was obtained.

He walked over to Eddie and said something to him, then put the money in his hands. With the condition Eddie was in, you could have put a pile of dog shit in his hands and he wouldn't have noticed it.

"Okay, Cadillac Man?" Billy asked.

"Okay, Billy. And, Billy, I would have done the same thing if it was happening to you."

He half smiled, said thanks, and walked back to the benches to sulk and maybe start taking bigger sips of juice. The other guy that borrowed money from Eddie was gone.

Now I had to deal with Eddie, had to figure a way to get him out of there. He was down for the count, contents of the bottle slowly pouring out into his lap.

I walked over. "Come on, guys, move the fuck over!"

Guess they thought I wanted to sit down. You should've seen the looks on their faces when I picked Eddie up and put him into my war wagon. Damn, besides reeking of juice, he had a load of shit in his pants. Oh, well, at least he was still breathing. Don't light a stick, whatever you do.

One of the guys in the park stood up. "Hey! What are you doing with Eddie?"

A few others standing around chimed in, "Yeah."

"Sorry, guys, but the party is over. I'm taking him home."

"He ain't got no home!" the first guy said.

"Yes, he does, his mother's place!"

"Bullshit! You're gonna take his money."

Now I was really pissed! I went over to the bench and grabbed Eddie's empty bottle by the neck and slowly walked towards Big Mouth. The others, seeing this, decided it was time to go, leaving him alone to deal with me.

"Don't worry about the bottle," I told him. "I'm not going to use it on you." Stepping closer, I said, "I'll show you a little trick. Watch what happens to the bottle when I drop it from chest high." I got closer.

During all this he was sipping away, I guess for instant courage. Bad move—it also dulls the senses and slows down the reflexes.

"Now watch very carefully and be amazed," I said, releasing the bottle. He watched its descent, followed it to the ground where it smashed to pieces, then waited for something else to happen. Something did.

Bang! Bang! Bang! Two shots to the face and one to the chest, causing him to fall backwards.

Here's a street rule to remember: once they're down, keep them down! I kicked him hard in the balls. Drunk or not, he would feel unbelievable pain and forget about having pussy for a while. Just be thankful if he can still piss. By the time he got up, Eddie and I would be long gone.

I heard a familiar sound. Eddie had sat up and barfed on himself. Terrific. No doubt it would seep into my bedding and clean clothes. I didn't know why I was doing this. Maybe I hope somebody will do the same for me.

I had to check Eddie's airway to make sure it was clean. A friend of a friend drowned in his own vomit, and nobody knew until it was too late. I pinched his nose shut and pressed down on his chin; looked clear. Then took a pencil and rolled it across his tongue, causing him to gag a little bit. Good.

Big Mouth was still moaning and groaning. Fuck him.

"Let's go home," I told Eddie.

Once we're going through the streets, all eyes are upon us, the outsiders passing judgment on the way we look. True, Eddie is in a terrible state, but he is still a man. He just needs help. Whether or not he gets it is entirely up to him at this stage. But I can state that the likelihood is that he won't make it.

Sounds cruel, right? Let me explain further. Most out here wouldn't change their lifestyles, why should they? You receive a check, then everybody is happy, it's party time! Your friends, wannabes, moochers, all gather together and soon the juice starts flowing. Everybody is bullshitting, laughing, singing, having a grand old time. Then someone has a slip of the tongue, one itty-bitty word explodes into an argument, and all hell breaks loose.

I remember two best friends arguing, and they pulled out blades and sliced and diced each other so bad they were both hospitalized. What was the argument about? Cartoon characters—who was better, Daffy or Donald Duck. Didn't see them for a while, maybe both bought a little jail time. Then one day there they were, back at their hangout, near Grand Army Plaza, partying and pointing, laughing at each other's numerous scars! Go figure.

Street people who drink together are friends to the end. You could be beaten, robbed, and stabbed and the next day forgive the guy who knifed you if he shows up with a six or a bottle of juice.

Looking down at Eddie, I was sick and sad at seeing a precious life being wasted.

As I was staring at him, he started gagging. I pulled him up just in time for an endless stream of vomit to gush out onto both of us. He fell back exhausted, looking about, confused, then looked at me with recognition.

"Where are we going, Cadillac Man?"

"Home."

"Good," he said, then closed his eyes.

His mother, coming back from grocery shopping, spotted us.

"Cadillac Man, is he okay?"

"Yes, ma'am, you go ahead and open the door and I'll carry him up. Come on, Eddie, up we go, you are home." I could actually feel his rib cage through his shirt. We entered the apartment. I heard running water, a bathtub filling up, then I saw her coming out of another room with a pair of jammies, waving to me.

Inside the bathroom, I stood him up against the wall.

"I'll stand here while you take off his clothes, ma'am."

"That won't be necessary, Cadillac Man, I have done this many times before, and you take your clothes off too."

"Ma'am?"

"I see that Edward got sick on you, and after I'm through with him, you can wash up."

"But, ma'am, I don't have any underwear on."

"Oh! Here, take this towel and don't worry, I won't peek."

I can't win this argument and I can't refuse a shower.

"Wait in the living room or kitchen," Eddie's mother said. "There is instant coffee in the cupboard above the sink, help yourself."

She didn't have to tell me twice. I made a beeline for the kitchen.

While I was waiting for the water to boil, I decided to look out the window and check on my wagon. I worry about the flags attached to it—I kept six American flags on the wagon at that time. If a group of kids grabbed them, I wouldn't be able to do anything to stop it. There I was, half-naked and hairy-faced. Sheesh! Oh, well, water is ready and my taste buds are in overdrive awaiting that first sip of coffee. Ahhh!

From the bathroom, I heard the sound of heavy splashing and something else, Eddie's mother crying.

"Oh, Edward, why are you doing this? Why?"

"I'm sorry, Mom," Eddie said. Then he started crying too.

That made three of us. Suddenly, I could taste not coffee but blood. Wizard blood!

He made a bad situation worse.

"Cadillac Man!"

"Huh? Yes, ma'am?" I came out of my reverie.

"We're finished, you can go in now."

"Thank you, ma'am."

What a sorry sight to behold, even though Eddie was cleaned up. Looked a lot older holding on to his mother.

I dashed into the shower and, oh, what a feeling. I could stay in here forever! Rarely get the chance, mostly it is bird baths in restaurant restrooms or water sprinklers in playgrounds if there aren't any kids around.

A knock on the door startled me. "Cadillac Man, I have some clean clothes that might fit you."

"Thank you, ma'am."

"When you come out, I'll have some fresh coffee made."

What is the quickest way to make me do anything—well, almost anything? Offer me fresh coffee. Good-bye shower. I must have lost fifty pounds of dirt. The clothes fit good, perhaps they belonged to her husband, the only thing I didn't put on was his underwear.

Then I made a mistake by looking at myself in the mirror. It had been a long time, and even with my hair combed I still looked like a wild man from Borneo. Beet-red face with a full beard and more gray hair, shit. More wrinkles, double shit. I used to be so cute, what happened? The streets made you this way, they did!

I walked towards the kitchen and I saw Eddie's mother sitting at the table, crying. She didn't see me so I took several steps backwards and coughed, waited a minute so that she could compose herself, then walked in. She was pouring the coffee and looked up.

"How are you feeling, Cadillac Man?"

"Much better. Please call me Caddy."

"Ethel."

I sat down, and on the table beside the coffee was a pile of money and, oops, my ice pick! Very careless of me.

"I put him in bed, Caddy."

Good, better here than a park bench, I thought.

"Where did I go wrong?"

"Don't blame yourself, Ethel, it was his choice to make. You can't change him back, it has to be his decision. Don't get discouraged. Now that Eddie will be receiving monthly checks, he is at greater risk," I told her. "But there is something you can do to lessen the chances of him getting hurt. Who has the mailbox key?"

"We both do, why?"

"Have the lock changed and you keep the only key. That way he can't get the check. Don't let him volunteer to get the mail, you get it. If possible, walk with him, and when his check is cashed, ask for at least half or more for safekeeping. If you hold most of it, he has to come to you, and the amount you give him depends on his condition. Chances are he will come back a second time, maybe the next day, then you tell him there is none left. Confused, he will believe you, after all, mothers don't lie. I have seen guys go through their entire check in a matter of days, then off to beg, borrow, or steal."

"What about this money, Caddy?"

"Sure looks like a lot."

"Oh, yes, fifty-five hundred dollars."

It was so hard to keep a straight face. I felt like screaming my head off. A difference of twenty-five hundred, and she doesn't know that the Wizard took a huge piece of the pie, at least two grand, my guess.

"Caddy, what is wrong, you look so angry."

"Huh? Sorry, Ethel, I was just thinking about what could have happened to Eddie if the others knew he was carrying so much money. Ethel, I need you to do me a favor."

"What do you need?"

"I need you to hide this money. Put it in the bank. Anywhere. Don't tell him you found it. If he happens to ask, just say there was only ten dollars in his pockets. I'm willing to bet he won't say he had more than that."

"Thank you for bringing him here. Is there something I can do to repay you, some money?"

"You already paid me, the shower, clean clothes, and coffee."

"I will pray for you, Caddy."

"Thanks, that means a lot to me, I pray every day. See ya, ma'am— I mean, Ethel."

When I got to the door, she called, "Caddy." She gave me a hug.

"Don't worry, Ethel, things will work out." Then I walked out.

We all know that she will worry, for that is what mothers do, at least some I know. I envy you, Eddie.

The next couple of days were boring and uneventful, thankfully. I didn't see anybody so I spent most of my time sleeping and canning. It was then I decided I was off to see the Wizard. I had a present for him.

I spread the word around and waited.

A couple days later, I walked past the park and who did I see sitting in his usual spot but Eddie. He didn't look too bad and was just opening a bottle of juice when he saw me.

"Hey, Cadillac Man!" he called, waving to me.

You're breaking your mother's heart, can't you see it?

"Hey, Eddie, how you feeling?"

"Good, good, and thanks for bringing me over to my mother's place. She told me you carried me up the stairs and that I got sick all over your clothes. Sorry. Before I forget, take this." He handed me a plastic bag.

"What is this?"

"Your clothes, cleaned and ironed. Mother told me to look for you and not to touch them."

"Damn, they look new with the creases! Thank her for me."

He took a big swig, spilling some down his shirt.

"Whoa, slow down, Eddie, it is fucking too early!"

I turned to my wagon and was about to leave when Eddie said something so softly I could hardly make it out: "Can you spare a dollar until I get my next check?"

Blood rushed to my head. I was going to bash his fucking face in, then an image of his mother appeared in my mind. I calmed down, smiled. She did the right thing by not telling him about the money. Way to go, Ethel!

I slipped him a dollar.

"Thanks, Cadillac Man, I'll pay you back when I get my check."

"Later, Eddie."

He got up, walked out of the park, and headed towards the liquor store. It was then I noticed he had pissed his pants. All my talk for nothing, in one ear and out the other. It happens a lot out here.

I knew the Wizard was around somewhere, others told me they had seen him. What was he waiting for? Maybe he was planning on sneaking up on me with his "fan club."

The next day I was walking past the park when I noticed Eddie sprawled out on the ground. The stupid bastard was snoring! And he stank like rhino shit!

"Come on, Eddie. Let me help you up."

From behind me came a greeting. "Hello, Cadillac Man."

I was startled for an instant, turned around, and there he was, the Wizard, along with two others from his club.

"I heard that you wanted to see me."

"Yes, I do, tell your kiddies to go play in the sandbox while we talk."

The two big shits with puffed-out chests looked at each other and one made a move towards me, but the Wizard stopped him.

"You go get me a diet cola and you go with him. Be back in fifteen minutes. Okay with you, Cadillac Man?"

"That's plenty of time, thank you, Wizard."

Passing me, one of the goons said something to the other that made him laugh. It was obvious they were dissing me.

"Go on, boys, go get your boss some soda pop," I said.

One charged at me. I flashed my ice pick, and the two shitheads reluctantly walked away.

I told the Wizard, "I'm leaving in a few minutes and chances are I may never come to these parts ever again." Boy, was he smiling. "And I know about the two thou you took from Eddie and I don't fucking like it. He doesn't know I know. It is our little secret."

"I told him what to do, it was his decision to carry out my suggestions," the Wizard said, still smiling.

I had started walking away when he said, "How much did you get, Cadillac Man?"

I turned back. Got real close to him and whispered, "Five thou."

His smile changed to a look of shock—then bang! Bang! Bang! Pain replaced the shock as he fell backwards onto the bench next to Eddie. He put up his hands in front of his face, gasping, "Don't hit me anymore, please!"

"I'm through with you, Wizard." He put his hands down.

Bang! Bang! Bang!

"Sorry, Wizard, I'm a rotten liar." Bang! "Motherfucker! Remember this, Wizard, if you fuck with Eddie while I'm gone and I find out about it, I'll come back for you."

Reaching in my pocket, I took out a piece of paper. "This is Eddie's mother's phone number. I'll call her from time to time to check." I didn't really have it, but he didn't know.

"See you, Wizard." I extended my hand to shake, and when the stupid bastard reached for it, bang! Bang! I popped him again. He let out a scream so loud the people in Hackensack were covering their ears.

On my way out I spotted the Wizard's cane and picked it up. Thought about keeping it, but instead I threw it out into the street and a car driving by snapped it in two.

A few weeks later I paid to have a shower and put on the clothes Ethel washed. Out here we can't change every day like you do. Inside one of the pockets was a thank-you note and one hundred dollars! Later, I bumped into one of the guys who hung out at the park. He told me that the Wizard disappeared and nobody missed him! Did his mystical powers make him invisible? Could be! Ha!

How I Got Here 2

I LEARNED ABOUT CANNING before there was canning. Let me explain. Back in the day a friend of mine taught me how to pick up bottles—soda bottles and beer bottles. We didn't have cans back in those days. But still, he taught me.

Joe the bum was a neighborhood fixture in Hell's Kitchen. I met him shortly after my father left, back in 1960. I was a little kid then, eleven years old, so it's hard to describe him now. He had to be at least six foot, in his thirties, red hair receding. He walked with a limp. He served in World War II. I know because one time he took me down to the Brooklyn Navy Yard. I wanted to go in but he showed it to me from the distance.

I liked him. Everybody was afraid of him, but when he was sober, he was a real nice guy. When he had a few in him, he would mumble and grumble and scare people off, but it didn't bother me. He got stopped by the police one night, filthy dirty, and everyone said he was a bum, but I never looked at a person that way. In my mind, he's an alcoholic.

One day he told me, I'm going to show you how to make some money, and we went to the garbage cans and picked up the bottles. The little bottles were two cents and the great big beer bottles were five cents. Oh, boy, I thought, this is *money* here. Back in 1960 if you gave me a quarter, oh, man, I was in seventh heaven. You know how much candy I can get for a quarter? Candies were two for a penny. Sodas were a nickel.

Everybody was a drinker back then, and beer was a cheap high, so there were always bottles around. Some days we would make a dollar, easy. We usually didn't have to go that far, there were places that would take bottles right in the neighborhood. I knew people at a couple places that liked me because I was a cute little boy with red hair and freckles. I looked like Howdy Doody. Joe would wait outside. They wouldn't let him inside the store.

So Joe would get his beers, or he would go to the liquor store and get a bottle of Wild Irish Rose. That was one of his favorites. Forty cents a pint, real cheap shit. And then whatever money was left over was for me. Although, once in a while I would say, get your cigarettes too, Joe. So I'd just be happy, number one, having the company, and number two, getting whatever money I made after he got his wine and his smokes. Eating was out of the equation. I never seen him eat anything, this guy. So he actually taught me about recycling. Thirty-four years later, I'd be glad for the things he taught me.

The first morning I was on the street, on the Upper East Side, the security woke me up and told me to get out of here. I must have had about two dollars. I remember getting peanut crackers that were twenty-five cents a pack, and that helped. For cigarettes I was picking up butts off the streets. I did that for many, many years, picking up butts off the streets.

That first morning, I'm saying, wait a minute, I need some money to survive. I knew I couldn't panhandle. To me it was a step down to go over and ask somebody, can you spare a quarter or a dime? But I knew about canning. Doing the walkabout in the hood, I noticed this beer distributor, there was a group out there and they were putting all these cans into one of those cardboard containers and they were going inside the store and coming out with cash. When I was living at home, it never really occurred to me to do something like that. Whenever I had an empty can or bottle, I just put it into the trash. But when I hit the streets, I was saying to myself, this is an excellent source of income for me. I went canning. My first time in thirty-four years.

I kept it up for a few days, getting enough money to eat, staying close to Hell's Kitchen. After a while I didn't want to go on anymore. I was so depressed that things weren't going my way. I was thinking maybe my family would come around. That's why I stayed local, hoping word would spread, they would see me and my condition. Perhaps I would even tell people that, oh, yeah, my wife threw me out, to make people feel sorry for me. I wouldn't give them the full story as to why.

Wait, you're thinking. Why didn't you just go straight to your family? Well, maybe my family's different from yours. I got three brothers, three sisters. I'm the third of seven. My sister Bess, my gosh, I don't even know her birthday, but I think she's six years older. Right now she should be sixty-seven, sixty-eight. She's living in a town called Carlisle, Pennsylvania.

All the kids were born to different fathers. Bess, I believe she never met her father. I could be wrong, but she never talked about him. His name was Green. The only thing I heard about him was that he was in the military during the big war. Other than that, there was no other mention. Jimmy is going to be sixty, I believe, sixty or fifty-nine. Growing up he had platinum blond hair. Now I remember I looked at my mother with jet-black hair and my grandmother with jet-black hair and my grandfather with reddish blond hair, and I said, what happened here? And face-wise, he didn't resemble anybody. A while back my brother applied for a job so he had to get his birth certificate, and when he got it, it said father unknown. He went ballistic. So why she took my father's last name, I don't know.

We lived in a big apartment at 421 West Forty-Fifth, between Ninth and Tenth. It was first registered under my grandparents' name. They were living at home too. But none of my mother's "husbands" lived there, never. The reason is anyone's guess, although when I was younger, she mentioned that she was on welfare, what they called home relief years ago. Once in a while we would get a visit from these people and she would tell me, go in the living room, I don't want them to see you. If you make any noise, they're going to come in and take you away.

My father worked at the Garden City Cafeteria, on 8th Avenue between 49th and 50th, right across the street from the Worldwide Plaza. Every so often I'd go over there and see him and hopefully get something to eat, but he would never give me shit. He would sit me down and smoke his Camels, and when it was time to leave, he'd say, well, you be a good boy, then he would go into the Garden City Hotel, which was only several doors down. I saw him several times and then, of course, the big day on my tenth birthday. My old man left when I was ten, right on my birthday. He told me, "My birthday present to you is that I will never see you again." But there was no real relationship there anyway. I didn't feel any love for him.

I look like him, though.

The next kid was Arlene, Miss Wall Street. She works down there, something dealing with stocks. I asked her one time if she remembered my father, and she said the only thing she remembered was the one time we went to the cafeteria and he gave me a honey-and-butter sandwich.

By my count, there were at least four men we considered fathers. All of them came and went. The last one was the father of my youngest brothers, Pete and Dan, though I never thought the two of them looked the same. They took his name, Hartmann, on and off over the years whenever it suited them, but my mother never married him. My siblings were saying, yeah, Ma got married, look at the wedding bands. Back then you could go into a pawn shop and buy a wedding band. Just say, oh, I got married, see, there's my band, and people would take you at your word.

I felt a little bit of closeness with Danny and Peter's father. I remember the last day I saw him was at Smith's Bar, on 44th Street and 8th Avenue. It's still there. He told me to meet him there and he came over to me, grabbed my chin. At that time I was twelve, maybe thirteen, but I remember it like it was yesterday. He said, well, I'm going to see you this week-end. I'm going to get you some new clothes. We all wore hand-me-downs. After that I never saw him again. I found out years later that he died an alcoholic.

Having brothers and sisters was like having friends, but not close friends. Once in a while Arlene and I used to play some games together. They had a game called Dinosaurs, where you'd write out *Tyrannosaurus rex* and see how many words you can get out of it. The only other time that she would be friendly with me is when her girlfriends were selling Girl Scout cookies. I never even kissed my sister. Except maybe at her wedding. The time I got the most hugs in my life was at my mother's funeral.

Where we lived, love wasn't necessary back then. Survival, that's all that counted, and that's why we were into our little things to make a few dollars here and there. Most of the guys didn't have fathers, or they didn't have mothers. Or they did have parents that were beating the shit out of each other or drunk or hiding from the cops or in jail or whatever. Still, most families, you had some sort of family gathering, midnight mass, Easter, something like that, where you would go as a family. Maybe the rest of the year you wouldn't bother, but at least once or twice a year you would be all together, a family. For us, whenever these occasions came about, we all thought, why would we go to church, for what?

My other siblings were close with each other. They had similar interests and they were younger than me. Later, they got money, and it seemed like they were competing with one another. But me, I was the outcast. I didn't have a house like Miss Wall Street or I didn't have the condo like my brother Peter had or I didn't have the house like my brother Danny has in upstate New York. Yet there were times when they needed my help, I helped them out within my power, a few dollars or whatever. Did they appreciate it? No, they still owe me money. I guess perhaps I can blame myself too. Maybe if I was a little bit more open.

And in a sense I let them down. For years, my older brother Jim was constantly beating the shit out of them. When I was little, he used to beat the crap out of me, nearly drowned me a couple of times, so when I got older, I wanted to do something. I wanted to beat the crap out of him so bad, and he knew it. When I came out of the military, they were all happy that I was going to kick his ass up and down the avenue. They knew how crazy I became in the army, because I was a lot bigger and stronger and more confident of myself with my fighting ability. But my mother was saying, oh, don't, don't, don't. You don't live here. You beat him up, when you're gone, he's going to take it out on us. She was so terrified of my brother. There were times where I tried to go over and see her and she'd say, oh, you can't go in the living room because that's where Jimmy has his stuff, and if you go in there, he's going to find out. It was out of loneliness, I guess. She had nobody else so she tolerated all this shit that he gave out.

Several weeks after I went out on the street I happened to see my younger sister Eleanor, who lives out in Queens. We were never really that close. In fact, the only time we really got close was when she turned to drugs, hard-core heroin. That was '74, '75, when I came out of the military. I got her to go into a methadone program. She knew that I was a volunteer officer and I basically told her, either you're going into this program or I'm going to kill you. I scared the piss out of her. I brought her over to the drug clinic and I waited downstairs. When she came out, I said, you got into the program? Yeah, I got into the program, she said. She'd go once a week, so I was happy about that, but little did I know it was going to be long-term with methadone. That stuff is poison.

So, Eleanor gave me a bullshit line that the family was looking for me. Yeah, right, they were looking for me. When she saw me, I was waiting in line at the soup kitchen, and she said, come to Astoria with me. Since I knew my brother Dan was there also, I said okay. I must admit I didn't look too good. Dan took one look at me and he was crying and I was crying and he was saying, you're staying here now. So I thought, I'm going to be getting off the streets—he's going to take me in, so maybe things will work out for me, maybe I've got a chance here. I stayed overnight, and the next day I was out canning and my sister came over to me and she says, you know something? You've got lice. Dan's two daughters, they got lice. I said, I don't have lice. But the street people, they're stereotyped, so all right, I got lice. I had to go to her place, and she got this stuff from the drugstore, some crap to put in your hair. Whatever it was, it stunk like hell.

Later on that day my brother came over and apologized, saying the kids got lice from some kids in school. So he told me I could go back to his place. I didn't want to go back. I knew that if it wasn't lice, it would be something else. That was what I thought—that he would get upset, maybe, by seeing me doing some canning, like Eleanor. She didn't like me canning. But it was my income, my source of income. And you know, whatever I made from canning I used to bring food home for her. We got into a big argument. I'm trying to do the right thing here by bringing in money and food for you. Well, these are my rules. I had to be home by a certain time and I could leave only at certain times because she would have to get up and lock the door. That really upset me, because as a canner you have to go out early. Canning was my income, and her embarrassment about it drove a wedge between us. So pack up the cart, I was back out on the street.

In the very beginning I was content with making five, ten dollars a day. But as time went on, I had a lot of time to kill, so I would spend more of it out there canning. It's something to do. So I could easily make fifty dollars a day, minimum. Most people they don't have any idea how much money you can make out there. I call it nickel heaven, five cents a can. There were times I made eighty to a hundred.

I found myself a nice, big cart, just sitting all by its lonesome on the corner near the A&P on 9th Avenue. I used it for canning. On any given day, I did at least fifteen to twenty miles, walk, walk, just load up the cart. I'd find the cans right in front of residences. You could get bags right out of the trash cans or from people at the redeemer after they were done cashing in. Later I would sometimes find some restaurants that would give me cans, but that was very rare. For the most part, I'd just stop in front of a residence, look in the recycle barrel, and also at the corners, the wastebaskets where people would be dumping. It's all tax-free income. But it takes time and energy. You want to make fifty bucks a day, you're going to have to work.

I'll give you an example. Later on I had a map of Queens from the Department of Sanitation. This map told you what days everybody put out the cans and bottles in any given location. So every so often I would walk from Astoria to Flushing, a little over three hours, collecting cans along the way. There were times I wouldn't even get to Flushing, I would have so much that I would turn back. I would go to a redeemer, unload some of it, and then go on to another area. Sometimes I would just work twenty-four hours straight because canning gave me something to do.

You know, one of your worst enemies out there is boredom. And the loneliness.

It hit me hard in the first couple of months out there. Nobody was talking to me, I mean nobody. When you're homeless, who would talk to you? People don't even want to *see* you. So sometimes you may not realize it, you'd be talking out loud to nobody. You're just getting it out of your system. It was like this guy at the meat market, Bernie. He used to work down in the freezer, and nobody wanted to go down there. Most of the time people would just call him down there and say, Bernie, put this on the elevator. But I would go down there on occasion and he'd be having conversations. I'd be looking in there and say, who is he talking to? Same thing on the street. It gets lonely out here. The closest I got to a conversation with anyone was when somebody was going by and they'd take a look at me and start laughing, laughing at me.

My first week after I left Dan's, I was sleeping right in front of this bank on Park Avenue, between 47th and 48th. Every night this guy would come over with a sandwich. He'd say, here you go, you bum, here you go. Nice, nice sandwich. And then one day I decided I'm going to see what this guy looks like. I opened up my eyes, and, man, I freaked out. He looked like something out of a horror movie—lipstick on, tattoos all over his face. I mean he looked like a complete psychopath. And I said that's it, I got to get out of here because this guy is going to kill me in my sleep one day. But still, it was good to have some kind of human contact, and I didn't have much. What really helped was that I started keeping a journal of my day-to-day activities. But mostly I went canning.

Finally, by word of mouth and then observing the other homeless, I found out places where I could get myself a hot meal, so I could save money there. It's hard out here in Queens, where I live now. There's no place to go to eat a hot meal unless you go way out to Jamaica. There's nothing in Astoria, Long Island City, Corona, Jackson Heights, nothing. But in Manhattan and parts of Brooklyn, my gosh, it was like every third or fourth block there was a place that you could eat, so it was impossible for you to starve. There were times where I would go to a restaurant. Some places would serve me, others wouldn't. I must admit I did look a bit like a maniac with my beard and everything else, but I was trying to keep myself clean, that was the main thing that worried me. Gosh, that was so hard.

But even after two weeks, I considered myself street. I liked the lifestyle. The first couple of days I was sleeping on a piece of cardboard, and thereafter in my travels I came across a dilapidated beach chair and I said, I could use this for a bed. And that same day I came across these banners that Macy's threw out. It was Macy's clearance day. I'm looking at them and I said, I could use these things as a blanket. It was perfect. I got myself a bed. I got a dilapidated beach chair and I've got a blanket, so what the hell else do I need? Everything was falling into place for me.

I found it very enjoyable that I could adapt to it. There were a few little inconveniences but other than that everything was fine. Washing was the biggest inconvenience going. I would go into fast-food places for a five-minute rub-a-dub, where you just take your shirt off and just wash your armpits and wash between your legs and that's it, out. It made the situation more bearable. All right, my clothes are dirty, but at least I've got a somewhat clean body, even though it's between my legs and under my armpits. There were even places, like along 6th Avenue, where they used to have these outdoor water displays. I used to go late at night. I would strip naked. I didn't give a shit. It was two or three o'clock in the morning. Who's going to be around? Go right in there, that's all. Boy, that water was cold, but during the summertime it feels good. And I had a bar of soap with me. I could be in there a good ten to fifteen minutes, wash behind my ears, wash my hair and everything, even dunk underneath the water, great. There were times where the square badges, as we called them, would come out, act rough and tough. They'd come out saying, what the hell do you think you're doing? In fact, one time they called the cops on me. The cops came and security was so proud of themselves and the cops told them we'll take care of this guy for you, and they would go in all proud. Then the cops would look at me and say, you've got two minutes. Get the hell out of here. But it was a convenience.

Little by little, I figured out how to do everything. I felt so free, nobody riding my back, saying do this, do this, do that. I did whatever I wanted to do and I didn't have to answer to anybody. I was free. I was free. You have so much freedom, so much time. Out in the streets I could basically come and go as I pleased. Like, today I'm going to be in Queens and tomorrow I'm going to be in Brooklyn, next day I'll be in Staten Island.

If I feel like sleeping the whole day, I'll sleep the whole day. Or if I stay up all night or I want to take a bath in the pond or whatever, who are you to tell me what to do? I had a camp stove and I'd open up a can of raviolis or whatever. I used to cook scrambled eggs. I used to make a meal for myself, right there on the sidewalk. Why not? When I first came around here, they told me that I couldn't do it because they said it was a fire hazard.

I could do whatever the hell I wanted. I could go swimming in a pond and I loved that. There in your world, you've got a lot of restrictions. You need a job to stay inside, otherwise you come and join me out here. You got yourself a wife, a girlfriend. There are more restrictions. You got to answer to somebody, right? When I was out there, I didn't answer to anybody but myself. That was the beauty of it. Not that I'm trying to glamorize homelessness, because it does have its bad points, but to me the beauty is there were no pressures. The only pressures I had was when people used to pick on me. Other than that, it was, oh, do I feel like canning today? No? I'll just pick a spot and take out my beach chair and just sit there wherever it was. It's quite a life.

There are some organizations that want to change my life. They say, well, we'll get you a job. Okay, you'll get me a job—minimum wage, right? How am I going to survive on that? If I get a job tomorrow paying six-fifty an hour, where am I going to live with the rents the way they are? Nowhere. Stay in a shelter? Un-uh. The shelter will only let you stay there for so long. And how much money would you have to save before you're able to get yourself a place? Do you think any landlord will let you take one of his places? Well, I work at McDonald's. I'm not going to give you this twelve-hundred-dollar-a-month apartment. No, you got to show me more. You get me a job that pays fifteen dollars an hour, twenty dollars an hour, I can get a place to live.

I wanted a job where I could take care of my family, where I could hold my head up high. I can't hold my head up high with a six-fifty-an-hour job. And if I can't get that, fuck it, I'm going to do what I want. It's all or nothing. That's the bottom line. Is that selfish? Yeah. I left a wife and kid behind. But that's how I was. That's the way I felt.

The alimony officers didn't see it that way. I was incarcerated at Bergen County Jail, in work release, for two years, October 31 of '95 to November 3 of '97. Nonpayment of child support. I'm not proud of that.

The work-release program was set up so they let you out of jail provided you have a job that garnishes your salary. I got lucky, I got myself a part-time job in ShopRite. But they couldn't cut me loose. I had no place to go. The thing is, if one of my siblings said, well, yeah, he can live with us, they would have cut me loose just like that. But I didn't have a place to go so I'd go to ShopRite every day and go back to the prison at night. Rather than garnish the check, I gave the whole thing to the wardens, and they would give me X amount of dollars each week for me to live on, for carfare or what have you.

When I was sentenced, I wrote a few letters. I called Dan at least on two occasions, but with these phone calls you can't really say much because they monitor them. I believe I was even trying to hit him up for a loan too. Quite frankly I was scared.

On the inside, I used to act crazy. I had a collection of hats, even women's hats. I used to put a hat on and go from bunk area to bunk area, and I'd be screaming at the other inmates, talking nonsense. They'd be saying, get out of here, you're crazy, and for the most part, that would save your life. After a while when they saw how crazy I was, most of the inmates didn't pick on me. Some of the COs were pretty cool too. I had been in law enforcement, so they knew that I wasn't going to be a troublemaker.

The COs got everybody up around six o'clock, then sometimes during the night they had check times. Other times they had shakedown, where they took our stuff and just tossed it all over the place, then they had the dogs come in and sniff around. The other ones within my area, these guys were happy to be in work release, even on the road crew, for the simple reason that they were able to work outside. There would be people that would kill for a juicy assignment like that. Me, I could come and go,

I could have escaped anytime I wanted to. But I had nowhere to go except the streets. Being in prison and being homeless, it's the same thing. You adapt.

I was a little upset with my family. I owed $3,550. You know, between my whole family they could have chipped in. Did they? My own brother, even though I don't like him, I would have put up the money. You figure it out: 733 days divided into $3,550, it's less than $5 a day. That made me a little bitter, especially when I see the other people coming and going, their families coming in with checks to release them, and the COs would be looking at me like, what's the matter with your family? Nobody came. My gosh, we had guys that were waiting to go to the max, and they got visitors. I was the only one that would never get one.

Sometimes the other inmates got some money from their girlfriends, wives, or whatever. I would have the circulars from ShopRite, and they would say, hey, Pops, could you get this for me? I was the oldest one there, in my forties, so they called me Pops. They would look at the circular and they said, oh, ramen noodles are on sale. They're usually like nine for a dollar or some shit, and I would tell them, all right, three dollars. Not for nothing, I'm using leather to go over there. So I had a sweet little thing going on in there. The one time I got busted was because somebody wanted a box of Cheerios, this big fucking box of Cheerios. I'm saying to myself, now how the hell am I going to smuggle this shit in? So I put it up my shirt in back. I got a curvature of the spine, but still that box stood out. This CO came over to me like, hey, how you doing, Pops, and whack, he slapped me right on the back. He said, just tell me it's for you. I said, yeah, it's for me. He says, get in there. Other times, you wouldn't believe how much stuff I was bringing in there.

It was in jail that I met Harold. He was in for alimony, had some money but tried to get away with it and got caught. Harold was a prankster. The first time I met him, he came over to me and he said, I'm taller. I'm looking at the guy, he's like five-six. I'm six foot two, so I'm looking down on him and saying, no, you're not. He said, you want to bet? I'm getting a little annoyed with this guy. Yeah, all right, I said, I'll bet you.

I'll bet you a pack of smokes. So he gave me this little-boy smile, went into his wallet, and came out with his license. He says, read the name on the license. That was his name, Harold Taller.

With that sense of humor, I fell in love with the guy. He was Austrian and me being German, he would tell me some of his stories from Graz, where he was from. Harold was a few years older than me, in his midfifties. He had a bit of a belly on him, but he was incredibly strong, good with boxing, hard drinker. He could drink vodka all day and still stay sober.

We got to be good friends. I was a little more experienced with jail, so I looked after him when I could. After about six months, he proved his point with his ex-wife and paid up, so he got out first. Before he left, he said, when you get out, I'll be there waiting for you. You know, you always hear that, but during my incarceration there were times when he would meet me at ShopRite and we would go to my favorite, Boston Market, for a chicken dinner, and he would give me a few extra dollars.

After two years and three days in, the warden came to me and said it was time to go. I wasn't released; in fact, I was kicked out. How many people you know get actually kicked out of jail? I even pleaded with them, said, can I stay a little bit longer? No, they said, you have to get out. I was institutionalized. I'm the classic example. I was used to that routine. It was great. So I called Harold and told him that they're thinking about kicking me out and I'm scared. And sure enough, on the day of my release Harold comes up the stairs and he spoke to the COs. Wait a minute, they said, he's going to be staying with you? Because Harold was a little crazy. He said, yeah, he's going to be staying with me. When I got out of the cell, there he was. He gave me a great big hug and said, come on, let's get out of jail. I remember it clear as day. November 3 of '97, he got me from jail and brought me up to Yonkers.

I worked for Harold about two years. He owned a Mercedes repair shop in Yonkers, on South Broadway. I found out several years ago that the place burnt to the ground. But at the time Harold was doing good. A few people would get a little behind with their bills, and he would say, Tomsky, go over there and ask them for the money. All I'd do is just stand there and look mean, that's all. Other times I would be in the garage answering the phones for him, or if some customers came in and they needed some work done on their cars, I would come out with a worksheet and fill it out for him. He would tell me what to put down. I'd also keep the place clean.

By court order I owed Kathy $129 a week, plus $25 in arrears for one kid. They based that on my meat-market salary at that time. Harold started paying me and I was giving her $154 a week religiously. As time went on and I kept doing little things for Harold, I increased it. I paid off the initial $3,550, but meanwhile the rest of it is getting interest on it. I'm proud to say that within a two-year period I paid it up, paid it all up. I was quite proud of that. I still got the receipts.

It was a beautiful job, all off the books. One time I bought a bicycle for Jessica for Christmas. You know, Kathy looked at me: well, it's $150, you sure you can afford it? I had a couple of grand on me and I'm like, yeah, I think I can afford it. We were actually starting to get a little friendlier. I guess it was the checks that she was getting. I thought it was awful strange that she got a new car within that year, but I didn't care.

I was crashing in Harold's garage that whole time. I didn't mind. I would just sleep in the backseat, or there were times where he would buy an air mattress for one of the offices. I wasn't too comfortable with that. He had these huge diesel space heaters, and he would heat up the office for me and it would get like two hundred degrees. I said, Harold, man, it's hot in here. And not only that, you got that stuff in your system, that smell of diesel. When he wasn't there, I would never have it on. It was an old building, cold. I'm surprised it didn't burn down sooner. It was a disaster in the waiting.

Harold was breaking my chops to get a place, but, no, I was just focused on taking care of Jessie. So what if I live in a garage, what's the big deal? So what if I'm sleeping in the back of a car or on an air mattress? I had everything I needed there. There's electricity, refrigerator, stove, all the amenities. There's food, TV. He eventually even put in a shower. So what's the difference? A garage, a roof over my head, a little damp sometimes, but holy shit, it didn't bother me none. I had a place to live. From time to time when Harold went overseas, I'd go back out in the streets because that's what I was most comfortable with, but mostly I was there.

After about a month, I contacted my family. I don't know why I did. I called Dan and told him I was out of prison, and he said, oh, that's great. You can come over and visit us for Christmas, and I did and I started to loosen up. I had reached out to my mother when I first got with Harold, but she still didn't trust me. If I tried to go in the house and see her, she'd say, no, no, you can't come in here. Jimmy will get upset. As long as I was working, they were happy, but I was still angry they'd let me be in jail all that time. So why did I go? Good question. I think maybe to see if they would accept me the way I was.

My appearance when I went over there, that shocked them a little bit. Harold dropped me off in one of his Mercedes and I wore a do-rag and had a beard. So I did look like what they call a *fucking maniac*. Maybe this was to make a point.

It was a turkey dinner, a traditional turkey dinner for the holidays. At the table, they wanted to keep their distance from me. You know, maybe I scared them. Let's face it, coming out of jail, you don't know how they might react to certain situations. We could be talking and then all of a sudden I'd just snap and take the coffee cup and throw it across the room. People handle ex-cons with kid gloves unless they were in themselves. My mother was sitting a few chairs away and wouldn't even look at me. I disappointed her. She had high hopes for me, the good boy, now I was the first one in the family to go to jail. That was a real black mark. Dan's two girls were there. They couldn't figure me out, either. They were both looking at me like, who is this? Later, when I went to my mother's funeral, my brother had to introduce me to them: oh, by the way, this is your uncle. My gosh, I was clean and everything, but the looks they were giving.

At one point my mother looked up at me, and if looks could kill, I'd be lying in Green-Wood Cemetery. I gave her a hug and I wished her a merry Christmas, then everybody else was just looking at me. They're all quiet because what do you say to somebody that just got out of jail? So what you been doing lately? How can you really bring up a conversation? I was cordial, thinking maybe I can get back into this life again.

Danny has one of those prefabricated houses, but it was in Cornwall, a nice house. Somebody from Hell's Kitchen with a house, it's unheard of. He's quite proud of it. Presents were already exchanged. I didn't have any. I got there in the afternoon, and I didn't bring anything. You know, by the time they invited me it's really too late to go out and do shopping, and then, too, I don't know what they like. It's been so many years. If I remember correctly, Danny got me a bottle of cologne. My other brother was there with his wife, Susie. She was cheating on him behind his back.

We all ate together, and afterward they counted the silverware. I could see them as they were cleaning up the table. Now I don't know if they singled me out, but they were just checking each fork, maybe thinking they should be careful because I just got out of jail. You know, you always hear those stories.

Harold called saying that he was on his way, because he figured I wasn't going to be there too long. When he pulled up with the Mercedes, everybody's looking outside. Wow, look at this guy, who's that? Oh, that's my chauffeur, I said. We promised that we would keep in touch again, but it didn't happen, didn't happen. In fact, I can't actually remember the next time we actually got together. I just drifted away from them. I drifted away.

The garage was beautifully situated between two houses of ill repute, and Harold patronized them frequently. The girls were all young, fourteen to sixteen years old, all Colombian. Harold, he would say, hey, Tomsky, you want to go with me? I'd say, no, no, no.

And he had this girl come over, Wanda, she was fifteen years old, though you wouldn't think it to look at her. She charged a hundred bucks. No problem for Harold. Anytime she was coming over, he'd sing that song, Wanda, Wanda's going to make you feel so good. Oh, boy. But the other ones, the street girls, they were like crackheads. A few beauties but mostly pretty rough. Sometimes they would come in and Harold was very generous with them. He would give them a few dollars if he didn't want to be with them, or if they were hungry, he'd make something to eat. In fact, a couple of times he would tell me, Tomsky, it's all right if so-and-so stays overnight in here. I don't care.

We used to feed the homeless in the area. They'd come in and we'd give them a few dollars or Harold always had extra food there for everyone. When troublemakers came in, I'd escort them out. So one day this guy came in causing some trouble. This was September of '99. I start walking towards him, Harold looked at me and said, don't worry about it, I'll take care of it. I guess it was a macho thing. Once in a while he had to prove that he still had it in him. So he walked towards the back of the garage. After a few minutes he didn't come back. Strange. I waited a few extra minutes, went out there, and I saw him on the garage floor with his head bashed in. This guy had grabbed hold of a pipe and smashed his head. Cops came, smelled a little bit of vodka on his breath, but that wasn't really the issue. The issue was the indentation in his face. So they took him to the hospital. They kept him there for a couple of months.

I didn't know diddly-squat about the business, but I tried to hold down the fort with these two other mechanics, who were pretty cool. The bills were mounting, and whatever money that was coming in, I had to pay the mechanics to keep them there. Then they started getting a little greedy too. There were times I wasn't there and I heard that they were bringing some parts home because they had keys. Or if I had to go into Hackensack to make a payment, they would close up. They said, well, I'm going home early. If Harold was there, he would have said, no, you can't.

When he got back, he wasn't the same. He had lost part of his memory. He was a master Mercedes mechanic with about forty years' worth of knowledge, and now he couldn't remember how to change a spark plug. He struggled. Finally he looked at me and said, Tomsky, I've got to go home. I couldn't argue with him. It was his decision. He begged, borrowed, and stole the money to get the plane fare, and right before Christmas '99 he went back to Graz.

I never heard from him again.

I was under the impression that this job was going to last forever. He was doing everything for me, feeding me, clothing me, everything. I would have died for him. That's how much I loved him. I still love him. December of '99, he told me, Tomsky, I'm leaving, see how long you can stick around here. My life was in the shop from '97 to '99. Those two years were paradise, sheer paradise. But I couldn't stick around. I had no money. The lights were off, there was no power, and we lost the customers. It was all downhill after that.

I went back to Manhattan for a little while. I talked to all my friends again to try to get a job, but it was the same old story: business is slow, we can't give you anything right now, maybe in another month or two. Here's a couple bucks. Big deal, right? I need a job. So I said, well, let me go back to the other thing I'm used to, the streets. All right, so I miss the washing and the food and what have you, but I quickly adjust. Indoors you get adapted. In prison you get adapted. On the street you're adapted.

After what happened with Harold, I said, I'm through. It seemed like everyone I ever got close to I lost. Same thing with the jobs, and after the garage closed, I said, that's it, I don't want to have another job again, never. I was terrified that it would happen again. After so many disappointments, how much can you take before you break? That's it, I said, enough is enough. I can't deal with this shit anymore.

Penny

Damn it's hot.

I must be brain-dead to be out here. What does it say? Shit, ninety-five fucking degrees. So that's why the rat with wings—the pigeons—are in the shade. The haze, the heat rising from the sidewalk, and you can smell the food vendors, car exhaust, and traces of cigarette smoke.

Why did I come here?

You know why, you drunk shithead. You need money, and you want to remember the old days in the hood. Yeah, I'm back in Hell's Kitchen, where I grew up. For those of you who don't know, it's midtown Manhattan, 35th Street to 57th Street, 8th Avenue to 12th Avenue. So much for the stroll down memory lane, everybody's all gone to the burbs, died, or went to prison. Back to reality. Got to hurry up and get canning. The nickels are calling me.

The day went doggingly slow with the heat. Some people were generous, giving food, a few dollars (I didn't ask for it). One guy gave me a pack of cigarettes, but I'm quitting. Hmm, how many times I said that? So now I got some smokes and a full wagon of cans and it's off to the redemption center.

On the way I come across two white guys kicking a homeless person on the ground. How did I know he was homeless? Easy, the bag. Some of us tie our possessions in a plastic bag to our wrists. That way if anybody tries to grab it, we go with it. The two guys are big and the homeless person is small, too small, no contest. Ordinarily I don't interfere, but this time is different. Two against one is not fair, especially when you can't fight back.

· Now I'm pissed off and I'm really going to hurt them, and believe me I know how. I'm a street fighter and I'll use whatever means to take you down and keep you down. If I have to use a weapon, it's usually disposable. Two unopened soda cans, wrapped tightly in several plastic bags or better a pillowcase.

Watch.

These two assholes are laughing, cursing, having a good old time—the fucks didn't see me coming. You, fuck-face on the left, will be the first to learn. Bang! The sucker's left side opened up. Blood and teeth splatted out, nose may be broken (hooray!), and he went bitch-screaming down. Ah! Ah!

Meanwhile fuck-face number two looks like he is in shock looking at fuck-face number one then slowly turns towards me. Bang! I didn't have as much momentum as before, but enough to open his right side. He too goes down screaming.

Hey how about that, a matching set? Left side, right side, they look pretty together.

Damn, the cans are broken within. Memo to me. One, replace them later. Two, clean pillow. It could have been worse; during the wintertime the soda freezes up, the pillowcase is shot, and then what are you going to sleep on?

"Hey, man, are you okay? Let me help you up. We got to get out of here before five-O comes. Don't worry about the two mutts. They aren't going to do anything to you."

(They're still on the ground looking at each other in disbelief.)

Shit, just my luck he can't get up or talk, and I'm not leaving without him.

So what do I do? I pick him up of course. Wouldn't you? You don't have to be a rocket scientist to figure it out. When the cops arrive, who will be arrested? Why me, of course. Two counts of felony assault and possession of a blunt instrument (bloodied pillowcase with soda cans).

After the two mutts are patched up, they would probably claim, "We saw him beating up on the little guy and tried to help, but this guy went berserk. Officer, we are good law-abiding citizens with good jobs and homes. And, officer, you know these kind of people are crazy." Not an exact quote, but close enough.

No job, no home, so off to jail I go—do not pass go, do not collect two hundred dollars, like the game says. As for the homeless person who is hurt, better pray that a city hospital is nearby. Why a city hospital? Private hospitals are in business to make money, right? So people like us with no coverage, unless it's a dire emergency, forget about it, expect to wait six to eight hours. Just look at the receptionist's face, see the expression when you say you haven't got any medical insurance. Meanwhile Mrs. Donna Reed who has medical card gold comes in with an ingrown toenail and gets triaged, treated, and sent home in time to make din-din for the kids.

Holy shit, this guy's a bag of feathers. My guess is four-eleven or five feet, about ninety pounds.

No time to check further, at least he's breathing, and we have to make like the wind and blow. Good thing I have a big shopping wagon.

Easy, pal. Placed a blanket on top of the cans and bottles, one on top of him, and an old coat for a pillow. I wonder what he looks like under that hat.

Later, time to haul ass. Good evening, ladies and gentlemen, this is the captain speaking . . .

Welcome aboard Cadillac Man Airlines, fasten your seat belts and away we gooooo!

Want to know something? As a rule I can't run for shit, a turtle could easily outpace me. But damn, this time I feel there's a propeller up my ass and wings on my kicks. Look at me now, weaving in and out of traffic and onto the sidewalk hollering, gangway!

People are cheering, yelling, cursing at some screwball racing a shopping wagon with what appears to be someone sleeping. So I start laughing and soon everybody is laughing and the motorists are honking their horns.

And people think *I'm* crazy?

Slowly the people and cars are thinning out and I'm approaching a rougher neighborhood, headed to my "house," a safe hideaway. This is no-man's-land. Land of people living in cardboard boxes, U.S.-mail and laundry baskets. Reeks of shit, piss, and cheap wine.

Do you feel it? The eyes, the eyes size you up and tell more. A white guy with a wagon with someone inside it. A lot of cans and bottles, he might have money and cigarettes and there's only one way to find out.

"Hey, man, youse got a cigarette?" I know that voice. Then a huge man stands up and everybody is grinning. Walking towards me, he's getting bigger, and, shit, man, if he doesn't stop growing, he's going to block off the sun! Sweet mama, this sucker is about six foot eight, must be 320 pounds.

"What, youse deaf, white boy? I asked for a cigarette."

"Sorry, man, but after I fucked your mother last night, she had the last one."

Whoa, it's so quiet now it seems time is at a standstill. His eyes narrow and, man, what big fucking fists.

Slowly he says, "Cadillac Man?"

"Yeah, Chocolate Milk, it's me, how the fuck are you?"

All of a sudden he laughs long and hard. I bet they can hear him in Cleveland. He picks me up in a bear hug.

"Yo, damn, take it easy, you're going to squeeze the shit out of me and I ain't wearing underwear."

"No drawers? Shit, Cadillac, youse so cheap. When was the last time youse went in youse wallet?"

"You oughta know, you 'borrowed' it."

"Yeah, nothing but flies. Shit, didn't nobody tell you? White boys have money. This white boy should change his race. Actually, nah—Cadillac Man, youse can never be a brother, youse ain't good-lookin', youse dick is too small."

"Yeah, maybe someday you'll lend me that black log of yours or at least some of it."

"Shit, I think every black woman in New York would follow you if you left town."

"Anyway, bro, I got to split, heading to my house."

"Who's the passenger?"

So I tell him what happened, watching the anger in the eyes.

"That's fucked-up, man."

"Here take these." I give him half of my cigarettes. I don't want to go without giving something for the cause. "Be careful, my brother, stay one step ahead of five-O." The others who were near my wagon part and I go on.

Got to check on my friend. Hmm, still has a pulse, breathing seems okay. Don't you worry, Dr. Cadillac will check you out further when we get to my house. Damn, no answer, those motherfuckers probably kicked him in the head. I hope there's no concussion.

If you want to survive out here, you should have several houses. Scope out the area, the more desolate the better. Check for signs of life: bottles, cigarette butts, bedding, means someone is living there and that means no trespassing, maybe booby traps. I ought to know. I do it too, to discourage new tenants from moving in. The more desolate the area, the better. A boarded-up factory is a palace—lots of nooks and crannies to hide in and sometimes running water.

More rules: Always set up an escape route just in case of fire, five-O, and predators. Secure the area if you can, but don't use new locks and chains, that attracts attention. Dirty them, wet them to get that rusty look. Scatter debris about making it look like nobody been there in some time. And most important, *do not* take a house where you find discarded needles. That means a crack house and that means junkies and that means trouble.

Ah! Here we are, home sweet home at last. I can't believe my eyes, everything is basically the same, debris field and all, and it's been a year at least. This is my Taj Mahal: an abandoned taxi garage with a steel-door entrance, an overhead folding door, and a trapdoor rooftop that I booby-trapped. Nobody can look in, the windows are blocked. You would need a lot of time and muscle to gain entry.

And the windows are booby-trapped, naturally.

Now for the piece de resistance.

What's this, you ask, dear reader?

Why, it's French.

Sacra blew! Cadillac Man is full of surprises.

Relax, I only know enough to get laid in a French whorehouse and order a cup of coffee.

This is the kicker: Last time I was here, I had running water and, get this, electricity. All these luxuries—all mine! Let's see if the key still fits, and, yes, it does and I'm inside. Now let there be light! And I hit the switch and thank you, Ben Franklin, for inventing electricity. And there is the shrine and the memories.

I lit the candles. "Hi, Irish, hi, everybody, I told you I would be back someday. I have another street person outside who is hurt. We'll stay at least a few days. Please watch over us."

Okay, pal, we are in my house, safe as can be, nobody knows about this place. Easy does it, this couch is very comfortable and don't go away, I'll be right back.

I put my wagon away, out of sight. Do I have everything? Yes, food, cigarettes, medical supplies, blood.

Blood! Holy shit, I'm bleeding, but where and how? I check myself, and, okay, no cuts, so where did the blood come from? Unless—dammit! I hauled ass back to the garage and sure enough there are massive blood-stains between his legs! Why didn't I notice it before? I'm fucking stupid, he could have bled to death in my wagon! It's not like me to be this fucking careless. I hope I don't have to take him to the hospital. Too many questions, then I would have to deal with five-O. I must work quickly and cut off his pants to see where the blood is coming from.

Relax, I'm not a homo or pervert. I'm only going to spread your legs to see how bad the cuts are, and don't worry, Dr. Cadillac Man will patch you up. Shit! I don't fucking believe it, blood everywhere! And somehow they cut off his balls and prick!

(Attention, Cadillac Man, this is your brain speaking. The reason why he's missing them, they weren't cut off, it's because he is a she! And that's not blood, she's having her period. You moron!)

Huh?

(That's right, he is a she.)

Damn! Just my luck to—

Bang! "Get your hands off me!"

Before I could react she leaped up and ran out of the garage office and over to the shrine.

"Whoa, take it easy, little lady, I'm not going to hurt you. If I wanted to, I would have already. Right? Just relax. I'm just going out to my wagon, I think I have some clean clothes that might fit you. I'll be right back, unless you want to leave without pants."

Man, that was a punch! Not bad for a little lady. And it's a good thing I didn't hit back, I hate to think what would happen. I don't discriminate.

Back inside: "Hello, is anybody home?"

There she is, trying to find cover behind the shrine.

"Okay, listen up. I have clean clothes I'll put in the washroom along with soap, a towel, and some gauze pads. Sorry I don't have any female napkins, I never use them.

"The washroom has a sink, it's clean, and I think it's big enough where you can sit inside, just let the water run for a minute first to get the rust out. I'm going into the office now to clean and afterwards make a hot dinner and you're invited. If not, you can leave. I won't stop you.

"Now I'm tired of talking. I've got work to do."

So I went to the office and within a few minutes I heard the washroom door slam shut and get bolted. The little lady is smart—you don't know me and I don't know you!

It sounds like she's swimming to China with all the splashing. I guess it's been awhile since she bathed last. Take your time, the water is free, just make sure you clean behind your ears. Might as well make dinner. I'm so hungry I could eat my underwear.

I'm making my favorite dish and—hey, look who's here. There she is standing by the doorway. I start to giggle. She's like a weight-loss commercial. Look at me! I lost sixty pounds using Cadillac Man's Super Enema Diet Plan. The smallest clothes I had and there is still room for another one of her in there.

Her face now that it's clean is pretty. A little-girl look but—I won't say it, I'm old enough to be her father.

"Well, are we hungry today? Chef Cadillac Man will serve you. Tonight's special is Beef Ravioli with Potato Chips. There is cold soda in the cooler, so help yourself."

Damn, I thought *I* was hungry; had to open two more cans.

"Slow down, you'll get sick and I'll have to clean it up."

She goes at it like she hasn't eaten in days. Then it starts, the heaves, and, oh, boy, I gotta work fast! I have a wastebasket with a plastic-bag liner I use for garbage.

"Okay, do it and get it over with."

I wait a minute or two. "Now go to the washroom and rinse your mouth out and don't gargle." She comes out looking pale but not too bad. "Feeling better? Here, eat those, and drink this slowly." I handed her some unsalted crackers and a soda. It helps to coat the stomach and sometimes avoid a second coming. She starts munching the crackers, a little slower now.

"No more food for now, it's late and I'm tired. You can use the couch, and don't worry, the blanket is clean. I'm moving the garbage to the other side of the garage to be taken out in the A.M., let me know when I get back of your plans."

And when I got back, I got her answer. There she was on the couch, fast asleep.

Rest well, little lady.

"Rise and shine! Sleep good? I made coffee, it's hot, and there are doughnuts. I have a busy day ahead, but if you want, I'll walk with you to wherever. Okay?"

Rolling up off the coach, still giving me those suspicious eyes. Can't blame her.

I grab the garbage, double-check everything, and out the door we go. "Listen up, my first stop is the redeemer to cash in this stuff. While I'm cashing in, it's important to stay by the wagon and don't move. If you have to go to the bathroom, try to hold it."

It's another hot one, the sun blazing down. The redeemer's place is crawling with punks. Like wolves circling for a kill they're eyeballing her and getting closer.

"Yo, you see something on my wagon you like?" I say.

"Huh, me?"

"Don't act stupid, asshole, away from the wagon."

"Yo, be careful, old man. Me and my friends take what we like."

"Yeah? You can't have it unless—"

"Unless what, motherfucker!"

"Unless you want to fight me for her." There are three of them, one of me. But that's okay, you don't have to win the fight, just have to make them think it's more trouble than it's worth.

"You're crazy, man."

"Yeah, I am fucking crazy! I'm so crazy I want to spill your fucking blood all over."

Reaching into the wagon like I'm going for a weapon. That's enough for them, talking some trash, they move on.

"Are you all right?"

Ah, shit! She has a death grip on the wagon and I see she pissed her pants. I can't get mad, she's scared.

"Relax, relax, little lady, they're not coming back."

Slowly life comes back to her face and she looks down.

"Don't worry about it, if I had a nickel for every time I pissed in my pants, I wouldn't have to can anymore."

(Ah! So that's the reason why you don't wear underwear, Cadillac Man.)

No, reader, it's not, can I go on please?

She giggled just a little bit but it showed a beautiful set of teeth. Damn, she could do commercials with those choppers!

"Come on, I know of a thrift store nearby, let's see if we can get some clothes that will fit you."

At the thrift store I tell her, go to the men's clothing and pick out two button-down shirts to conceal your—you know—and two pairs of pants. If you don't see anything, go to the young men's section. The saleswoman is eyeing us. I haven't shaved in a while and the little "man" has on the urine-stained pants.

She goes through the racks and finds something she likes. One white shirt, one blue, a pair of corduroys and some jeans. She gives the clothes to the saleswoman to ring up. "Anything else, sir?" she asks me. No.

"Okay, we have two shirts at a dollar each, right, sir?" Yes.

"And we have two pants at fifty cents each, right, sir?" Yes.

"Lastly, two woman's panties at twenty-five cents each. Right, sir?"

I look down at the little lady and she is grinning. Oh, well.

"Here's the money, and have a nice day."

Here we are at our next stop, a fast-food joint.

"You're going into the men's room to change and wash up. Don't shake your head. It's the only way, if you go in the ladies' room, people will notice. Here's soap and a towel, make it quick, and don't worry, I'll be standing outside to make sure nobody goes in."

Man, I feel like a big brother, or maybe a father. No, not a father anymore.

Then on to do the laundry. As a rule I throw everything into the washing machine, but the little lady took charge and separated the clothes, washed and folded them like a pro. All without saying a word, just head down and about her business.

Everything's all in order.

"Well, it's early and I can walk you to the train station or bus terminal."

She shook her head no.

"You still want to hang on?"

She shook her head yes.

"All right, little lady, just for a little while, and remember this: if you get in my way or slow me down, I'll kick your ass, okay?"

She nodded and smiled. God, I wish I had her teeth, but they don't last out here.

I'm low on cash, and if we're going to eat tonight, I have some serious canning to do. I chose an area that was safe and the pickings good—on 12th Avenue, between 42nd and 43rd, near where the cruise ships let off.

But I have to hurry, the other canners will be here soon. There's lots of money out here, and lots of people wanting to get it. Sometimes I see the woman I call Mama-San, a Japanese lady who has a place to live but just cans for extra cash. Always smiling that big smile. Other times it's the South Americans, coming around in vans, mostly women and always real organized.

As I'm picking up, she's trying too. I gave her a plastic bag and we each do one side of the street, that way we cover both sides more quickly.

"Don't worry about your hands being dirty, we'll clean them when we're done. I have Handi Wipes."

We're going from corner to corner, stopping at waste cans, working through barrels and bags in front of residences. Every can you pick out is another nickel in the bag. Man look at her go, racing to each trash basket. I could see she's having a good time at it.

"Whoa! We're almost done, slow down!"

She did good, damn good, and I told her so. Her face lit up like a Xmas tree. Still not a peep out of her, though.

Sheesh, I hope she talks soon and I hope she isn't a blabbermouth. You know the type.

I knew a girl named Shirley (sorry, no last name here) when I was a kid. She talked so much on the phone, I had to put my phone in the freezer to cool it down. One time she called and I was in a bad mood to talk. She'd be talking, and every other minute I go uh-huh and soon I got the urge to take a crap. I couldn't interrupt her, so the hell with this. I'm not going to crap myself. I said one more uh-huh and put the phone down. Oh, much better, and now I'm hungry but first let's see if she's still on. Yep. So I do another uh-huh and go to the fridge for a sandwich. After I eat I remember the phone and race back to hear her say, thank you for listening, bye for now. I said uh-huh. Don't ask me what she talked about.

"Come on, I'll show you how to use the redemption machines." She's a quick learner, pumping the machine with cans and bottles as I hand them over. I stood back like a teacher watching a student work. Between the two of us, we made more than forty-five bucks—fantastic!

I told her we can eat anywhere she wanted and pointed across the street to Pizza Heaven. Good pizza but the owner is a troublemaker and deaf as a post to boot. Well, if my partner wants pizza, she'll get it, and let's hope the owner's in a good mood.

"How many slices?" She holds up two fingers. "Plain?" Nods yes. "Yeah?"

"Yes, we would like three plain slices and two colas please."

"You got money?" the owner says.

"No, I got food stamps, you idiot."

"What you say?" Like I said, deaf as a post.

"I said, yes, sir, here you go and thank you."

So me and the little lady sit in a booth and start to enjoy our pizza when he comes over.

"Is the pizza good?"

"No, your mother's crusty panties taste better."

"What you say?" His favorite line.

"The best pizza in the world!"

She's giggling and I started to laugh and it got louder until the owner and somebody else came out of the kitchen. I think they're related, their belly is the same. He's coming our way.

The new jelly belly says, "You're disturbing the customers. You go on now." I look around and see that there's only one other customer, an old guy who's probably been here since Columbus discovered America.

"Listen, pal, we just finished and will be leaving in a minute."

"You go right now! I call the police."

And that's the way it goes. Try to clean up fast and leave with some pride still intact.

Last, we go grocery shopping. The little lady gets those female things and then we're finally back at the garage. Whew, what a day, and now, some quiet time. I'm tired, but it's early, which is good. I have to tell the little lady it's time to go away from here. Sooner or later they'll shut the electricity and water. Sooner or later they'll break down the door. The longer you stay in one spot, the harder it is to leave.

She's in the washroom. That's it, splash all you want. It's going to be a long time until the next one, unless we get lucky.

"My, my, aren't we squeaky-clean." Man! Those teeth. I hope in my next life I have teeth like that. And a bigger pecker too.

Kidding.

"Sit down please, we have to talk."

I didn't talk about yesterday's first encounter and I hope in time she'll tell me what started it. "It's time to go now."

She looked scared.

"Relax, not just you, both of us, we leave in the morning. You worked like a pro today."

There she goes again with that smile again. Sheesh!

"We need to make money, and the only way is to go to other canning areas further away. Tomorrow I'll get a wagon for you, I know where they are."

I want to tell her about the ways of street life, what to do and what not to do. How to make do with what you got. I tell her there are times we don't bathe, use the streets discreetly as bathrooms. There are weather conditions, street people, and outsiders. I tell her we sleep outside with the night crawlers and stray dogs and conceal ourselves if necessary. I tell her that if we get into a fight not to interfere. "Remember, little lady, *run* and they won't bother you, they'll think you cut out on me."

I put my hands on her shoulders and she shuddered.

"Are you sure you want to stick around here?" She nodded yes.

Okay that's that. And I'm still hungry. "How about some of my famous dish, macaroni and cheese with lima beans? Sound good to you?"

Man, did she shake her head no.

"Doesn't matter, we're going to have it with eggs in the A.M." Is she turning green? Nah, just my imagination. And green, white, or pink, she's hungry enough to eat too. Ah! The belly is full and there's one more thing to do before beddy-bye time, I have to check the wagon.

She's watching TV. Good, I'll be gone for a few minutes. TV? you say, dear reader. Why not? I have the juice, and everything I found when Irish was alive is still here. TV, hot plate, microwave, coffeemaker, all discarded by people like you because they were chipped or you bought a fancier model. It's a shame I have to leave them behind, they're useless to me in the street but easily replaceable on recycle day.

I go outside to double-check my wagon, I do it every day. I like to be prepared for anything that happens. I know the areas we're going but still have to be careful, expect the unexpected. Looks good: bags for canning, clothing for all weather, bedding, first aid kit. We've even got pots and pans, a camp stove, and some emergency food. Everything we need.

A noise.

Somebody is coming behind me.

It's dark here and I don't know who it is. I shut off the penlight and reach in the side pocket of my pants and take out an ice pick.

When he sounds like he's just a step off, I whip around with the ice pick up and shine the light right in his face.

It's the little lady! She lets out a scream, turns, and starts to run.

"Wait it's me!" I yell.

That stopped her halfway down the block. Man, can she run!

"I'm sorry for not telling you that I was going to check the wagon." She's crying, probably thought that I split without her.

"It's okay," she says.

She's talking! Sheesh, just about had to stab her through the heart to get her to say something. "Hey, you're talking!"

"I'm sorry."

"For what?"

"For not talking sooner."

"It's okay, when you feel like talking, talk. Besides, I have plenty of throat lozenges."

We both laugh.

"Cadillac, my name is Penny."

"Makes sense."

Get it, dear reader? Penny makes cents! Sheesh! No sense of humor.

"If you want, you can call me Caddy, just don't say it when people are around.

"Tell you what, to make up for the big scare, you don't have to eat the macaroni with the lima beans in the morning. Okay?"

She grabbed on to me and started crying again.

"Come on, let's get back inside."

I took my last bird bath (I'm too big to sit in the sink), and, yes, I did clean behind my ears! Penny's asleep, hat still on and wrist bag off. As tempting as it is, I'm not going to look in the bag. It's personal, period. Lights out—nighty nite.

She woke me crying, went on for a few minutes. I wanted to hold her and say you're safe with me, but I backed off.

Ah! The smell of coffee in the morning. I decided to give Penny and my-self a special treat after what happened last night: cheese omelets, sau-sages, buttered rolls, and coffee! I see that she's stirring, about to wake up, the aroma is strong like a greasy spoon.

"Wake up, wake up, you sleepy head, get up, get up, get out of bed," singing. "Chow is now, last call for chow! Dig in, I'm making seconds."

She's up off the couch in a flash, eating so fast it's like her hands are blurring. A big omelet, three sausages, and four rolls. Sheesh—you want a side of brontosaurus with that? She's just sitting at the table and yawning.

"All right, before we get fat and lazy, we got work to do. You clean up and I'll put everything away." Even though we might not come back, we have to keep the house clean. She handles the dishes and I put everything back in place.

Last chance to use the ladies' room. And out the door.

Open your eyes, Penny, and welcome to my world. Watch, listen, and learn, for final exams are given daily. You fuck up lightly, I'll holler and show you the right way. You fuck up royally, I'll put my size-thirteen shoe up your little ass, and I mean it.

I find a beauty of a wagon near the A&P, same place I found mine. I show her how to tie and separate the recycle, making it easier to handle and redeem. At cash-in time we did great and I told her to keep half. Every-thing fifty-fifty, fair is fair. Keep a few singles on you and hide the rest and don't tell me where, because I won't tell you where mine is. Don't flash the cash, you never know who's watching. We'll take turns buying provi-sions, concealing them in dark bags, that way nobody can see what we have.

If we cook on the street, pour the contents of your pan onto a paper plate, then take the pan and a gallon jug of water over to the sewer grating, rinse it out, and wipe with paper towels. If you have to take a dump or piss, try to hide and use the basin I have in front of the wagon. There's a jug with bleach and water mixed, and when you're done, rinse out the basin and don't be bashful. I don't want my wagon to smell like a shithouse.

We aren't on any time schedule so it's around-the-clock canning, and just because we just cashed in yesterday doesn't mean to stop. There'll be days when the pickin's are slim. Our good days will make up for them. We'll be getting up early, before dawn, so that the outsiders won't see us napping and complain to five-O. Weekends are different, the outsiders are in their pretty homes and we can sleep a little longer. Once in a while she would stop and have a puzzled look, still shy about talking, and I would explain this or that.

More than a week goes by like that—canning in the daytime, eating and sleeping at night. She's still sticking with it, even though we're staying out on the street now. With each day that goes by, she gets better, a fast learner. Her talking in her sleep is still a problem, and now she's tossing and turning being that we're lying on a hard surface. It takes a little while to get used to.

I don't like the area we are right now, up in Harlem, near Marcus Garvey Park and the projects. I could have gone around it but we would have lost two hours of recycle time in the canning zone. Yeah, I don't like it, it's shadowy and quiet and we're in the land of crackheads. You can see the spotters on the rooftops watching for five-O while the sellers are working the white guys in their out-of-date cars, buying what they think is good shit only to find out later they were ripped off. Good, the fucking assholes may live to see another day. The sellers won't rip off the crackheads, that's bad for business. I told Penny to work the avenue where I can keep an eye out. The side streets are too dangerous and anything can happen.

It was slower than expected due to caution and the hot temperatures. I stripped down to a T-shirt but Penny couldn't because—well, you know why. We went into several fast-food joints for bird baths and that helped for a while. Eventually we're going to need to shower long and hard to feel fully clean. Bathroom washups suck, but you make do.

We took plenty of breaks in the shade, Penny with water and I coffee.

"You drink too much coffee, Caddy," she said. She's right, I do prefer it over water or soda anytime. Everybody tells me you need water and they're right to a point. As you know, two things will happen. One is sweat, which is healthy, so you go home, take a nice shower, come out smelling like a cheap whore, and put on clean clothes.

But what about me? If I sweat and there isn't any bathroom around, I'll stink like a dead rhino left to rot, and even if I had clean clothes, why put them on a stinky body, right?

Second, what happens when you drink too much and feel bloated? Why you go pee, of course. You piss at your job, at home, in your neighbor's backyard, in your boss's coffee because you didn't get a raise, at your mother-in-law's with the seat down, etc.

But what about me? Same as above, but during the daytime with people around, very discreetly. Pretending to look in garbage cans, between parked cars, trees, etc. Remember this if you have to pee outside. Conceal yourself, remove object from pants, aim, hands free and looking straight ahead, whistle, and fire! And so what if you piss on your shoes, it will only be a few drops. For women, I'm sorry, you're going to have to ask Penny.

By evening, we're ready for a break.

"Here we are, come on, let's eat, I'm so hungry I could eat a moose!"

I do a once-over, and, man, this place was at one time a beautiful diner and now they have to beg for the business. I went over to the table and banged it a couple of times with my fists, causing customers to look.

What am I banging for? she wants to know.

"It's a table for two and I'm not paying for our uninvited guests—look."

Pardon the pun, but she got buggy-eyed looking at all the crawlers.

She's happy and I want to keep it that way as long as I can. I decided to try a silly little joke. Usually I order sausage with my eggs, but this time it's just eggs, coffee, toast, and french fries.

"No sausage today, Caddy?"

"Nah, I'm in the mood for something different."

I reached into my bag and took out a can of . . .

"Dog food? You can't be serious!" she says.

"Oh, yes, I am, watch me. You know Penny, dog food is quite tasty. Think about it, every time you open up a can, they come running. Now I prefer the beef chunky with brown gravy, it goes great with eggs. Watch as I mix it all together, Ah! Looking good. You want some?"

"Ewww, no way."

I look around and I see money changing hands, and, wow, even the cook, they're placing bets, and one guy is wide-eyed and his coffee cup seems like it's stuck to his face.

"Mmm, this is delicious and damn I wish I had another can."

The best part came when I licked the plate clean. That's when the guy with the coffee cup coughed and sprayed coffee out his nose. Never actually seen that before.

She's giggling. "I can't believe you did it!"

"Why not?"

"It's dog food, and dog food is for dogs."

"Yes, true, but if you're really hungry, you would eat anything."

I tell her: I remember when I was first out here I came across a real-life hobo. (Yes, they exist but they're rarely seen, always on the move.) It was a cold night and he was cooking something that smelled so good the aroma attacked my senses saying, "Hey, that's food and you haven't eaten in days." I cautiously approached him and offered some cigarettes for food. He reached into his bag and pulled a coffee can out and filled it. It was hot and delicious, loaded with beef chunks and vegetables, and, hey, how about that, I really am eating hobo stew! I was so hungry, I gave more cigarettes to have seconds, then he smiled a wide, toothless grin and started to sing, "How much is that doggie in the window? Woof woof."

I looked at the stew, then at him still singing, "The one with the waggly tail! Woof woof."

Then I figured out what was in it and started to laugh. I didn't care, it was so good, I would have arm-wrestled Lassie for it.

I put some paper towels on a plate and dump the french fries on it to absorb the grease. Ah, that's better. These fries were so soggy they looked like they swam the English Channel!

"Take what you want, Penny, and don't use the bottled ketchup, it's watered down. Here take these ketchup packets." I never use diner utensils, you always find the previous meal on them. Plastic is the way to go, use once and throw away.

"Here you go, my dear. Always have a bag full of condiments and utensils for occasions like this or if you have to eat on the street. End of lesson, time to chow down."

The waitress comes back. "All done I see, would you or your friend like some dessert? I have apple pie and chocolate cake."

I look over at them and, damn, they look like they should be in the Smithsonian Institution.

"No thank you, just the check.

"Well, we might as well use the bathroom. Penny, you go first. Here's some paper, and remember, do not sit, just squat." There's probably so many crabs that they cook them for Friday's seafood menu.

"Let's split while we can. Ah, fresh air, Times Square."

"Where are we going now?"

"It's beddy-bye time. I know of a place not far from here, an office building with a deep vestibule."

"Is it safe?"

"Yeah, I know some of the square badges who work there."

It's not a long walk. A big place, with nice pillars. We can sleep behind them, and if anybody walks by, they won't be able to see us. We just finish spreading everything out and put the wagons together when we find out we have company.

"Hey! What do you think you're doing?" asks the square badge.

"Hi, Maurice, it's Cadillac Man."

"Oh, hey. Wait, don't move, I'll be right back," and he went inside to use the phone. "Okay, you and your friend can stay, but remember, leave early and clean up."

"No problem and thanks.

"Well, Penny, we had one heckuva day, let's get some sack time."

"Caddy, can I ask a favor?"

"What?"

"Can I sleep next to you?"

"What, are you crazy? I snore like a bear and my farts break the sound barrier."

"I don't care."

Okay, okay.

It was awkward at first getting into a comfortable position, but we finally settled down with her head on my chest.

"Caddy?"

"What?"

"I'm nineteen years old."

Damn, yeah, sure, and I'm twenty-three. Yet she has no reason to lie, I think.

"Go to sleep, Penny."

"Good night."

As of that night and thereafter we slept together and she stopped talking in her sleep too.

But Penny, when you talk, I'll listen.

"Rise and shine, buttercup, a new day is breaking."

"Ugh, Caddy, what time is it?" It's still dark out.

"It's four A.M. and we have to get ready to leave before the outsiders arrive. If you have to use the bathroom, do it now, just knock on the glass door and put your hand between your legs, the square badge will show you where it is. There's no ladies' room, so act natural, and if he comes in with you, go in the shitter to do your number and I'll put everything together while you're gone. Oh, and take these bottles and fill them up at the watercooler, we'll need them today."

Ah! There she is, looking ten pounds lighter and her jugs are full. I mean her bottles. "Here, have some hot coffee and cookies courtesy of Cadillac Man diner."

"All right! Where did you get it?" At this hour not even the roosters are awake and there aren't any diners to be found.

"Cookies are from the wagon. The coffee I made." Here's how: While she was in the bathroom, I took my thermos over to the watercooler, pressed down the red tap for hot water. Then back to the wagon, added instant coffee, instant milk, sugar. Then shaken, not stirred. The name is Man—Cadillac Man.

"Okay, Penny, coffee break is over, time to saddle up the wagons. I hear the calling of distant cans waiting to be picked up, and let's not disappoint them."

And so we leave, alone in our thoughts, absorbing the stillness, the sanity of the street this early A.M. Where are we going? I decided to rest Penny for a few days, not from canning, a mental rest. She has to keep busy in a safe area. And, yes, I need it too.

We walk the carts over to the edge of Central Park, and we can all day, smooth and easy. By late afternoon we've got the carts piled high, and Penny's messing with her shoe, looking at park benches like she wants a rest.

"Come on, just because we got a little money doesn't mean we stop. There's still more work to be done, then to the redeemer, and finally supply shopping. No rest for the weary, my dear."

At first she gives me a little-girl pout, then comes that toothy smile. Damn, she should audition for toothpaste commercials. Sheesh.

Late that afternoon, luck is on our side again. We find a huge piece of foam-rubber padding, big enough for the both of us to lie down comfortably. It fits perfectly under my wagon, and, hooray, no more hard surfaces for a while. We're staying tonight at a construction site on 78th Street, an apartment building going up, which is good, lots of hiding spots. There isn't any security because there's nothing to steal, and our wagons are easily concealed, ready to go by our escape route just in case. We're all tucked away in a cozy corner of a floor that's half-finished. We're going to sleep good tonight.

"Caddy?"

"Hmmm."

"I'm really nineteen, honest. I'm a runaway."

"Penny, you're of legal age."

"No, you don't understand. I'm a runaway. I had to run away to protect myself and sisters."

"What do you mean?"

"From my father."

"Go on and talk, Penny."

She starts to cry again, I could feel the tears on my chest and kissed her forehead. Let it go, Penny, get it out in the open.

She talks for a long time, like she'd been holding a lot in. I'll tell you the whole thing, as close as I can remember it. She said:

My father was abusive towards the end. But I remember the times we were happy being Daddy's little girls. Then the factory where he worked closed down and moved to another state. He tried to find work, even my mother offered to look and he said more or less to stay home with the kids, he was the provider. With a family to support, the unemployment checks weren't enough, so we used our savings and soon they were gone. My mom told him the money was gone and we would have to go on welfare.

My father went ballistic, saying welfare is for poor people, people in the slums. My mother told him, "Wake up and smell the coffee, some of your best friends are on it, I know, their wives told me." Then he slapped her and walked out, slamming the door. It was the first time, I think.

I ran over crying into her arms and said, "I'll quit school and find a job." She pulled me away and said, you're staying in school, period. "And don't be mad at Daddy, he didn't mean it, and watch, he will come back and say, 'I'm sorry.'"

She gave me a hug and a smile. "Go check on your little sisters." Dad came back that night and the fight resumed. It got worse day after day, and now he's drinking more. Sometimes when I got up for breakfast, I would notice a bruise or mark on her, and if our eyes met, she would look at me as if to say, "He didn't mean it." I did some babysitting jobs for our neighbors, and every time I tried to give her the money, she said no and to save it "just in case."

"Just in case of what?" I asked.

"You'll know when."

I didn't understand then, but later I did. I graduated from high school with honors, my mother and sisters were there cheering me. Needless to say my father wasn't, still in bed after boozing all night then coming home to beat the hell out of my mother. She tried to cover up the bruises with makeup and big dark sunglasses and keeping everybody from getting too close, but it's a small town, everybody knew. My mother aged twenty years before my eyes. At night I prayed for a miracle, for all this misery to stop and to see my parents being happy again.

One day, my mother took us grocery shopping. The weather was miserable, raining, lightning, and thunder outside, and inside we were having a good time making jokes about the food and silly girl talk. We talked about going to college, but I told her I needed more time to think it over. Secretly, I didn't want to go. I was afraid for my mom and my sisters.

We went to the checkout counter and she started making funny noises from the mouth and waving the arms up and down. My sisters thought it was another game to play and started guessing out loud who or what the character is. They were all laughing. I was embarrassed. All those people looking at her, talking.

Cool it, Mom, everybody is looking, I said. It got worse, she was flailing around, then suddenly she stopped, collapsed to the floor. We all started to scream, and a woman who was an off-duty nurse tended to my mother and told the manager to call for an ambulance right away.

The police asked me why she had so many bruises. I said, I don't know. Where is our father? I don't know. I guessed they figured I was in shock and drove us to the hospital.

At the hospital it was the same, questions, questions, questions. And when I asked about my mother, they would say, wait until your father gets here. Hours went by, a social worker gave us food, then a priest, nurse, and I think everybody from the hospital visited us at least once. I lost my cool and said, "Why doesn't someone look in the fucking bars for my father?"

Heads turned in my direction but I didn't care who heard it, even my father, who just walked in with the police. I don't know why, but we all ran to him, hugging and crying and saying that something happened to Mommy. I'm hoping—no, praying—that our father would comfort us and say, "Don't worry, everything will be all right."

He said nothing, rigid as a statue and reeking of alcohol. One of the doctors waved at him and they went into a room where others were waiting. I can see them behind the glass doors talking, the priest that spoke to us is now speaking and has his arm around Dad. It's bad news, I know it is, Mom is in bad shape. I have to stay calm for my sisters' sake, after all, I'm the oldest, right?

They came out, my father with the priest by his side, the doctors behind them, and the social worker sits down by my sisters. I'm standing alone when they stop in front of me.

Dad spoke first. "Penny, your mother is dead."

Just like that, no remorse, no nothing.

The priest is talking but I'm not listening. I'm focusing on my father, waiting for a reaction, nothing!

"You bastard, you killed my mother!" I started punching him. They took me aside and I can hear them asking my father if he's all right, and it's so funny, like a fly trying to hurt an elephant. I'm laughing and they're probably thinking she is going into shock. A nurse offers me a pill with water and it's just what I need, a chill pill.

A doctor introduces himself, Dr. Devlin, and sits next to me.

"Penny, I'm sorry for the loss of your mother. If you have questions, I'll try to answer them."

"What happened to my mother, doctor?"

"Penny, your mother was already dead when she arrived at the hospital."

"Why?"

"We suspect it was a brain aneurysm, but we won't know for sure until we run some tests."

"Did she suffer?"

"No. An aneurysm, in simple terms, is a blood vessel that grows to a point then bursts. Death is almost immediate. The autopsy would confirm it."

"No! No, no autopsy, I heard stories where you cut the person up."

"Yes, Penny, we do, but only where it's necessary for us to learn the cause of death. And we do it in a humane way to treat the body with dignity.

"Your father agreed to it and signed the papers."

"That bastard, he killed our mother."

"I can't comment on that. The autopsy results will determine whether or not to further the investigation. Be strong, Penny, your sisters need you now more than ever. I have to go and continue my rounds. Here's my card. Call me if you think of any other questions."

"Thank you, doctor."

The police drove all of us home.

Then something strange happened, he stopped drinking and started to act like a father again. I was leery, but my sisters were thrilled. I decided to keep an open mind. I still didn't trust him for the way he looked at me and especially them.

The doctors were right, it was a brain aneurysm and she suffered very little and wasn't even aware of anything and died in minutes. Natural causes they called it, and the police were satisfied. But I know in my heart, he helped speed up her death with all those beatings.

Mother had an insurance policy we didn't know about, and it came in handy to use for the funeral. It was beautiful and all the relatives we haven't seen in so long were there, a sad reunion. My father, acting like the grieving husband, greeted everyone, and in some instances he received cash. I saw him quickly put it away.

You phony bastard!

I'm not the only one who thinks the same way. My aunt Clare, my mother's sister, a year older, would call my mother once a week and they would talk for hours and my father didn't like it. If he found out she was coming to visit, he wouldn't be there. Something happened between them, I never knew what.

We buried my mother and everybody left except Aunt Clare, standing by the grave, and I went to her. She said, "I still can't believe that your mother is below us instead of your father. God forgive me."

I was shocked, speechless.

"Maybe someday I'll tell you why I dislike your father. In the meantime I'm not trying to scare you, but be careful and watch out for your sisters. Come here and give your aunt Clare a big hug and kiss."

I did and she took my hand and I felt something slide in. She looked me in the eyes and said, "Just in case."

I got a sudden chill and for a moment there I thought it was my mother talking.

"You better go now, your father's watching us."

I gave her another kiss and said out loud, "Bye, Aunt Clare, don't forget to write us."

She waved and grinned to my father and sisters and was gone. I slipped whatever she gave me into my pocket. We drove away in silence and I can feel his eyes on me. I didn't dare look at him and I think he knows!

When we got home, I went to my room and changed clothes and hid it in a secret spot in my room. I made dinner for us—I'm a good cook, mother taught me—and sat down to eat. It was so quiet at the dinner table, we were waiting for someone to break the ice and it was my father.

"Penny, you were with your aunt Clare a long time. What did she have to say?"

"We talked about Mom dying so young and how much we're going to miss her."

"You lying bitch!" he screamed, and hit me so hard it lifted me off the chair and onto the floor. I was in so much pain and I tasted blood!

My sisters were screaming and he told them to shut up and go to their rooms or else. He was facing away from me and waved at them to go.

"Daddy, please don't," they said.

Last chance! Leave now! And they did, running to their room and locking the door.

"Penny, what did you and Aunt Clare talk about?" Taking off his belt.

"I told you before, we were talking about Mommy and how much we're going to miss her." Without saying a word, he lashed out with the belt and hit me. I curled my body inward so my back would take the worst of it.

"Tell me, tell me, you stinkin' bitch, you're just like your mother!"

"Daddy, please stop, it hurts! I'll be good, I swear."

Again and again, so many times. After a while I didn't feel it. I went numb, maybe in shock. Then he stopped and reached down and picked me up off the floor. My feet were dangling in the air, his hand holding the shirt tightly, his face so close to mine it was scary.

"If you or your sisters talk to anyone about this, I'll kill all of you! You understand me, girl?"

"Yes, Daddy."

"I'm not finished with you." He dropped me and went out the door.

God help us.

I go to the bathroom to check myself in the mirror. My lips are swollen and cut, though the bleeding stopped and the teeth are okay, but when I took off the shirt, I almost screamed. The back looked like a game of tic-tac-toe, marks all over, gashes with dried blood.

I went into the shower. Pain, unbelievable, like a thousand needles in my back, slowly subsided, and I was able to wash with a sponge. Afterwards I took aspirins and went to bed, then a knock at the door.

"Penny, can we come in?"

Can't let them see me like this.

"No, I'm tired. I'll see you guys in the morning."

"Are you okay?"

"I'm fine, go to sleep."

He didn't come home that night.

Sometimes he would go right to bed, pass out, and the next day eat breakfast and go out the door without saying a word. Those were good days.

Other times he'd come home with slutty women. It was kind of funny, hearing them laugh, then the bed squeaking. At breakfast while we're eating, my father would say, "Take a good look at my friend here, girls, you'll never have tits like these in your entire life!"

His girlfriend would blush and playfully hit him, and when it was time to go, his hand was up her dress for all to see. Those were the tolerance days.

Then the dark days where he would ask the same questions and I give the same answers, receive the same beatings and threats.

One day everything came crashing down. I was tired and went to bed early. In my dream, crystal clear, my mother and Aunt Clare were together having tea at the dinner table and spoke in unison, Penny, now is the time, just in case, just in case.

I woke up and heard my sister crying, "Daddy, please." Then: "Don't touch me!"

My father is in her room doing something! I quietly close my door and see that hers is open a bit. I peek inside and see my father lying next to her, touching her. I kneel down and slowly crawl into the room.

"Come on, don't be a baby, everybody your age is doing it."

"No, I don't wanna."

I'm almost there, luck is on my side, her bed is high, and even though it's almost dawn he can't see me crawling. I reached up with both hands and grabbed his hair tight and said, "You fucking pervert!"

He let out a little scream and fell on top of me, but I still hold his hair trying to yank it out! Harder and faster the punches come, the pain was enormous.

"Let me go, Penny." Anger and pain in his voice.

"Fuck you!"

Somehow he was able to get off the floor and hold me at the same time.

"Penny, dammit!"

"Fuck you!" I still held on.

I look at my sister and see she's not moving, in a state of shock I guess. Then he shoved me into the wall with all of his weight, over and over, until I loosen my grip and let go.

"So, you like pulling hair? I'll teach you a lesson."

He grabbed my hair and pulled me away caveman style, and I managed to get up, only to be tossed in the bathroom. He went over to the medicine cabinet opened it, smiled, and took out scissors!

"I'll give you one guess what I'm about to do. Snip, snip, snip, Penny."

He can't be serious! I have beautiful long hair past my shoulders, and the last time it was cut was years ago. He lunged and I fought, kicking and punching to no avail, he's just too big! I'm exhausted and sore, can't go on much longer, and start pleading, "Please, Daddy, not my hair."

"Snip, snip, snip, Penny." Laughing.

Then grabbed, twisted, and put me in a headlock. I was helpless.

Struggling, I can feel the scissors cutting and close my eyes. I want to talk, but his arm is on my throat and I'm crying.

"Open your eyes, bitch, I'm done."

"No."

"Open your eyes or I'll snap your fucking neck, right now!"

My God, it's gone! My long hair cut short like a boy. I scream.

I feel his slap. "Shut up, little boy."

I fainted. I don't know how long I was out, but when I came to, there were my sisters kneeling beside me.

"Where's Father?"

"He's gone, left a few minutes ago."

"Girls, go to your rooms and pack one piece of luggage, of only the things you'll need."

"But why, Penny?"

"Because we're leaving and not coming back!"

"Where are we going?"

"Not now, I'll tell you later. Get packing, lock yourselves in, and don't come out until I get back. I have to go somewhere, be back in a few minutes. Now go."

But first to my room and get the money just in case. Oh, Mother, I understand, just in case of emergencies!

I almost forgot Aunt Clare's note:

Dear Penny

For bus fare, just in case.
Call me (607) 555-3478

Love,
Aunt Clare

Thank you, Aunt Clare.

Good thing the bus terminal isn't far away. I bought the tickets and ran back fast. I used to run track, have always been a good runner.

Got back to the house, I called Aunt Clare.

"Hello."

"Hi, Aunt Clare, it's Penny."

"Penny, what's wrong?"

"I don't have much time, Aunt Clare, but in twenty minutes my sisters are boarding a bus and will be by you at one fifteen." Six hours from now.

"What happened?"

"I can't explain, the girls will tell you everything."

"What about you?"

"I'll be along later. I want to make sure they're safe with you first. Gotta go now. I love you, Aunt Clare."

"But, Penny, where—"

"Remember, one fifteen. Gotta go, bye."

One more thing I have to do. I went to the bathroom to pick up my hair. It will take years to grow back and won't be the same.

I knock on their doors. "Come on, girls, we've got to hurry!"

"Where are we going, Penny?"

"To the bus terminal, I'm sending you to Aunt Clare's. You'll be safe there."

"Aren't you coming?"

"No, I'm catching the next bus. I don't want it to look like we're all leaving together. Let's go, the bus is leaving in fifteen minutes."

One of the hardest things I have ever done was to put my sisters on that bus.

"We're scared, Penny."

"Don't be, Aunt Clare will be there waiting for you. Girls, tell her everything that Father did, I mean everything."

I handed over a bag and said, "Especially this."

"What's inside, Penny?"

"My hair."

When it was time to go, we hugged and kissed each other. The bus driver interrupted us by saying he's on a time schedule and will leave without us.

"Go on, I'll see you soon, I love you."

The bus slowly pulls out and I can see them waving from the window. I waved back and wondered, will I ever see my sisters again? Okay, got to go back to the house and pack quickly. It's quiet, that's good, it means he's not home. The first thing I take is mother's address book, it has Aunt Clare's phone number and home address.

Next, the letters from my friend Lois in New York City. We're best friends since the first grade until last year her dad's job relocated there and the family moved. We still keep in touch by writing, talking about our innermost feelings, boys, etc. At times she would talk about city life, it sounded so exciting.

She always said, if ever you come to New York, come see me and I'll show you the sights, just the two of us. Lois, I'm taking you up on your offer. In my pocket is a bus ticket, and I hope if your parents don't mind that I can stay with you for a few days. We have to talk and, no, my father doesn't know I'm here and my sisters are at Aunt Clare's house. Oh, what fun we'll have!

Wake up, Penny, you still have to pack.

Yes, you're right, the quicker the better, and I don't like it, it's too quiet, like a tomb!

I've got to leave here fast, I'll call them from the bus terminal right before the bus departs. Let's hustle, girl, the next one is in fifteen minutes. I grab my bag and take one last look at the place with all its memories that I'll never see again.

There's no turning back, New York City, here I come!

Wow! It was unbelievable!

My town is so quiet, but here it's so big and so loud and crowded. People and cars everywhere I turn. How can you live in a place like this? I wonder. People bump into you and don't apologize and keep going. I see a taxi stand and wait in line.

A taxi pulls up, the driver gets out and tries to take my bag, we're having a tug-of-war.

From what I can figure out, he's saying that my luggage goes in the trunk, taxicab rules. But I don't want to, it has all of my belongings! Everybody yelling, then a man with a yellow hat with the words TAXI DISPATCHER came up to me.

"Hey, buddy, give him the fucking bag and get in the cab, you're holding up the line."

"Okay, okay, you win." Gave him the bag and jumped in and told him Lois's address.

The driver is a maniac, weaving in and out of traffic, cursing, screaming at the other cars. I could be wrong, but I think we went by the same buildings twice, or maybe they all look alike? We made it in one piece and I don't know how in twenty minutes. It's beautiful, has a doorman and a huge park across the street.

"Twenty-six dollars, plus tip, please."

I gave him twenty-seven dollars, and what a look I got. He sneered and said something in a foreign language. Then he got out, opened the trunk, and handed my bag to the doorman, who opened the door for me. The driver must have been in a hurry to get back to the bus terminal, screeched out and went through a light.

Wow! Wait till Lois hears this, she'll probably laugh and say, "A typical New York experience." I'm almost broke, that ride cost more than the bus ticket, and I hope I can borrow some money. She'll understand, she's my friend.

The doorman brings me inside to the lobby's front desk. There's a young woman standing behind it.

"May I help you?"

"Yes, I'm here to see my friend Lois, Lois Foster."

"Is she expecting you?"

"No, it's a surprise visit, we're friends."

"One moment please."

She has a quizzical look on her face. I guess with this baseball cap on and my size you might think I'm a boy, but when I speak, you can tell. She goes through a file on the desk, then looks up at me.

"I'm sorry, but the Foster family is away on vacation."

"Are you sure?"

"Yes, it says right here, they left last week and will return in three weeks."

I'm stupid, stupid, stupid, should have tried to call her before I left! But there wasn't enough time.

"Excuse me, miss, are you all right? Would you like a glass of water or something?"

"No, I'm fine, I need fresh air. Thank you for helping me."

"Would you like to leave a message for your friend?"

"No, I'll come back."

"Be careful."

I can see that she has a scared look in her eyes and I'm scared too, alone in the city, no place to go. What am I going to do? I walked for hours, only stopping to buy cheap snacks to stretch my money and using the bathroom.

So many people staring at me, then my bag, and probably thinking, I don't want to get involved, and kept going. I'm getting tired, it's night-time and where am I to sleep? A church! Perfect! I'll tell the priest I'll be gone before morning mass.

I pound on the door, no answer. Back home the church is always open, day and night. So sleepy, can't go on, and I hope nobody will say anything to me if I only lay down for a while. Oh, how do campers do it? Sleeping on hard surfaces, it's so uncomfortable, and what I would give to have a nice soft bed, my bed, right now.

"Come on, get up!"

"Huh?"

"Let's go! You're blocking the church entrance!"

It's a policeman and it's early morning. He gets into a police car and is staring at me, I better leave fast. I don't want to go to jail.

"Don't let me catch you here again!"

I lower my hat a little more to cover my face and walk away.

How long did I sleep? Not enough, I'm still tired and ache all over. And hungry too.

Down to my last few dollars.

Walking, walking, until I see a group standing in line in front of a church. The people are filthy, dirty clothes, and some have shopping carts. I heard about them from neighbors back home who visited New York. They said they're crazy and dangerous.

"Hey, man, get in line, they are almost out of food."

"No seconds today, damn," an old man said, walking past me.

He wasn't wearing any pants, only underwear. But he said *food*. Yes, I see others receiving something at the door.

Stand in line and when it's my turn, a nun hands me a bag.

"Bless you child, next."

"Bless you too, sister."

She was surprised, then smiled.

Then I walked two blocks away because I also heard the homeless are thieves. (Sorry, Caddy. Not you.) Open the bag and find one ham sandwich, an orange, and a small container of milk. Got to remember that street number and what time it was, just in case.

I started to cry. "Oh, Mother, Aunt Clare, I miss you so much." I didn't know I was talking aloud, people are staring. "Leave me alone," I screamed at them, and ran away. I kept running for a long time, then I stopped inside a park. Catching my breath, and my God, they're here too.

This group seems to be happy, they're laughing.

They're leaving.

The sandwich and orange were good, not filling, I need more. I just spent my last few dollars on a lot of snacks and a bottle of soda. If I'm careful and don't get piggy, the food will last a couple days, more if I find another church that serves food.

Up ahead is a park.

It's beautiful.

There are park benches facing a river, in the distance an island with factories, and off to the left are two huge bridges where I can see the traffic. Joggers, bicyclists, lovers holding hands, and water fountains with cold water!

I feel at rest here, listening to waves gently touching the pier walls and watching the sun slowly go down, it's breathtaking. I stretched out on a bench to relax more.

Something is poking me in the back. I must have dozed off, it's nighttime and very quiet.

There's that poking again and it's a finger, maybe a policeman coming to tell me to move on.

I start to get up and a voice says, "Don't move, don't make a sound or I'll kill you."

I thought I was going to have a heart attack, my throat went dry.

"If you are nice to me, I'll let you live."

I used to read my mother's magazines and now remember the articles about the women found in parks raped and murdered. My back is facing him so I don't know if he has a knife or gun.

"You better be fucking nice," he says, and is pulling my shirt out. "Unbutton your shirt."

My God! What is he going to do? I do as he says.

"Be nice and you'll live."

Suddenly I feel a hand on my breasts, I stiffen.

"Well, well, this is my lucky day."

His hand is hard with calluses, rubbing me all over and pinching my nipples.

"Mmm, that's so nice."

He's breathing heavier, starting to moan. Then I feel something on my face, it's his penis!

I should bite it off, sick pervert, but can't, I don't have the nerve. He is rubbing it faster, squeezing my breasts harder, then it's all over my face!

It's disgusting.

He slowly released his grip on my breast and took his hand away.

"That was very good, give me your hand!"

I put up my hand slightly and a piece of paper slides in.

"For services rendered. I'm leaving and don't turn around, count to one hundred.

"If you don't do as I say"—he reached over and grabbed my breast hard—"I'll kill you here and throw your body in the river!"

I believe him and start to count out loud, one, two, three . . . At one hundred I turn, sit up, and look in all directions. He's gone.

"You bastard, I hope you rot in hell!" I screamed, feeling queasy, and tried to reach the water fountain. Instead I fell down on all fours and vomited.

What is that I closed my hand so tightly on?

A twenty-dollar bill.

I crumple it and throw it into the wastebasket and go to the water fountain to wash up. As I'm trying to get stuff off, I start to cry. What else is going to happen to me?

Got to get out of this place, I never want to see it again.

I left the park.

Go back, Penny!

What, are you crazy! What for? I almost lost my life!

The money, Penny.

The hell with it, it's dirty money.

You went through a terrifying ordeal and came out alive.

You're broke, sooner or later there won't be any food left!

Get the money, Penny.

I did.

I wanted to get rid of it fast so treated myself to breakfast. It was expensive but worth it and my stomach felt full for the first time in days.

I try not to think about last night. I was careless and know now, never go into a park tired unless there are people around and it's early.

It's so boring, walking back and forth with nothing and nobody to talk to. I keep thinking about a stranger coming. I can't see his face, he's coming to help me and getting closer. I'm not into that hocus-pocus stuff, but if I get a feeling that something is not right, I won't do it. This time though it's right.

Does it make sense to you?

Please come quickly, I need you.

Hey! This is just what I need to cheer me up.

To my right and midway in the block I hear music and see people dancing on a stage! It is some sort of song and dance rehearsal and everybody is having a good time. I walked into the crowd and before long I was singing and dancing to the music. They had this really, really old song my grandmother used to listen to, "Let's Do the Twist," and everybody was exhausted afterwards.

(Thanks, Penny, I feel like a fucking dinosaur! Extinct!)

I felt great until I looked down to see my bag is missing. At first I thought maybe it was kicked around during the dancing. But it's a heavy bag and maybe somebody moved it out of the way. Maybe it was found and brought to the stage. Maybe it was stolen!

No more maybes, it was.

My bag is gone!

I starting screaming, "Did anyone see a brown traveling bag?" over and over.

People were leaving, I was looking, nothing!

Oh, please, please, I'll do anything to get it back!

My clothing, pictures of relatives, phone book, money, everything.

I was stupid and why did I put it down?

Because you wanted to dance, you jerk!

I went to the corner of the street and watched everyone leave, thinking perhaps it was picked up by mistake by someone carrying luggage. No luck.

My last chance, back to the stage area. They are taking it apart, could be it slid underneath. I looked and asked the workers and they all said the same thing, "No, sorry."

That's it, for sure it's gone.

My last piece of sanity and now I don't care what happens to me and the stranger who is coming, don't bother with me, just keep on walking.

I wandered the streets with no direction, just feeling sorry for myself.

What did I do to deserve this kind of life and nobody should live like this and—

My bag.

I see my bag leaning against a wastebasket. Ran over and picked it up and it felt very light, then I noticed it was cut open on the side. Everything gone and I see in the wastebasket all of my pictures and papers torn up!

I found a plastic shopping bag in the trash can and gathered up all the pieces. I screamed and started running and running. I was running so fast, I wanted to have a heart attack and die, but I tripped over something on the sidewalk and went down.

I'm in pain, but when I see the object, laughter replaced the pain. A plastic soda bottle!

I can't believe it, of all things, it's so funny.

Then laughter turned to sorrow, I cried.

An emotional roller coaster going up and down, then for some reason I fell asleep right there on the sidewalk.

I don't remember dreaming but I slept for a long time. Waking up, I find myself in an abandoned car with my pants down to my knees. How

I got there I have no clue, maybe some pervert picked me up, had his fun, and left.

I seem to be okay and I would have known if we had sex. We didn't, and even if it happened, I just don't care anymore.

I give up, I surrender, I'm waving the white flag.

I'm hungry and, fuck it, let the flesh rot and fall off.

Are you listening, God?

I quit!

Do whatever you want with me. Please take me. I closed my eyes and stretched my arms to the sky.

Waiting and waiting, nothing.

Please end my suffering, again I wait.

Again, nothing.

Okay, have it your way, I ran.

Running is good for me. I have no time to think about—oops.

"Hey, little man, watch where you're going."

I accidentally bumped into him so hard that I went down on the sidewalk. He barely moved at all.

"Hey, little man, apologize!"

I kept silent.

"What's the matter, cat got your tongue?"

"Charlie, this little man has no manners. He must be deaf and stupid."

I didn't see the other man standing behind him, and they are big, really big like my father but a lot younger.

"Nah, he is deaf and real stupid!"

Both are laughing.

"Come here, little man, I want to see if you have a tongue." Laughing, reached down with his hand, and I came up and bit down hard.

"Oww! Shit, let go of me, let go!"

His friend came around and kicked me in the chest. I fell down and couldn't catch my breath.

"You son of a bitch!"

Then another kick, this time to the stomach, and as much pain as I was in, I'm able to breathe again. They're kicking me and laughing. When is it going to stop?

I curl my body inward to protect my face and chest.

Where is everybody?

It won't be long now, I'm getting dizzy and my heart is racing.

I love you, Aunt Clare, my sisters.

And that's when you came.

"Caddy."

"Humm."

"What are you thinking about?"

"Wishing I was there at the time to help you and your sisters, to talk to your father."

"Talk to my father? About what?"

Holding up my fists, I said, "These would be doing all the talking."

She hugged me, crying but not so bad now. I hold her for a long time and look out at the sky. Finally she goes soft and starts to breathe easy, and soon I do too.

Sometime in the night, she's suddenly there with me. This is the type of dream you don't want to wake up from. The softness of her skin, the scent and the taste of her. I could have easily tossed her off and ended it, but, God, it felt so good and it's been a long time.

I looked up and saw the tears flowing and tenderly kissed them. She looked at me with those blue eyes. I didn't know why I was crying too.

We locked in a lovers' embrace. I thank you, Penny, for making me feel like a man again. She's sleeping. God, I can feel her heartbeat.

In the morning, using our escape route, we almost made it out, but before we did, there they were, the whole construction crew!

"Hey! What are you guys doing in here?" said the guy in front.

Damn he's big. They all are.

"Sorry, sir, we're homeless and just looking for soda cans and bottles to cash in to get something to eat."

He looked at the wagons and said, "Why the flags, are you a veteran?"

"Yes."

"I am too."

Then came the question-and-answer session, the only true way to find out if someone is truly a veteran. I told him I was in the service from 1968 to 1971, in the army. I was in Fort Jackson, South Carolina, and then in several other stateside posts. I finished my time overseas and came out an E-5. Satisfied, he said, "Wait right here."

He went back to the group, he's talking, they're listening.

She whispers, "Caddy, what's going to happen?"

"I don't know, but look." There were all reaching in their pockets, pulling out cash, and they handed it to him and he walked towards us.

"One last question," he said, looking in my eyes. "Do you or your friend here drink or do drugs?"

"Only coffee and no way."

"I believe you, and here, this is from the boys."

As a rule I can control my emotions out here, but not this time, I cried. I shook his hand and said thank you.

"Your friend doesn't talk much."

"No, something happened to him."

"So where are you going?"

"For sure to get a bite to eat and then look around later to find a safe place for us to sleep."

"You can sleep here if you want, it's safe."

"Huh? Where?"

"Out front in the trailer."

"You trust us?"

"Yes, and besides, we had a couple of break-ins. You'll be our security team."

"But what about the police?"

"Don't worry, I'll tell them. The key will be under the stairs. All I ask is that you leave early and don't touch anything on the desks. Stay as long as you like. Ah, we have been talking all this time and I didn't ask, what's your name?"

"Cadillac Man."

"Everyone calls me Big Sal."

"And I can see why, you're big as a house."

"It's my mama's cooking." Laughing. "Anyway, Cadillac Man, think it over."

"Thanks again, Big Sal, and thank you guys, we really appreciate your kindness."

"One more thing, we leave here at five."

"Okay, Big Sal.

"Come on, Penny, let's get something to eat."

"Penny?"

"Oops, sorry, Big Sal, that's what I call him because he has a pocketful of pennies."

"That makes sense."

Oh, no, please don't say it.

"Let's go, my stomach is growling."

The waitress saw us and put down two cups of coffee without saying a word and left. After a few minutes she came back over and we ordered extra eggs, pancakes, French toast, and sausages to share.

Oh, man, am I stuffed, too much!

I paid the bill and left a generous tip. Still more than a hundred bucks left, between what I had and what Big Sal gave us.

"Okay, Penny, let's go."

"Where are we going?"

"To a canning zone. Today we have a lot of work and won't be able to cash in."

"Why not?"

I tell her that not too far from here there's going to be a street festival. It's going to cover a large area, a lot of people and wastebaskets—can heaven. We can do it twice, in between breaks.

"This is your first time, so you'll be wearing surgical gloves."

"Why?"

"It's a dirty, slimy job. The cans will be mixed in with food scraps and who knows what else. We don't have to worry about the wagons. I know of lots of hiding spots that are safe. If you run into trouble, put your hat on backwards, anything else come over to me. When our bags are full, stay put and I'll bring them to the wagons. We'll eat, have fun, and make money too! What do you say to that, Penny?"

"Let's go, Caddy."

Everybody sing along:

> *A canning we will go*
> *A canning we will go*
> *High and low for cans we go*
> *A canning we will go.*

Hmmm, that's strange, I didn't hear the reader. "Hello, reader!"

It's been a while, maybe he's taking a long dump.

Oh, well, back to the story.

Penny looked so funny trying to wear the gloves. Her hands are too small for them, they kept sliding off. Finally I had to cut them down to size and tape them to her wrists. Not bad, the first time around produced two huge bags and Penny found a five-dollar bill in the wastebasket. It was sticky, but we didn't care, a little bit of water and it comes right off. So what if it's a little wet? Money is money.

At the street fair, so many gave us food, I guess they saw us canning. Must have tasted every ethnic cuisine in the festival. These people didn't look down at us. They cared, you see it in their eyes and voices. At that moment all earthly problems were forgotten and everyone was having a good time. This is the way it should be.

Usually for an area this size I do twice, one up and one down, but with Penny, we picked it clean and she found more money, a few dollars in change. Oh, Penny, we make quite a team. But I wish you would stop looking at me the way you do sometimes, it warms my heart and that shouldn't be. Out here, if anything happens to a friend, it takes longer to heal because you can't express feelings to others. Keep them in check, all of us here can spot weaknesses and use them to our advantage. You don't belong out here, people don't survive.

"Penny, I don't get it. You have an aunt who loves you. Why don't you call her? You've got a place to go."

She turned to me fast and glared at me, biting her lip, her eyes so full of anger and shame. But why?

"No!" she said, and went back to the trash can she was working on. A minute passed and then she looked at me again, gave me that big smile. "I want to stay here with you."

How can I say no? There's something she can't go back to there, and I know what that feels like. Plus it gets so lonely out here. "Okay, Penny. You can stay." The smile again, then she quickly turned her head back to her cans.

We went back to work, not talking much, and by the end of the day had six huge bags, a real good day's work. As a joke I tied all six to Penny's wagon, one on top of another. She didn't say a word, just started pushing, struggling to look over and to the sides of the wagon. Didn't complain once.

I stopped to light a cigarette and she crashed into me.

"Hey!"

"Sorry, Caddy, why did you stop?"

"To light a cigarette. Come on, let's go."

I stopped for a traffic signal.

"Hey!"

"Sorry, Caddy, why did you stop?"

"Traffic signal."

This went on and on, until my joke backfired.

"Okay, okay, you win!"

"You mean I passed the test?"

Test? "Ah, yes, with flying colors!" Go along with it, see what she says.

"When you piled up the bags on my wagon, I said to myself, this must be a test to see if I can handle a big load. I couldn't see, but you were making so much noise I listened and followed."

"Noise? What noise?"

"Your wagon going *clickity-clack, clickity-clack.* And your farting."

"My farting?"

Everybody sing along!

> *Beans, beans are good for your heart*
> *The more you eat, the more you fart.*
> *The more you fart, the better you'll feel*
> *So eat your beans at every meal.*

"Eww, that's gross."

"Like Jimmy Durante used to say, I got a million of them."

"Who?"

"Never mind, before your time. Here, let me lessen your load, the joke's over and—"

"Joke?"

"I mean—"

"What joke, Caddy?"

Ouch, my ears, so I explained, laughing with it. After all, Penny can take a joke good-naturedly. Right?

Wrong! And guess who winds up with all six bags? Me!

"Come on, Caddy, hurry it up, we have four miles to go," she said.

You slave driver! See what happens to you after I tell my union delegate!

Ah, here we are at last, the construction site! Perfect timing, after five and we're exhausted. Penny is quiet, it's been a long day, and we'll probably go to sleep right away. The trailer is huge and I see an AC unit attached with a portable bathroom to the side.

Oh, please, let the key be there. It's there.

Thank you, Big Sal!

We go inside to find it's still cool and a box on one of the desks with our names on it.

A note:

Thought you would be hungry. Sodas in the fridge. Remember,

keep the place clean, don't touch any papers on desks, and leave early.

Big Sal

Sandwiches and potato chips inside the box, in the fridge there's enough soda for a small army but we'll just take what we need and thank you again, Big Sal. I feel refreshed, alive—a most pleasurable evening for us with no outside interruptions.

In the morning, the construction crew is off—it's the weekend. We have the entire day to cash in at two redeemers, the sooner done, the sooner we can relax. It will be easy because we have all cans and that means one machine instead of the usual three. And if we find anything along the way, an added bonus.

Penny took half of the load, so that we could walk side by side.

"It's going to be a scorcher, Penny, slow and easy."

"Caddy, we need to find a place to shower soon. I need to take care of myself."

"Are you sick?"

"No, silly, feminine hygiene."

Oh, that, of course. It's been a long time for me. I think the last one, Carter was president. Or was it Eisenhower?

"Penny, we're going to shower today!"

(Bravo!)

Keep out of this, reader, and go play with your rubber duckie!

"Are you sure?"

"Yes, absolutely." I hope.

Here we are at the redeemer and it's not too crowded. I hear a familiar voice and see a big blocky guy pushing everybody away from the can machine. Yep, that's him, Maurell. An ex-boxer with a glass jaw. He's Eastern European, speaks very little English.

When he's not canning, he's panhandling and he doesn't have to speak to get attention, just look at his hands! Cripes, they're fucking huge! It reminded me of fresh hams in a butcher shop.

The story on the street was, one day Maurell was twenty-five cent short of buying a pint of vodka. One of the guys told him he would give him twenty-five cent, on the condition that he takes a crap in his hat. Maurell really needs the twenty-five cent. Sure as shit—no pun intended—he took off his hat and put it on the ground. He grunted, he groaned and produced one helluva crap and brought the hat full of crap to the guy.

The guy looks at it in disbelief. Then Maurell said in that heavy accent, "See, it's fullll."

He got one dollar.

What happened to the hat full of crap? I don't know, I didn't ask.

"Penny, start doing the cans. I have to talk with Maurell."

"Okay."

He's sitting on someone's overturned wagon and they're cursing at him. He's just ignoring them, counting change, and I have an idea.

"Hey! Maurell."

Looks up. "Cadillac Man, it's fullll." Showing me his change, thirty-five cent.

"No, it's emptyyy."

He smiles.

"Maurell, do you have a place to stay with a shower?"

"Yes, Cadillac Man, it's fullll."

"Holy shit! Did you say yes?"

I hope that's the only word he learned. I hate blabbermouths.

"All done with the cans, Caddy."

"Thanks, Penny. This is Maurell."

Whispers, "Gosh, you weren't kidding, his hands are huge!"

"Yeah, he probably can juggle watermelons."

"Okay, Maurell, I need a favor."

He nodded.

"My friend here and I need to take a long shower and don't rush us. While we're showering, you'll be standing outside guarding the wagons. Do not, I repeat, do not touch anything on the wagons or leave for any reason. After we come out and everything is okay, all of us are going to the liquor store."

His eyes widen.

"To show our appreciation, Maurell, we're going to buy you two fifths of vodka!"

Son of a bitch, the eyes are ready to pop out.

"Is it a deal?"

"Yes, yes." With laughter. "Cadillac Man, it's fullll, it's fullll!"

What are we waiting for? Let's get the hell outta here!

Maurell is happy, he's singing and dancing. And, no, I don't know the language, the dance may be the cha-cha. One, two, cha-cha-cha.

Anyway, we stop in front of this beautiful four-story walk-up. I love these type of buildings, they have so much history. We're in luck, his apartment is on the ground floor. He opens the door.

"Remember, Maurell, stand guard and don't touch anything."

He smiled, saluted, and stood by the wagons.

Going through the foyer, the air was stale, reeking of mold and old cigarette smoke. To our left, a kitchen that hasn't been used in years, judging by the dust and cobwebs, and next to it the bathroom and what a pleasant surprise. An old-fashioned wrought-iron bathtub with a shower attachment and it's clean, too clean for Maurell. Where does he eat and take a dump? Out, of course!

Okay, now let's see if the shower works. Water knobs turn and moan into life. Brown, rusty water at first, then deliciously hot and clean.

"Okay, Penny, you're first."

Ah! What a beautiful sound, the splashing of water. Outsiders have no idea what it's like to walk around and sleep feeling half-clean. Try it for a week, just use the sink only. It will give you a small taste as to what we go through out here.

Enough talk, time to snoop. I'm not nosy, just curious. Lots of old furniture, worth a small fortune. A dresser filled with pictures of Maurell's younger days, in boxing poses, military uniform, and his wedding. She's beautiful and where is she now?

I found out in the next room, the bedroom. She's dead.

A made-up bed and on the one side is an open Bible with a funeral card dated ten years ago. On the floor is a makeshift bed, numerous vodka bottles, an ashtray, and her funeral pictures. He is still grieving and I feel his pain. Vodka is his solace.

Sorry, Maurell, my new friend.

"Caddy."

I made the sign of the cross and prayed for Maurell and his beloved wife.

"Caddy."

"Comin', Mother!"

"Oh, Caddy, I feel sooo good and sooo clean."

"Is the water still hot?"

"Oh, yes, it's wonderful."

"Gangway!"

Man, this is great.

"So what did you find snooping, Caddy?"

"Nothing but old furniture and old memories."

I don't know who was more shocked. Penny and I looked so different, not homeless but like outsiders wearing mismatched clothing.

"Caddy, you look so handsome!"

"Like Clark Gable?"

"Who?"

"Never mind, before your time."

"I wish we could come here every day, Caddy."

"Me too." The chances of meeting up with Maurell again are slim. We move around a lot and so does he.

"Come on, we've been here long enough, let's not abuse it. He's probably grown grass under his shoes, the amount of time we spent in here."

I don't believe it. There he was, standing at attention next to the wagons.

"At ease, soldier!"

"It's fullll."

"Okay, Maurell, you know the area, take us to the nearest liquor store!"

"Yes, yes, Cadillac Mann, it's fullll!" Laughing.

So off we go, and Penny and I are having a good time. Beautiful day, so clean.

It's fulllllll.

Back at the trailer I secured the wagons, then covered them with construction tarp.

Rain is coming, I can tell.

"Well, my dear, it's time for you to visit Cadillac Man the tailor! He uses only the finest garbage bags to make quality raincoats. And you're in luck, no appointment necessary!"

A double check of what I'll need. Oh, this is good. The only thing missing is a camera!

"Okay, Penny, we'll start from the top and work downward. Hat please."

Take a supermarket, plastic shopping bag and insert the hat. Then stuff the bag into the hat, keeping its shape.

"See how easy it is? Try it on for size."

"It's a little snug."

"Good, you can't have it too loose, it would fall off as soon as you bend down to pick up something."

Now for the raincoat. For this I'll need a large, heavy-duty garbage bag. I have to compare her size next to the bag. Okay, for her I have to cut off at least six inches to start.

Cut across the bag opening. On the bag bottom cut a half-circle opening in the center, this is for her head. I made a mark where her elbows are and again cut a half circle, slightly smaller, for the arms to slide through. It's done, but before she puts it on, we do the shoes.

This is the easiest, two plastic shopping bags, one for each foot. Slide in foot, put shoe back on, and pull up the bag tightly and tie to ankles loosely.

"Now you're ready to put on the raincoat. Go ahead."

She wiggles into it, smiling.

"Hey, not bad, just one more item. A belt, I don't want you to do a Mary Poppins on me."

Sometimes the wind blows under and inflates the bag; if you wear a belt, most of the draft is eliminated. Maybe the pants legs and your arms for sure will get wet. Better that than the whole body. With a steady rain you'll stay fairly dry.

There's one disadvantage to wearing all of this. On a hot, muggy rainy day the raincoat will cling like a rubber suit, making you sweat so much, you want to take it off.

Sometimes, I would find a place and get naked, then on with the raincoat. The beauty part is nobody knows, you can't tell by looking.

"Put on your hat and step back." Perfect.

"How do I look?"

"Like a garbage bag that came to life!" Laughing.

"Really?"

"No, you look great! A genuine foul-weather-equipped street canner! I salute you!" Kissed her cheeks French-style. "We'll test everything tomorrow, depending on how heavy the rain is."

"But, Caddy, it stopped."

"Not for long, the air is thick and you can smell the river. Open the door and take a deep breath."

"Ewww, it stinks and it's hard to breathe."

"Too much moisture, we're going to get a lot of rain. We're lucky to be in here, these types of nights are miserable and depressing. I call them blue nights."

"Blue nights?"

I try to explain: Nights like this, being out there wet and miserable, alone, looking at the houses. Imagining the families inside warm and dry. The sound of laughter or a child calling their parent coming from an open window. The memories of a life I once had come flooding over me and I'm drowning. I scream loud and long, don't give a fuck who hears me, then the memories fade away.

"So those are blue nights, Penny."

"They're gone, Caddy."

"Huh? What are you talking about?"

"The blue nights are gone because we're together."

Oh, Penny, I wish you were older or I younger. Things would have been so different for us. There is so much more to do and see in life! But not with me.

Penny was restless that night.

I woke up hearing her cry. Sit up to see her sitting behind a desk, hands over the eyes.

"Penny, what's wrong?"

No answer. As I got closer to the desk, I knew. On the desk were two piles, remnants of her family photos. I must have brought back the memories of her family during our conversation about blue nights.

"I'm sorry for talking about my blue nights."

"It's not your fault. I think about them every day. And I don't know what I took these out for, so depressing."

"Never forget the ones you love, Penny. Pictures reinforce the love, making it stronger."

"You're right, even though they're ruined, I can see them in my mind. Might as well throw them away."

"Why?"

"Caddy, they're all in little pieces."

"Give me a chance and I'll try to fix them."

Years ago one of my hobbies was jigsaw puzzles. The smaller the piece, the better I like it. Make the puzzle almost impossible and I love it!

"Start making the coffee for me. If you want to, see if the TV works and watch something. With a little bit of luck I should be done in a few hours. Wish me luck."

She smiled and came over and kissed my cheek, her breasts brushed across my arm.

"You better get dressed and make the coffee, you're distracting me."

So I started.

The first thing I did was to turn over the pieces, the black side facing me, and found some sort of letter mixed in. I picked the pieces out. I'll repair it later.

Next separated the corners and margins. It took some time, but after a while I'm ready to fill the inside of the pictures. Very tedious task, just like a jigsaw puzzle. They're filling in rapidly, though.

Penny is watching TV, and every time she brought over coffee, she would turn her eyes away and not look at my progress.

I tape them carefully so that the pictures wouldn't be lopsided. I turned them around and stacked according to size.

Done! Now for the note. Took less than a minute, it read:

Dear Penny

For bus fare, just in case.
Call me (607) 555-3478

Love,
Aunt Clare

I hit the jackpot.

"My, my, what beautiful pictures you have here."

"You finished them? You really finished them?"

"Yes, I did!"

"Yippee! Yippee!"

If they had an award for the biggest smile and happiest face, Penny is the winner.

With tears flowing, she sat down. She pointed out her mother, Aunt Clare, sisters, and lots of baby pictures. None of her father, no surprise.

"The first chance we get, we have to buy a small, compact photo album."

"Come on, let's go back to bed for a few hours."

It's still early and raining heavily.

It didn't take Penny long to fall fast asleep. I gently touched her face, which brought a little smile. It saddened me.

Soon you will be gone, Penny. I must savor every moment with you.

When we got up, the sun was shining and Penny was a little disappointed that she couldn't try out the rain gear.

"Don't worry, Penny, there will be times where we won't be able to take them off, this month's weather is so unpredictable."

A typical weekend day, the outsiders are at the parks or beaches. And the redeemer is closed, so we're able to can at a leisurely pace.

A blue pickup truck pulls up beside Penny, and I see the driver talking to her. She didn't give the signal for trouble, so I guess he's asking for directions. But she doesn't know the area. I do, so maybe I can help him. As soon as I start to go over, he sees me and takes off. That's odd.

"What's up, Penny?"

"Wonderful news! His name is Joe and he owns a building three blocks from here. He fired the super and was cleaning out the basement when he noticed about twenty big bags of cans and plastic bottles. It all has to be taken out today because the fire inspectors are checking the boiler tomorrow and the bags are a fire hazard. Joe said I can take as many as possible. Caddy, the both of us will get a lot, maybe all of them."

"No, Penny."

"A lot then."

"No, Penny."

"How many?"

"None, not a one, Penny."

"I don't understand? Why?"

"It's a setup, a very dangerous one to lure you into a trap."

"Are you sure, Caddy? It's a lot to pass up."

Do we know this guy? No. Do I believe him? No way.

"Penny, I've been out here a long time, and when something smells bad, it stinks, and Joe stinks!"

I heard a story about this, about two brothers. Both alkies, both homeless. One night a guy drives up saying he's a contractor working on a basement for a landlord. The building's super was fired and he left behind a load of bags filled with plastic soda bottles and cans that the contractor was going to throw away in the morning.

He said they'd be doing him a big favor by taking them so that he can spend more time on his work project. "You need the cash, I don't need the trash," he said. "Is it a deal?"

When they got to the basement, there was a guy waiting for them with a huge knife. A big, hairy motherfucker, wearing only a mask and leather briefs with his cock sticking out. Then his buddies came in, locked the doors on them. You can imagine the rest. The story is that they were held down there for days while those perverts had their fun.

True story? I don't know. I heard it from a few different people. But then, you hear a lot of things out here. Maybe it's bullshit. Bottom line, why take the chance? Who would protect you if someone wanted to take advantage?

Took Penny by the arm. "Let's get back to work."

We did pretty good, at one location three full bags of cans, must have been a party.

When we went to eat and tried to pay the cashier, we were told that somebody paid for our meals and left. It would have been nice to thank them personally, so instead left a generous tip. On the way back we're going to pass a department store and I suggested to Penny to buy a photo album.

Nothing fancy, just as long as it's waterproof, and don't get pink, it's a girlie color.

Goes in and comes back out a few minutes later with an album—pink, of course. Sheesh. There goes my reputation.

And wouldn't you know it, on the way back home it started to rain. At first a drizzle, then a steady downpour. Penny was thrilled, putting on the raingear. Any street person going by and looking at her, they would say she's one of us.

It's not rainwater falling from my eyes, its tears for a young woman with an awesome smile walking proudly wearing a garbage bag.

Does that make any sense to you?

We're home at last, I let her go ahead while I secure and waterproof the wagons.

When I get back, she already started on the pictures, inserting them with great care. She doesn't even know I'm there. With tears flowing, she tenderly kisses each one.

It's obvious she misses her life. How many times do we think about home? Everywhere we go there are constant reminders. Children at play, a song, an aroma, a color. It sneaks up on you suddenly and just as quickly disappears. If I get started thinking about my life again, I won't be able to help Penny. Have to distract her.

"So, Penny, do you have enough room for the pictures?"

"Yes, Caddy."

"Whew, that's a relief." The thought of going back to the store and getting another is scary.

"Penny, in the morning we're leaving for Cleveland."

"Cleveland?"

"Yeah, they don't know me there and I hear it's safe to own a pink photo album."

The body feels great, the sun is shining, a perfect day so far, and I hope nothing spoils it. To go through a day without something happening is a blessing. In some areas it's like the Wild West and others so boring you could hear the grass growing.

"Cadillac Man is feeling very generous right now and he wants to buy you ice cream."

"Vanilla with sprinkles."

"You will have it, my dear! For me, chocolate! I feel like singing the ice cream song!"

"Ice cream song?"

"Follow me, all together."

> *Ice cream, you scream*
> *We all scream for ice cream*
> *Hip, hooray!*

Acting like little kids singing along to the ice cream parlor. We didn't care what people thought of us, we were having fun.

At the parlor we were having a good time enjoying the ice cream and watching the children on a miniature merry-go-round outside.

Then trouble came a knocking.

Two teenage boys were eyeing us and came over to our table.

"Hey, man, you're sitting at our favorite table."

"Really? Well, that's too fucking bad, you'll have to wait until we're done."

"Huh?"

"Get lost, boy wonders!"

"Stand up, old man, I'm going to kick your ass."

Everybody looked at me.

Penny said, "Caddy, let's go canning."

We pick up and go.

Besides Penny canning is the only thing that keeps my sanity. We live day to day and couldn't care less about politics, the economy, or world issues. The door is closed, that's fine by us. Street news, who went to jail or died and, the best, who got decent housing with benefits, that's all we want to know, and sometimes meeting old friends who survived another harsh winter and had stories to tell. It's sort of like a family reunion, meeting up with a long-lost brother or sister.

You listen and you learn little tidbits of survival. Looking at Penny, it would be an uphill battle with my help. Alone, she would surely die!

Why am I thinking this way?

She will be gone before the winter sets in, I promised myself. It's hard for me to accept the fact that I'll be alone again. I have lost partners in the past, but this is the first time it's a woman, and I truly care for her. Just look at her canning right now, she's a natural, born to live in this world.

Bullshit! Nobody is.

With all of our hardships, she's quick to smile and so full of passion. Quick to react if I go too far with someone and stop me in time. You have to go home, Penny, before it's too late. I'm trying so hard not to fall in love with you!

"Caddy!"

She's waving and pointing into the wastebasket.

"What's up?"

"Look in the garbage bag, eww!"

I was thinking maybe she found a dead cat or dog, that happens. Instead it was porno tapes, gay porno tapes, and lots of them in mint condition.

"No *eww*, Penny. *Eureka!* is a better word. Money in the bank, we're rich."

"What are you talking about?"

"I know a place I can sell all of these instantly."

"Where?"

"A gay bar, the Pink Slipper."

"You are going into a place like that to sell them?"

"Why not? I know the owner, his name is Harold."

"Why do you think they were thrown away?"

"Haven't a clue, perhaps a jealous boyfriend? Let's boogie, lady, we got a lot of traveling to do."

It's almost dark by the time we get there. My dogs are yapping and a barking, while Penny looks fresh as a daisy, ready to do more. Sheesh!

Up ahead I see the neon sign, a big pink slipper kicking up and down.

Here comes Harold. He's something to see, Maybe five-seven, and dumpy, about three hundred pounds, with this crazy hair dyed bright blond like Liberace. "Cadillac Man, darling!" Arms out to embrace.

"Harriet, don't you dare!" He likes to be called Harriet.

"Oh, Cadillac Man, don't be a fuddy-duddy."

Fuddy-duddy? "Let's sit at a booth and I'll show you what I got."

"Ooo, sounds interesting!"

"Knock it off, Harriet."

We sit down and I place the garbage bag on the table. "Take a look-see."

Eyes widen, reaches in, grabs a handful, and starts waving them. "Ladies! We have goodies!"

Everybody was whistling and howling.

"Cadillac Man, perfect timing, I was down to my last two."

"How much, Harriet?"

"Two dollars each."

"What! Are you fucking crazy? That's top dollar? The sign behind the bar says twenty dollars each, three for fifty, and, look, all of them are in mint condition. Five, Harriet."

"Here." Hands me an envelope. "For the tapes, top dollar."

"Harriet, if you were a woman, I would give a kiss on your lips." So I kissed the hand, gentleman-style.

"Ooooh."

"Crème cookies."

"What do you mean by that, Penny?"

"Never mind, before your time."

Sheesh! That's my line.

It was miles to the trailer, and we only have three hours before the crew comes back. No problem, I know another place. There's a secluded spot in a park on the way, so I take us there. I secure the wagons and put a blanket down for us to rest on. The outsiders are all asleep, and there are no other street people here. Trees all around and just one streetlight showing the soft grass.

"What a beautiful, peaceful spot, Caddy."

"Indeed it is."

"How many of your lovers came here?"

"None and only you."

"Were there any?"

"No, you are the first and last."

I was looking towards the heavens when I heard her little snores.

Sleep well, Penny. Dream of the life you once had and the better one that's still to come, and sadly without me. She reaches out to touch me and smiles. I can just barely see her in the light from the street lamp.

"Go back to sleep, it's late."

"She turns away from me, then I hear her say, "I love you, Caddy."

"I love you too, Penny," but no response.

I stayed awake through the dawn, fully at ease absorbing the early sunshine and feeling the gentle breeze.

"Caddy?"

"Hello, sleeping beauty."

"I'm sorry for sleeping so long."

"No big deal, you were tired, and every chance your body gets to rest, it heads towards sleepy land."

Most of our people sleep to fight boredom or just to be left alone. You don't see us so much during the day, too many outsiders. So we hide and hide deep until the twilight slips away.

"What did you think about while I was sleeping?"

"Thinking about leaving here."

"Huh?"

"Next week we go to a new area."

"But why, Caddy. We like it here."

"That's why we have to leave, remember what I told you once before. Never get used to staying in one spot, something always happens. Sooner or later Big Sal and his crew will leave, their job done, or maybe one of the big bosses decides to have a late-night inspection. We don't want to get him into any trouble. Right?

"Still got two good days to can, let's pick this place clean."

Double-checked ourselves for creepy crawlers, those sons of bitches deliberately wait until bedtime and come out of hiding, then head for the crack of your ass or, worst, the front. At one time it felt like I had a colony of ants living down below, and I knew what had to be done to get rid of them. Gentlemen, use this method as a last resort.

Ladies, turn your heads please.

I still get the shakes thinking about it. Brrr! You're going to need rubbing alcohol or aftershave lotion and most important a lot of water, sink or shower or bathtub. I'm in the streets so I don't have your luxuries, made do with something else.

Okay, here we go.

I was in agony from itching and scratching so with no one around I took off my pants and shoes. Next I poured a generous amount of aftershave lotion onto a washcloth. Held my breath and rubbed in both places.

What fucking pain! My balls and ass crack were burning like they were on fire! I screamed so loud all the pigeons left the park, then I ran into the lake. Sitting in the cool water eased the pain, and after a few minutes I got up, walked to the shore. Never again!

When I got back, my pants and shoes were gone. I was careless. Fortunately, my wagon was nearby with extra shoes and clothes. So now you know what to do with ants in your pants. Burn them! Drown them! And hold on to your pants and shoes!

Okay, ladies, you now can turn around, thank you.

"What's the matter, Caddy, got ants in your pants?"

Sheesh! Why did she have to say that?

"No, just counting my change."

We met up with tourists who wanted to take our pictures.

This happens from time to time. Usually they come up to you with this cheesy smile and say, "Do you mind if we take your picture," looking like they're trying not to pee. Some of them are slick, though. One guy will run behind the wagon and wave at the camera while the other one snaps the picture. I call that a "drive-by shooting." When they ask, I always say the same thing: "Five dollars apiece, payable in advance."

So these four came up with the twenty dollars and started snapping away.

Posing behind the wagons. "Hey, Fred! Look at me. I'm homeless." Laughing.

One of the guys wanted me to pose with an empty beer can in my hand. No way. Another tried to put his arm around Penny and I gave him a hard stare and he decided not to. These fucking morons. If I was a predator, I could have easily taken their cash, cameras, even the wives' underwear, and who would have stopped me?

I can imagine the story they'll tell the neighbors back home while passing the pictures around. Maybe even have a few laughs. Satisfied with the amount taken, they said thank you and headed toward the subway.

"Caddy, I didn't like the way the women were looking at me."

"I know."

No offense, ladies, but your behavior towards us needs improving. You'd expect men to be the tougher ones, but it's not always that way.

I remember my first year out here, trying to survive the pouring rain and bitter-cold weather. A cardboard box or garbage bags to keep me warm and dry while I tried to get some sleep. I would hear you. Usually in a group, your laughter at my misery would stand out from the others.

You couldn't see my tears. I was amusing to you, a novelty in your eyes. To the tourist we're part of the city, like Times Square. We're stereotyped as crazy people to approach cautiously with a soothing voice and never alone.

Outsiders don't understand why we are this way. They fear us. And don't say bullshit, I've seen it many times in your eyes or the way you step back when talking to me.

"Why the angry look, Caddy?"

"Never mind, let's can."

Penny came over and gave me a hug.

"Thanks, I needed that, and how did you know?"

"You're crying."

"Shit! Anybody looking at us?"

"Don't be afraid, Caddy, let it out."

It was a struggle at first, then uncontrollable tears. I'm grateful that Penny was there comforting me. The heartache subsided, so did the tears, but I felt weak and drained. Penny, bless her, went to a store across the street and came back with coffee. She didn't say anything, just rubbed my back. I felt much better.

"I owe you big-time."

"You don't owe me, Caddy."

Kissed her lips and smiled.

"Come on, we're losing money standing here."

The rest of the day was busy for us, good pickings, and even found a jar of pennies discarded in a trash can. On one of our breaks while she was with the wagons, I went into a deli to buy some refreshments and a calling card. I put it with the phone number, ready for the right moment to come.

"Caddy, are we going to do any more canning?"

"Nah, our wagons are full and we have pennies to wrap. Plus my taste buds are saying cheeseburger, french fries!"

"I'll buy if you fly."

"Where'd you learn that?"

"Never mind, during your time."

Sheesh! So we picked up the munchies and were nearing the trailer when I spot the telephone. Now's the time. Have to think of an excuse fast.

"Penny, one of my wheels is coming loose, I better fix it now. It's going to take a while, so you might as well eat first."

"Take your time, I'll be wrapping the pennies, and when you're done, we'll eat."

I secure the wagons and creep back to the trailer; radio is on, the pennies will keep her busy. The telephone is on the other side of the street where I can see if the trailer door opens and she can't see me. Oh, please, let it be a working phone.

A dial tone! So far, so good. I punch in the numbers and a phone is ringing on the other end.

"Hello?" a girl answers, probably one of Penny's sisters.

"Hi! Can I talk to Clare, please?"

"Who should I say is calling?"

"My name is Cadillac Man and I know where Penny is."

She put down the receiver. I heard her yell, "Aunt Clare, another one. He says his name is Cadillac Man."

Another one?

"Okay, Mr. Cadillac Man, no reward unless you give me some credible information."

About my age, I'd guess, on edge and tired from receiving crank calls with false leads.

"Just 'Cadillac Man,' and I don't give a damn about any reward. I want Penny to go home before it's too late."

"Just tell me what you know, sir!" Raising her voice.

"Take it easy. First of all she has two younger sisters living with you, mother died recently, abusive father who cut off her blond hair, and this note just in case. Aunt Clare and phone number."

I heard some sobbing, then she blew her nose and came back on nasal-like.

"I'm sorry for yelling, sir."

"That's okay." She's under a lot of stress.

"Is she all right? Can I talk to her?"

"She's fine and right now is wrapping pennies. She doesn't know I'm talking to you."

"Why?"

"I don't have much time to explain everything to you."

"Give me your number then, and I'll call later."

"Yeah, sorry, Clare, I can't give you the number because I'm calling from a pay phone with a calling card. I'll come right to the point. Penny and I are homeless and living on the streets in New York City."

"What? New York City?"

"I found her about a month ago and she has been with me ever since."

"Why didn't she call me? I would have come and got her."

"I don't know, you'll have to ask her."

"How did you find my number?"

"It was in with some torn pictures of Penny's."

"Torn pictures?"

"Again, she'll have to explain, it will take too long."

"Okay. Okay. What's your plan?"

"Are you willing to come to New York City?"

"Yes, anywhere, I want to bring her home."

"Me too. Now listen. On Wednesday morning at nine Penny and I will be at the Greyhound waiting area in Port Authority Bus Terminal. It's located in midtown Manhattan. If you come by bus, even better. We'll be on the first level. Wear a green baseball cap."

"Why green?"

"It's going to be crowded there and that color will stand out from the rest. Don't worry, I'll be able to see you. When I do, I'll wave, and Penny will be next to me. Then take her home.

"One last thing: if possible, bring her sisters along with you, no green caps though."

The recording comes on telling me I've got sixty seconds left, saves me from having to explain: I think our fondness is turning to love, and that's why I want her to leave now. Sooner or later one of us will die, and I don't want Penny to be alone out here. "Do you follow me?"

"Yes, I do. And thank you. I'll see you Wednesday."

"With a green baseball cap, Clare."

Laughs a little wet-sounding laugh. "I won't forget."

I better dirty my hands, make them look like I was working on the wagon. Penny, I like your aunt Clare, wish I had one just like her. She'll never replace your mother in some ways, but she'll try. One down and one to go.

"Hi, Caddy, perfect timing, I just finished the pennies."

"How much?"

"Six dollars and three cents."

"Not bad for found money."

"How's the wagon?"

"Good as new for another thousand miles. Did you eat?"

"No, I waited for you."

"Let's chow down. I'm so hungry I could eat Harriet's underwear."

My sweet Penny, how much I will miss you so.

Got over to the redeemer the next day, and while Penny was cashing in, I mingled with the others. The word on the street was two wannabe gang-bangers were shakin' down the homeless and canners through threats, gestures, and pushing around, everybody is scared.

They are in an area where Penny and I are headed next to can. I sure hope we don't meet up with them, for their sake. Now it was my turn to cash in.

The others went over to talk to her. They accepted her, not because of being with me. She is "street" in the way she talks, handles the machines, etc.

It's going to be hard on me telling them she's gone. They'll be sad yet happy knowing that she's back home. We all wish for it, and a few are lucky to be accepted back to the family fold.

She's unaware that this is the last time here and seeing them. It's better that way, not knowing, right?

"All right, ladies, enough chattering about your sex lives, Penny and I have to hit the road."

That brought on laughter.

"Caddy, guess what?"

"What?"

"Wanda is pregnant again."

"I have an alibi."

"Huh?"

"Never mind. Hmm, let's see, that makes number seven."

"Wanda has six kids already?"

"Yep, and all by different boyfriends. Give her some cheap wine and reefer and she will drop her drawers, then take advantage of you."

She has a sweet setup, I explain. She makes a couple hundred a week from canning, receives PA (welfare) and food stamps, which she sells at half price. Then she hits up the fathers of the kids demanding food, diapers, and money or else be reported to PA. They gladly pay up, rather than doing the right thing by being a parent to the child.

Look at her now wearing hand-me-downs pretending to be homeless and panhandles too. More money. Anyway, she likes to party at night and dresses to the nines, no cheap shit, designer clothes and flashy jewelry and off to the nightclubs, get stoned or bombed, somebody always paid. Go home with the dude, drain his balls, then cry, saying she has so many bills. More money.

She's friendly with her super and rents out the boiler room in the winter to the homeless at ten dollars a night. More money.

If you're receiving a check and got into her pants recently, watch out. You just cashed the check and guess who appears crying, saying I'm pregnant with your child and I want to get an abortion. More money.

Or I'm pregnant and need to go to a specialist. More money.

She's a beauty, the ultimate scammer!

I would love to find out where she stashes the cash, probably has an offshore account somewhere. Sooner or later her luck is going to run out, though, it always does out here. What the street gives, it takes back from you twice.

· · ·

The area we're going into is slowly changing for the better—if you are new generation from suburbia or out of state. The poor are leaving, running away from high rents or just plain dying. Fancy stores with fancy names doesn't impress us, just keep it plain and simple for us!

I could never fit into this new way of life.

"Penny, we have a lot of canning to do, so we'll be up late. Being that tomorrow is our last day using the trailer, let's get extra hours of sleep and rest. The next canning zone is far and we have to leave early."

"How good do you know the area?"

"Like the back of my hand, I grew up in the neighborhood."

"Do you still have family there?"

"Yeah."

"Do you want to see them?"

"Nope, I already tried to."

"What if we meet up with them on the street?"

"Say hello and then good-bye, period. Come on, let's get busy, I'll stroll down memory lane with you when we're in the new area."

We really worked our butts off, covered a lot of ground today, and we're tired.

And would you believe that Penny found more pennies, a sackful that even I struggled to pick up.

"That settles it, Penny. On Monday morning we're going to court to have your named changed to Dollar."

It took every ounce of strength we had to make it back to the trailer.

"Oh, Caddy, I'm sooo tired."

"Me too, our last full day here and we're going to get a lot of extra sleep."

"Make our bed, I'll be right in."

Tomorrow a day of rest and maybe a little canning. I get back and she's sound asleep with her clothes on and I won't disturb. Another day done, another day closer to going home, my Penny. We slept about ten hours and I was awakened by her kisses. I feel her hands.

Our lovemaking was so full of tenderness.

"What do you want to do now, Caddy?"

"Even though it's late, I would like to buy my lady breakfast."

"Oh, please do, kind sir."

"Let's go."

"Caddy, you are forgetting something."

"What's that?"

"We're naked."

"Oh. Did you whisper in my ear when I wasn't looking?"

"No, Caddy, we're both awake."

"Oh, yeah, that's right."

We had a lot of fun window-shopping, going into several stores, the best was women's clothing.

"Penny, are you sure you want to go in there?"

"Why not?"

"The way you are dressed."

"I have men's clothes, but underneath I'm a hundred percent female who likes to dress up on occasion. Come on, let's go inside."

"Sheesh! Heaven help me!"

"What's the matter?"

"I'm going to be surrounded by women's underwear, my reputation will be ruined!"

"Stop it, Caddy."

"Can I wear a disguise?"

"Stop it, Caddy."

"What if I come in through the back door?"

"Caddy!"

"Okay, okay, but if I see Harriet in there, I'm splitting."

As soon as we step inside, every eye is staring at us. A salesgirl cautiously approaches.

"Can I help you gentlemen?"

Gentlemen? It never fails, I think everybody should have their eyes checked. Penny is too beautiful to be a man.

I must admit at first glance I thought so too, but it was different, she was dirty and her street clothes were way too big.

"No, you can't help me, but my friend here wants to look around."

She goes through the racks, selecting a dress, placing it against her, then looks at me. I would shake my head no, pretend to barf or pinch my nose. Then she picks this green floral-patterned dress. That's the one! She smiled and nodded in agreement.

"Caddy, can I buy it?"

"It's your money, Penny."

"Do you really like it?"

"I love it!"

"Caddy, they have a cosmetics counter!"

"Why put on a phony face, Penny, you have beautiful skin."

I hate that stuff. Women put on so much makeup and perfume they look and smell like a two-dollar hooker. She's not listening.

We approach the cosmetics counter and there's a salesgirl with a big grin, pointing a perfume bottle at me. A nightmare from hell!

"Sister, if you squirt that on me, you won't live to see your firstborn!"

I must have really shocked her, she did a juggling act before finally catching it.

"Caddy!"

"I'm sorry, I get edgy when anything is pointed at me." To the shop-girl: "My girlfriend wants to sample the perfumes."

"Girlfriend?"

"Well, she ain't my mother!"

"Caddy!"

"I'm sorry, not used to being in these kinds of places."

"Okay, Caddy, I want your honest opinion."

"Believe me, you will get it."

"What about this one?"

"Smells like a wet dog."

"Caddy!"

"You told me to be honest."

"Fine. This one?"

"Sweaty socks on a summer's day."

"This one?"

"Cheap hooker."

"This one?"

"Expensive hooker." Turn back to the salesgirl. "Excuse me, miss, do you have anything that's vanilla-scented?"

"Yes, here you go, sir."

"Ah! Perfect! Take a whiff, Penny."

"Mmm!"

"I was told by an elderly grandmother that when she was a young bride, she couldn't afford perfume. To smell nice and in the mood for 'hanky-panky,' as she called it, she used something her mother mentioned for the wedding night. One drop of vanilla extract behind each ear will excite your husband and you will get pregnant that night."

"Vanilla extract?" said the salesgirl. "Did it work?"

"Must have, she had eight children."

"Gee, I should try it, my husband and I want to have a baby."

We all laughed. I hope it works.

The lipstick was the easiest to pick, a light shade of red, then Penny kissed my nose.

I looked like a clown with a big red honker.

We leave the store. "Okay, Penny, let's go shoe shopping."

"But, Caddy, I spent a lot of money."

"No, you saved, today everything in the store was half-price."

Went to at least a half dozen places, the shoes were too nerdish, gawky, or flat-out overpriced! We were not looking for designer names, just shoes that are nice and fit comfortably. Finally found just the right pair.

"Come on, Penny, let's go home."

"Do we have to? There's still plenty of sunshine left, it's early."

"Yes, we have to, the trip is long, we need to rest up for it. You know, Penny, now that you have these clothes, we should dress up and go to a nice restaurant this week."

"Really? No kidding?"

"Yes, I'll even shave and put on a clean pair of socks!"

"Caddy, I don't think I'll be able to recognize you."

"With clean socks on?"

"No, silly, after you shave."

"Clean-shaven, people say I resemble Errol Flynn!"

"Who?"

"Never mind, before your time."

Penny, I'm sorry for lying, but the dress and shoes will only be used on the day you go home. I can't see you leaving with street clothes on, back to your world.

I was trying to figure a way to get you to buy some clothes and you beat me to it. Thank you.

"Caddy, you look deep in thought."

"Thinking about how beautiful you are going to be all dressed up."

She didn't say anything, just came over and hugged and kissed me.

When we got back to the trailer, we stretched out and immediately fell asleep. I got up first and started to clean our weekend mess, fast-food wrappers, coffee containers, etc.

Penny is right. I'm going to miss this place too.

Just another memory, a fond one at that, to look back on and shed a tear.

Knock it off, stay focused, there's two more days to deal with. Better write the note now while I feel up to it.

Dear Big Sal and Crew,

Penny and I are leaving today. I wish there was some way we could repay your for your kindness and generosity.

We will never forget you guys.

Thank you,
Penny and Cadillac Man

I tape up the note to the water cooler, that's the first thing you see opening the door.

"What are you doing, Caddy?"

"Just finished the note and placed it where it can be seen."

She got up and read it. "I'm going to miss them."

"Me too."

"Caddy, do you think we'll ever meet up with them again?"

"It's a big city, anything is possible. Let's get ready."

"Wow! It's dark outside, how long did we sleep?"

"Long enough, about five hours, and I'm hungry, let's go."

We get to the door. "Don't look back, Penny."

"Why?"

"It will hurt, just think of the good times we had here."

"So long, guys, so long, Big Sal."

"Let's hit the road."

We went out canning, not getting that much, winding up way into East Harlem. Then the long walk down into midtown with all our gear, since I had promised to show her my old neighborhood. By taking a shortcut I know, we can knock off some walking time, but we'll have to go through one of the meanest hoods in the city. I know a few street people, so maybe get safe passage.

Penny, have an open mind and see what it's like to be poor. Listen, you can almost hear them crying. The children growing up in these deplorable conditions, because the landlords, if they can find them, refuse to make any repairs and their reasoning is, it's too dangerous. I bet their children don't have to worry about rats, peeling paint, no heat or hot water, etc.

The area is drug-infested and that means a lot of crime. So many precious children and their parents died. Mostly innocent bystanders, going to the store or in the playground, good people who had nothing to do with drugs, just wanted to lead a normal life. It's a shame, amongst these buildings inside is a future doctor, lawyer, politician, if given the chance.

Gunshots far off. Not far enough for me.

After another hour of walking, we come out in midtown Manhattan. I always liked this area. So much to do, so much to see. The pickings are good, thanks to the lunch-hour crowd and the vendors.

"Caddy, this reminds me of the first area we worked together."

"You're right. We're on the outskirts of Hell's Kitchen, a stone's throw from Irish's place and my neighborhood."

"You're kidding! Do you come here a lot?"

"I always meet up with old contacts, friends, a little taste of nostalgia, and let my presence be known. There are some who save up their recy-clables, for when I see them, I pay top dollar."

"Why don't they go to a redeemer, Caddy?"

"Can't, for several reasons, one is that they have jobs as porters and don't want their bosses to find out they're making money off the building's recycle, have no time to wait at the redeemer, and I think they are embar-rassed to go there. We got time, we don't have to walk as much, plus we make a nice profit. It's a beautiful setup and worth every cent I paid for it."

"You paid for it?"

"Ain't nothing for nothing. I paid cash and a quart of scotch for the loca-tions from an old-time canner suffering with arthritis of the knees. He took me around to meet everyone, and with a handshake it was a done deal."

"Remember that you promised to show me your neighborhood."

"Word is bond, Penny."

So we're going along for about an hour when Penny drops back abruptly.

"What's wrong, Penny?"

"I think my friend Lois lives on this block. Look, there's the canopy, and across the street is the park I told you about. Let's go in and ask for her."

"Penny, what's her address?"

"What do you mean? It's right there."

"Look, Penny." Pointing my finger down the block.

As far as the eye could see, on one side the park and on the other side a dozen or more canopies sticking out.

"Oh." She's so disappointed, I hate it.

"Tell you what, Penny, let's walk slowly down, and if you see a canopy or number that looks familiar, we'll stop, go in, and ask for her. Okay?"

We have one hundred dollars plus what's inside the wagons, the can-ning can wait.

"You think we have a chance of finding her?"

"There is always a chance."

I didn't want to tell Penny, but our chances were slim to none. There are several avenues in this area that have similar settings, dozens if not hundreds of buildings. But maybe we'll get lucky. Let's hope so for Penny's sake. For about an hour and a half we walked in and out of all these fancy buildings, suspicious looks from everybody, and Penny getting more discouraged. No luck. When she came out of the last one, I could see that she was hurting and went to her.

"Caddy, I just don't understand it."

"This is a big city, and there are a lot of places like this, we had to try."

"It's hopeless, isn't it?"

"No, and I truly believe that someday we'll find your friend's place."

"You mean that?"

"Absolutely! Let's get back to canning."

She smiled, "Okay, Caddy."

God, I'm going to miss that smile.

Penny, the next time you talk to your friend Lois, it'll be from Aunt Clare's! The clock is ticking louder now, can you hear it? Less than twenty-four hours to go. Lord, hear my prayer, give me the strength to get through this and deliver Penny safely into her aunt Clare's arms.

Voila, Penny, my old neighborhood. There really isn't that much to see, a few remnants of my past, and now with all the newcomers, it turned into a yuppieland.

"I want to see where you played as a little boy."

"Why?"

"I just want to. Please, Caddy?"

Okay, but there is hardly anything left, it has changed so much.

"Here we are, Penny, this area used to be called Hell's Kitchen." Thanks to modern times, yuppies, and landlords, this once thriving neighborhood with so much history was destroyed. Oh, there are a few old timers hanging on, but when they die, it's a fresh coat of paint, a rent increase, then the newcomer from Frostbite Falls calls their friends to look-see what I got in Hell's Kitchen—oh, sorry, I hear it's called Clinton now. When you ask them about the area, they just say, "I'm several blocks from Times Square." Big fucking deal!

Ah, what the hell, I'm judging them too harshly. Everybody has a right to live wherever they want to. I guess I wanted my neighborhood to remain the same way always, growing up here. Not that it was any funpark. It was predominantly German-Irish, and the main source of income around there was the docks, plus the railroad yards and the slaughter-houses down 11th and 12th avenues where the Javits Center is. There was a lot of crime in the area. Jobs were hard to come by. Growing up, we used to break into the railroad cars and take fruit, then sell it to the fruit stands or what have you.

Now my friends and even my enemies and the local hangouts are gone! But I'll show you some places that are still standing. Come on, I'm feeling generous today. (Maybe a little sad too.) Took her to my grade school, first job, where I had my kiss.

"How was it, Caddy?"

A disaster! I was eleven, crazy in love with Terry Snow. Same age, and believe it or not she said she loved me too! One day she asked me to kiss her. I had been practicing, kissing my pillow at night, waiting for the moment to come. So I was ready, not nervous at all. I closed my eyes and kissed her ear!

Oops, tried again, this time the chin. Well, at least I'm getting closer.

"Let's try it with our eyes open," she said.

Okay, I'm game, it should make it easier right? Then I kissed her nose, then cheek, and finally the eye! She was laughing and said I'm blind as a bat. I walked her home and never saw her again ever. My first chance and I blew it. How hard can it be? Grown-ups do it all the time.

It wasn't until two years later a tomboy kissed me by surprise and I said, "Now it's my turn," and bull's-eye, right on the kisser! The rest is history.

Hey! How come you aren't laughing? Everybody else did when I told them.

She came over to me and tenderly kissed my lips and said, "Caddy, Terry's loss is my gain."

"Goodness, gracious, great balls of fire!"

"What do you mean by that?"

"Never mind, before your time."

The park was a few minutes away, and when we got there, I got pissed off and couldn't hide it. "Look at this shit, Penny, will you? A fucking play-ground for inmates!"

This used to be a place for families. Kids everywhere, playing together. Now the park was surrounded by a high, iron, spiked fence with en-

trances on both sides. Fortunately for us it is early and there are kids playing inside not knowing the meaning or purpose of the fence.

Look over there, this is supposed to be a public place. So why is there a
sign posted with the hours from dawn to dusk? I remember when they installed them, the local community leaders thought it was a great way to keep
the riffraff out. Riffraff, what a fucking joke, a few teenagers at night drinking beer and smoking a little pot and fighting amongst themselves, never
bothered anybody. I knew these guys from the neighborhood and their parents, we all watched out for each other. The homeless were nonexistent, we
had a few winos and left them alone or gave them a bottle to move on.

We got to the other side of the park. This part I remember the most, and
everything is gone except the comfort house and the flagpole. Playing
marbles, bottle caps, and hopscotch, what memories.

"Did you have a lot of friends?"

I tell her: I didn't have any. The only time I played with other kids was
when they needed another player. But that was okay, I was used to being
alone and my imagination was my best friend. I daydreamed about Su-
perman. To leave here and fly through the clouds, never to come back,
not even to see my family. The happiest moments of childhood were my
daydreaming.

We go about a half a block down, stop, and look at a building.

"This is where I grew up."

"Anybody still living there?"

"Yes, my mother and brother."

She grabbed my arm. "Come on, let's go see them. I bet they would be
happy to see you."

"No, they would not."

"Caddy, how can you be so sure?"

"I know my family, Penny."

At this time my brother is at work; before leaving, he told my mother
not to let anyone in, especially me. He thinks I would steal things of his.
I could care less what he has. My other siblings were afraid of him growing up, even I was subject to his beatings. As I got older and bigger, I
wanted to kick his ass, and my mother stopped me by saying, "You don't

live here anymore, and if you do anything to him, when you leave, he will take it out on me."

Even now I saw him in the street on occasion and I wanted to hurt him just as bad as I did back then, and thought of what she said and changed my mind.

"What about your father?"

I have almost no memory of him, pretty much dropped his load and left. My mother was there but not there. Never once did she say she loved me or give a hug or words of encouragement. She would write letters or cards signing them "With love," but I don't think she knew what the word meant. Something was wrong, all the men in her life left and nobody knew why or didn't ask, and I bet she would not tell me or anybody else.

Our grandparents lived with us and I loved them, very caring and affectionate people. After my grandfather died, I saw changes in Mother, she was making my grandmother cry a lot. There was too much tension in the house, I wanted to help but my mother said no, and it was then when I moved out.

I'm shaking like a leaf, telling Penny all this, and I know she can see. She pushes me towards the wagon. "Come on, Caddy, let's go across the street, I need to sit down." There's some sort of church with a place to sit down across the street.

Why do I come here? Sometimes it is homesickness or hoping to see my other siblings and/or an old friend. I never end up seeing anybody I knew. It is then the old daydreams kick in, whoosh! Able to leap a building in a single bound!

There are a lot of street people around here, but they mostly do their canning at night and like to stay out of sight as much as possible. They all know me. This is my "backyard," my home stomping grounds.

"Well, now, I'm feeling better and there is one more thing I got to do before we leave here. You want to come along with me?"

"Sure."

"Take my hand, please."

We left the wagons and walked back across the street so we were standing again in front of my mother's building.

There's the window, with the shade drawn.

"Come on, Penny, let's get out of here."

"Hey, Cattalack Man!"

There is only one person I know who can't pronounce my name.

"Hey, Detroit! Get your raggedy, bony ass over here!"

Detroit is a sicko and would do anything for a laugh. One time, he found a huge rubber dildo, put it on a table with a sign saying FOR RENT, SPECIAL RATES FOR HOMOSEXUALS!, and sat down on a busy street during rush hour. Got arrested again and he said, "I'm offering a service to people who don't have the time to get laid!"

"Hey, hey, Cattalack Man, whatcha doing?"

"Hey, hey, Detroit! Where are Chicago and Philadelphia?"

"In Florida with Las Vegas and San Francisco."

Penny has a puzzled look and I started laughing, Detroit too.

"Penny, say hello to Detroit."

"Hi, Detroit. Real or street name?"

"Real as can be, and Penny?"

"Real."

We talk a little and Detroit starts to tell Penny about his family. He tells everyone. He would tell the pope if he was standing here.

He says, "My mother was the finest, sweetest, lovingest whore money could buy."

Penny looked at me and I nodded yes.

"She loved us all, all eighteen of us."

"Your mother had eighteen kids!?"

"Yep—eighteen kids and eighteen different fathers. But we didn't mind, she was so good and caring to each of us. Mother had to travel a lot and every time was coming back pregnant. We had a lot of fun trying to figure out the baby names beforehand. Mother stayed home for a while, then back to business. We lived in a huge house, out in Detroit, of course, with three aunts—they weren't really our aunts, understand, but they fed and clothed us while Mother was away.

"Then one day the police came and spoke to our aunts, who got us all together. It was bad news, Mother died in a car accident. Social services came a few days later and took us away. We were spread out to other agencies throughout the state.

"I wasn't adopted and at the age of twenty-one I was released to the outside world. With no money or job I drifted up here. I made a few friends out here, and we were all planning to move down to Florida. One of them knew somebody there and said life was real good in Florida. So we decided to save up enough for us to go down there.

The day before we were scheduled to leave, I was involved in a car accident where both my legs were broken, sent me to the hospital. I told them to leave without me, I'll be down as soon as possible. That was two years ago. When I got better, I sued the driver and now finally the case is over. I'm waiting on a cash settlement from the insurance company, then off to be with my brothers."

"So what's been happening around here lately, Detroit?"

"You know Crackers?"

"The one whose old lady always beats on him for not making enough money canning?"

"Yeah, yeah. Him. He's in the hospital with a fractured skull and she's in Rikers."

"What did she hit with this time?" Last time she slammed him with a coffeepot.

"A toaster." Laughing.

"Was there any bread inside of it?"

"How the hell do I know?" Laughing more.

"First time coffee, second time toast. The next time it's gonna be a frying pan with eggs. Breakfast anyone?"

"Caddy, don't start again!"

"Sorry. What else is new?"

"Same old story at the machines, store workers want a tip to fix and empty them. Greedy-ass motherfuckers! And Sandy is still around, acting big."

"Son of a bitch! Is he still driving that flashy red car?"

"Nope, a newer one, bigger and all white."

"I'd like to throw him in the trunk and drive into the fucking river."

"Be cool, man, you know he's got friends. Man! Look at the time! I got to leave, someone I got to see!"

"A sweet honey?"

"You know it, Cadillac Man. Shouldn't keep a lady waiting."

"Then go, man, go."

"Thanks, man, be seeing you. Later, Penny."

"Later, Detroit."

"I hope he gets a lot of money from the insurance company."

"Me too, Penny. He deserves to go home."

Penny's smile turned to sadness. Don't worry, my darling. Happiness will be yours tomorrow, I swear.

Word up, word is bond. And please, God, I need your strength, please help me.

"We can can at a leisurely pace, or not can at all. I know someone around here who owes me money." I'm lying.

"Who is he, Caddy?"

"One of my contacts, Franco, a porter. He keeps his building's cans for me. We'll meet him early in the morning and take it all before his bosses come in. Even with a sixty–forty split in his favor, we stand to make at least a hundred dollars, not bad for a few hours' work."

"And he trusts you?"

"We shook hands and that is as good as signing a contract."

"So can we walk around and enjoy the day, Caddy?"

"Good idea, we'll check in a hotel."

"A hotel?"

"Why not? Let's treat ourselves and declare today a holiday! We'll rent a room, you dress up in your new clothes, and we'll go for a nice Italian dinner! I'll even wear a shirt and tie!"

Is it my imagination or did everything stop all of a sudden and people are staring at me? Nah.

To get to the hiding spot for the wagons we had to do a wide arc, purposely avoiding the bus terminal. In the morning, I'll take her in from the back side of the station and hope she won't recognize it until the last minute.

. . .

Our last night together, I want it to be special. We packed up what was needed and headed to the hotel.

"Ah! Here we are at last."

"This is a hotel?"

"Sure is, they just don't advertise, it's word of mouth. It is a one-nighter, safe and discreet. The manager, I know, is a piece of shit but minds his own business."

"But why here, Caddy?"

"I wish I could have taken you to one of those fancy ones on Broadway, but let's face it, we have no ID or credit card. This building is old and so is the furnishings, but it is clean and well kept. Come on and meet the Weasel."

"Weasel?"

Go down to the basement, ring the buzzer, and there he is.

Short, dumpy, with big eyes and a long nose. The only thing he is missing is the long nose hair sticking out to the sides.

"What the fuck do you want?"

"Hello, Weasel."

"Who the fuck are you?"

"Put on your glasses, you blind fucking bastard!"

"Cadillac Man, is that you?"

"Of course, you fucking moron!"

"Shh! Please, Mother is watching her soaps."

"How is she doing?"

"Getting better every day, thanks, and what are you doing around here?"

"My friend here and I want to use the honeymoon suite."

We go up the steps, door one opened, door two, and behind the final door I'm stunned!

The whole room is pink, the walls, the furniture, everything. Penny with a big grin on her face is enjoying this. Sheesh!

Oh, well, it is only one night. While we're unpacking, Penny asks, "Caddy, where is the bathroom?"

"Out in the hallway."

"You are kidding me."

No, Penny, these buildings were made this way, single-resident occu-pancy, one or two rooms on each floor with one bathroom. There are some places that have three rooms, but they are smaller, I ought to know, I lived in them for years.

Years ago this was a hideout from five-O, a place to go if you wanted to disappear for a while. Later Weasel's father realized he could make a lot more money converting it into a lovers' hideaway and charging daily rates. When he died, Weasel took over and installed TV/VCR with porno movies, sex toys, the works. It got very popular.

"How did you find out about the place, Caddy?"

"I never patronize and that is the truth, and as I said before, by word of mouth."

"What about Weasel?"

"When I was a kid, his mother used to give me cookies and a dime all the time." It would kill her if she knew that Weasel is a fucking crack-head.

"Come on, let's wash up, dress like outsiders."

Penny gets to the bathroom first, looks in.

"Caddy, you are not going to believe it!"

"What? No toilet seat?"

"No."

"Goldfish in the bathtub?"

"No."

"Harriet's underwear hanging up to dry?"

"No." Opens up the door wide enough so I can see in.

Fucking pink everywhere! Even the crap paper!

"Penny, look at the toilet seat!"

It had a pink lint covering, and it's a good thing I don't have to take a dump, I would wind up having that pink lint on the crack of my ass. Sheesh!

While Penny was in the shower, I took a long-overdue shave. No longer looking like a grizzly bear, I noticed the wrinkles. Why can't the face be like the ass, wrinkle-free? We sit on our asses most of the time and not one little wrinkle! My face is a road map of wrinkles, this way and that way. Some women may call it the rugged look, to me it is the prune-face look. Cadillac Man, you are getting older. In ten years your balls will be down to your knees!

"All done, Caddy, and—oh, you look sooo different!" She's never seen me clean-shaven.

I'm sorry, Penny, it will grow back fast.

"Caddy, you wait here, I want to get dressed first, but I'll leave your clothes on the hallway table."

Not a problem, pretty lady. I guess there are times like this a girl needs her privacy.

Who is that person I see in the mirror? Is it me wearing a pressed shirt and tie? Damn, can't remember the last time I dressed like this, and I must admit I don't look too bad.

"Caddy! You can come in now!"

The first thing that struck me was the sweet scent of vanilla. Then there was Penny. Dressed before me for the first time as a woman, she is radiant and I begin to cry. Not out of sadness but joy, knowing that the woman I love will be safe and secure, even if it means being in another man's arms.

The clock is ticking even louder now, have to maintain my composure. My Penny.

"Come on, Penny, let me show you off to the outsiders' world!"

We left holding hands.

At some point we went past a large storefront window that caught my image passing and I had to step back again to look. Blue shirt, red tie, black pants, and green sneakers. Perfect. This is not me, an image of the life I once had and don't wish to go back to. I lost everything, and to try again with the chance of failure, I won't risk my sanity. The past is dead and my future is in God's hands. Whatever he has in store for me, I accept willingly with open arms.

"What are you looking at, Caddy?"

"They have a sale on canned tuna fish today."

"Huh?"

"Never mind, let's go."

On impulse I went inside a florist, bought for Penny a single red rose.

She smiled and we hugged each other, even the outsiders passing by were grinning at us.

Someone is tapping my back. "Excuse me, sir, can you spare any change for a homeless veteran?"

I turn around and—son of a bitch.

"Mac! What the fuck are you doing putting on a scam like that? You weren't even a Cub Scout!"

"Cadillac Man?"

"Yes, and don't ask, it is none of your fucking business! And leave while you can. I don't mind you scamming the outsiders saying you're homeless, but never ever mention again about being a veteran too."

This guy lives with his mother, collects SSI, and drinks away the check in three days, then goes scamming for the rest of the month. To look at him you'd think he was homeless. If the outsiders only knew that what they give with good intentions most of the time is spent on booze or drugs. "Sorry, Penny, Mac just rubbed me the wrong way."

Why get aggravated, the day is young, let's have a good time!

We went into the park, and at this time of the year it is bursting with activity, a sightseer's delight. That is how we acted, going to the zoo, feeding the elephants, on the carousel. Penny was driving me crazy, saying let's do this and we'll do that next. I really didn't mind until she bought me a balloon. A cartoon character with big ears to match mine and a goofy smile. Do I have one too? Then Penny tied it to my wrist. This is ridiculous. I hope we don't meet up with anyone we know! Sheesh!

It's a good thing being clean-shaven and wearing a tie nobody will be able to identify me. Though wait—what about Mac before? People are staring, laughing, pigeons hanging above like they're waiting to attack. Is it my imagination?

Indeed it is.

Loosen up, Cadillac Man, this is the last full day together! Make it memorable.

We sat down on a park bench and Penny is trying to feed peanuts to squirrels.

"That's not how you do it. Watch and learn from an expert."

She handed them over.

I put a peanut in each nostril and one in my mouth, making sure the squirrels could see them. Then I lay down on my end of the bench and wait.

Penny is laughing and so are others, but I will have the last laugh, I saw someone do this once and it worked! Waiting and waiting, pointing to the nuts, come on, guys!

Now there is a crowd over by Penny's end of the bench, and I don't know if they want the squirrels to get the nuts or not because everybody is having fun. They are looking at me like some kind of nut (no pun). Please, guys! I'll give you five dollars! Ten? A roast-beef sandwich!

A roast-beef sandwich?

Nah, the heck with it, I took them out.

"Peanuts, anyone?" Everybody started laughing again. I threw them away, and son of a gun the squirrels came over then and ate the peanuts. They had the last laugh! Sheesh!

"Come here, Caddy."

What did I do now?

She grabbed me by the tie, I went down, then she kissed my lips.

"Thank you, I'm having a wonderful time."

"So am I. Hungry yet?"

"Yes."

"Good, I am going to treat you to the finest Italian dinner in the neighborhood."

"Look, Caddy, the squirrels are following us."

No way am I shoving pizza up my nose! Let's get out of here!

Dark drapes drawn across the storefront window, inside it is dimly lit. About ten booths for four people, four smaller tables center aisle, a bar the size of an old token booth, and there is Bruno drinking a glass of wine. Short and stocky, the man is a genius in preparing Italian food. Pay him a compliment and he will grunt at you. In all the years I have been coming here, I've never seen him smile or say a word, just a what-are-you-bothering-me-for? look on his face. We're being stared down by others, "second-generation neighborhood." Maybe I know their parents. These are not yuppies. They are here to eat, not to brag about themselves. Music is low and soft just like the conversations going on.

It is perfect.

A waitress approaches. "Yes?"

"Two for dinner, and has Bruno smiled recently?"

She laughs. "Almost."

"Damn, I wish I was here to see it!"

"You from the neighborhood?"

"Yeah, Forty-fifth."

"Then you know the Kellys?"

"Yeah, I do. But they lived on Forty-seventh."

"Table or booth?"

"Booth, please."

I waved to Bruno, and he gave me that look just as the waitress was coming with the menus.

"Appetizers?" said the waitress.

"Penny?"

"Whatever you are having, I'll have some of."

"Well, then let's have an order of antipasto and garlic bread. For drinks will have two colas please."

She comes back with a big plate of cheese and salami, so beautiful, and a loaf of garlic bread as long as my arm and smelling like heaven. No one hassling us, just treating us like human beings, like two people in love. The waitress comes back and we're ready to order. Penny?

"I'll have the lasagna."

"Make that two, another order of garlic bread, and two glasses of red wine."

"Caddy, I thought you didn't drink."

"I don't anymore, but the occasion calls for it. And besides, if you eat like an Italian, you better drink like one."

The waitress bought over the food. "Here you go, guys, enjoy."

"Mmm, looks and smells soooo good; thanks."

"A toast: may our friendship be everlasting, Penny."

"It will, Caddy."

I saw Penny turn a little red.

"Not used to drinking wine?"

"This is the first time."

"Take little sips like." I'm doing the same. "You don't have to finish it."

The company, the food, and the surroundings are such a joy, I feel totally relaxed. Tomorrow it will be a memory just like all the other times spent with Penny.

She is smiling at me right now.

I smile back.

Oh, Penny, if you could see through my smile, you would notice my heart breaking.

Walking down the street hand in hand, we may appear to be father and daughter, but get closer and you will see that it is not. For we are lovers, for all to see.

Shaking with anticipation, I must have dropped the keys at least half a dozen times, Penny is anxious and I felt like kicking the door down.

Clothes went flying off, I even ripped my shirt getting it off, but I didn't care, wasn't going to wear it again ever. Our bodies emitted so much heat, our pores opened filling the room. Let the world come to an end now!

Never have I experienced such pleasure before, and this woman, my Penny, made feel anew.

"Thank you, Caddy, for the wonderful day, and I hope we get to do this more often."

"Okay, you're right. From now on, one day a week we'll set aside for ourselves."

"To do whatever we want?"

"Yes, indeed, my dear."

This is insane! Why should I throw away my happiness by bringing Penny to the bus station tomorrow? Am I being selfish? Yes. I love her but she doesn't belong in my world, and there is so much for her to experience in life yet. Once you are used to my lifestyle, it is hard to leave. To be alongside the outsiders again would be learning how to walk again one step at a time. Always worried that you might fall down, and the pain is far greater the second time around.

Tick tick tick. It is so loud, surely you can hear it by now. Keep me awake, which is what I want, a blessing of sorts. To feel her every movement, breath and warmth from her body. Her silly snores and facial expressions with those awesome teeth.

Please, God, protect my Penny. Let something happen to me instead of her. Give her a good life, job, husband, and children. And please, Father, help her to forget about me and this life.

Oh, I want to hold her in my arms right now, but I dare not awaken her for in the darkness she will most certainly feel my tears. Sleep well, my darling, my Penny.

Tick tick tick, riiiingggg!

"Wake up, Penny, wake up."

"Oh, Caddy, did I oversleep? I didn't hear the alarm go off."

"No, I turned off the alarm a few minutes ago, I didn't want it to wake up the whole place."

"It's still dark out."

"Yes, we have to see Franco the first hour of his shift before the bosses arrive." Be calm, Cadillac Man, you told another lie.

She's looking in the mirror. "Caddy, I look so different with my street clothes back on again."

No, you don't, you are so beautiful to me, no matter what you put on.

We're up earlier than usual, just need a cup of coffee to charge my batteries.

Let's get out here and be on our way before the outsiders wake up and ruin the day.

Dropped the keys in Weasel's mailbox. Some of the street people are hanging out by an all-night deli hoping to score change from the morning crowd. We weren't bothered going in or coming out with our coffee because street people know who they can try to scam. Just one glance and eye contact and they know we're street people too. Get to the wagons and nothing has been touched, and why not? Because I knew this area like the back of my hand.

"Caddy, how far is it to where Franco works?"

"Not far, about ten minutes away."

We're practically on top of the place when Penny stops suddenly. She looks up at the overhead ramp leading in the terminal just as a bus is leaving. Standing there watching one after another go by, without looking down she said, "I know where we are. The bus station, right?"

"Yes."

There is sadness in her voice. Her head down now, chin on chest, I could see the tears falling and gently pull her into my arms.

"I'm sorry, Penny, but this is where Franco works. Tell you what, we'll see Franco, get the goodies, then leave lickety-split, okay?"

"It's all right, Caddy."

"Come on, we have to find a spot to hide the wagons, then wait for Franco." After we hid the wagons we went inside. It is still early, the place is fairly deserted, and for now the arrivals are slow coming in. In a few hours the place will be a madhouse.

I hope Clare didn't forget the green hat!

"Might as well sit it out while we wait.

"Why so quiet, Penny?"

"The gate we're sitting in front of is the one I went through."

I put my arm around her. "I'm sorry, Penny, I didn't know. Come on, we'll find somewhere else to sit down."

"No, I'm fine here. When do you think we'll see Franco?"

"Well, he has to come this way to get to the storage closet, so my guess is within the hour."

The terminal is starting to fill up, friends and family are greeting the arrivals with hugs, screams of joy, laughter. Penny looks at the commotion and puts her head down.

I know what you are thinking about. Please be patient, it won't be long now.

Or will it? I have this nagging thought in the back of my head that

Clare had to take a later bus or it broke down and she's waiting for a replacement!

Calm down, Cadillac Man, and, oh my gosh!

Can it be?

A woman wearing a green baseball cap with a long peacock feather in it, flanked by two teenaged girls looking to and fro, headed our way. Clare, you are a genius! The feather in the cap!

I stretched my arms out behind Penny and waved. They started walking faster. Yep, no doubt about it, it is them!

"Hey, Penny, take a look at the woman coming toward us! That is some crazy hat!"

"Shh! She might hear you."

"Nah, she is too far away. Come on, take a peek, it is soooo funny."

She slowly lifted her head and I think their eyes met 'cause Clare tossed the hat off.

"Penny!"

"Aunt Clare?" Then turned towards me, tears coming, looking puzzled.

Struggling to talk, I finally said, "Time to go home, Penny."

She was about to say something when:

"Penny!"

"Penny!" Her sisters in unison.

Penny leapt up. "Aunt Clare! Judy! Sandy!"

And everybody started to run at the same time.

What a sight to behold, a family's love. I wish I was blessed with such happiness as theirs.

And now it is time for you to leave too, Cadillac Man. Your true emotions are showing, tears of joy knowing that Penny is back with her family and tears for losing the woman I love. The one I would never see again.

Oh, Penny, please be happy.

Now is my chance to slip away, the place is getting too crowded. As I'm going up the escalator, eyes are on me. I felt like yelling, "What is the matter with you people, never seen a man cry before?" but didn't. Must hurry and leave this place. I never want to come here again.

"Cadillac Man!"

I turn and see Penny running.

"Penny, hooray!"

"Cadillac Man, yippeeee!"

Yippee.

But the escalator's moving, and I am too.

I waved to her and softly said, "Good-bye, Penny, my darling. I will miss you so."

Oh, Penny, please be happy.

The memory of your smile and the feeling of togetherness we had will be everlasting.

Lord, I need your help to ease this pain. A moment of happiness in my life is gone again. Why do I always let it go?

I must get out of here fast, I grab my wagon. I'm about a hundred feet away, then suddenly stop and turn and look at Penny's wagon. It looks lonely. I walked back to touch something that was once a part of my Penny's life, then I kissed the handlebar. I reached into my pocket and took out Clare's phone number, ripped it into small pieces.

"Remember me, my love."

Took a deep breath, exhaled.

Oh, well, the day is young.

Look out world, here comes the Cadillac Man!

How I Got Here 3

FROM '99 TO 2002 I MOVED AROUND A LOT before I really settled down. I went back to Hell's Kitchen for a while and then I went to Brooklyn. I was out there for a couple of months—in Coney Island for a while, Brighton Beach, Bensonhurst. I was in East New York too. I stuck out like an Oreo cookie, but I got along good with the people over there. In Manhattan I went to look for some old friends, but no luck. We're like nomads for the most part, but I was slightly disappointed when I got over there and nobody was around. Of course, I went to Central Park and there were new street people over there. I really didn't want to make their acquaintance. So then I went to Brooklyn and hung out by Prospect Park.

From Brooklyn I went up to the Bronx, over by Van Cortlandt, and I was there for a little while. From Van Cortlandt I went back to Hell's Kitchen again, then from there I came out to Astoria. In those years I'd just be free, one place one day, another place the next. I slept everywhere.

There were times where I'd be sleeping underneath trailers, behind the big wheels, and nobody would notice me there because I've got dark clothing on and dark blankets. Anything not to bring too much attention to myself. I'd sleep in garages. You can hide in people's backyards, provided you conceal yourself very well. I spent a couple nights in the old maintenance rooms under the Triborough Bridge. If nothing else was open, I'd be over at the cemeteries.

I think I've visited every cemetery there is. I like the Calvary Cemetery in Woodside or Saint Mike's in Astoria. There are several nice places in Brooklyn. Green-Wood, that's a perfect place. Who's going to bother you? The dead are not going to bother you. With some cemeteries they have security guards, but at night they don't want to go out there and check the grounds. They're staying in their shed. So a cemetery is a perfect place to hide and you get plenty of rest.

At Saint Mike's I slept in the mausoleums. One time I slept between two coffins. No big deal. All right, there is a little bit of a musky odor in there, but other than that, no problem. Then there were some times in Brooklyn that I was just so tired I even slept in open graves. It's just like when you're in the army, right? They made you dig a foxhole, and you sleep in it. What the hell is the difference? You know, they're going to put somebody in there the next day, so in the meantime I might as well go in there. Believe it or not, it's warm. Well, not *warm* warm, but it's comfortable enough and there's no draft. Though you would obviously put something down first.

Cemeteries are good places to stay. Parks too. Central Park is ideal because it's so big, and the precinct over there doesn't have enough manpower to cover the whole area. And the Parks Department doesn't have that many people. In fact, I don't think they even work at night. Just name your spot and you can hide in the shadows.

Prospect Park was another great one. The bigger the park, the better. Astoria Park is no good. It's not that big, and they patrol it. In fact, I remember when I used to go canning there, the cops used to yell at me for going down there after midnight. Said, what are you, crazy, coming down here canning, with all the trouble that goes on over there? They do a good job at the 114th there patrolling it, but still you hear stories what goes on over there when the cops leave, the little get-togethers, lovers trysts, and the drugs, maybe on occasion a mugging.

With Central Park back in the seventies and eighties forget about it, your life wasn't worth a nickel if you went through after dark. Now it's like Little House on the Prairie over there. But still a lot of people won't go in there at night, so that's a plus for the street people because they know they won't be hassled by one of the outsiders going jogging. You know, I just saw a street person sleeping over behind those bushes there.

That's what I love about Astoria, there are so many cubbyholes and places to hide. I settled here in 2002, underneath the viaduct where I live now. Before that I was just going two months here, three months there. When I first hit the streets, I had no particular destination in mind. You know, I got to the place where I felt tired and I said, well, this is a good place to plop down. All I was focused on was just getting some sleep. But now with the wintertime here I have several places that I stay at where I'm away from the elements. I feel safe there. That is the key, to feel safe.

The viaduct is on 33rd Street and 23rd Avenue. It's painted yellow, with murals on both sides. One side is a big blue-and-white Greek painting, with some statues and the word *Athens*—there are lots of Greek people in the neighborhood. The other side, where I park my cart, used to have a beautiful mural of firemen and policemen holding up American flags. Last year, some kids painted over it with some political thing, with Bush and Hillary fighting it out. I don't like it as much, but still, this is my place. This is where people come to see me. In the evenings, all the birds that live in the railway trestle above the viaduct start to sing as they're getting ready to sleep. You wouldn't believe the noise. In the mornings too.

Astoria is my comfort zone. We're very territorial, my people, absolutely territorial. When I planted myself down underneath the viaduct, I said, that's it, I'm staying right here. No way am I leaving, especially the way I was treated by the people. You know something, I like it here. Seeing these people, how concerned they were. And it was no bullshit, it was genuine concern. A while back, I finally cemented the back wheels of my cart in place. I'm not going anywhere.

Not many people make it for eleven, twelve years on the street. The average is about two years. Summertime is a piece of cake. It's the winters that get to everybody. You find people on the street frozen to death. Half the time, the ones that you find like that simply wanted to die. Drinking was the biggest downfall years ago. Alcohol gives your body a false sense of warmth, but the minute you go to sleep, you're never going to wake up again.

The reason I'm still out here is stubbornness, and partly my background. Working in that meat market was a real plus. For a number of years my day consisted of working in an icebox that was at thirty-two degrees constant. If I wasn't there, I might be working in the freezer downstairs, which would be set at zero. I became used to it. I would just have a heavy sweater on. I was comfortable wearing the sweater and a light pair of gloves. If you have too much clothing on, you really can't handle the stuff. You got to stay loose. If you had four sweaters on, you couldn't pick up a side of beef; it would just slide right off you, so just have on a good sweater and an inexpensive pair of gloves. You can't grip a box if you have a bulky pair of gloves on. It's the same thing if you're getting into a fight with somebody—it's almost like having boxing gloves on, so they're not going to get the full effect. I put light gloves on, you can still see my knuckles. When I hit you with these gloves on, you're going to feel it.

Also, wear a hat. They had this study years ago that said that by wearing a hat you retain your body heat, and it's true. Look at all the street people during the cold weather. They're all wearing hats. There was a time I had about twenty hats, baseball caps that people gave me. Now I'm down to about eight. The woolly hats I wore on several occasions. I didn't like them that much because with my long hair, they have a tendency of riding up on your head. A baseball cap is more comfortable, although the wind will blow it off. Just keep your head warm and your hands warm.

Don't wear too many layers. They're too bulky, and if you go in some place that's really warm, you're going to start perspiring and it's most uncomfortable. A lot of people ask me if I wore long johns. I tried them once or twice, but let's face it, they're itchy. And I like to stay loose. I got a hooded shirt on, flannel shirt underneath here, I'm comfortable.

For people that hit the streets for the first time, I would highly recommend that they wear a lot, then after a while your body becomes conditioned. People always say how cold it is out there, and I tell them the reason you're cold is that you spend too much time inside. Think about it. You're at your job for eight or ten hours, nice and warm, you go outside for a few minutes and that winter chill hits you, you're like, holy shit, I got to get back inside. Whereas, with me, I'm out there twenty-four/seven in the cold. You adapt. Now when I go inside, it's too hot in there.

The one good thing about the wintertime is most people won't detect a body odor. In the summertime if you get within five feet of somebody, you know that person. But during the wintertime you can get away with it because most of the time people's sinuses are so frozen they don't smell anything. You could wear the clothes until they fall off you. And what's the big deal? Why should I change every day? That would mean that the clothes would pile up and then I'm going to have to wash them. I do laundry once a week, and that's expensive enough. I was content at times to wear shirts and pants for weeks, even months. If somebody came over to me and gave me a nice sweater or nice coat, I would put it on to show the people that I appreciate what they gave me and out of respect for them. But otherwise, I like to stay loose.

Right now I'm wearing a gray sweatshirt. I got this last Christmas from somebody. Underneath it I've got a flannel shirt that I've had for about four years. The black pants I have on, I've had for I don't know how many years. The shoes, I believe they're called Sketchers. I got them from the producer of the documentary they made about me. He gave me two pairs. He wasn't sure of my size so he bought me one size thirteen and the other fourteen. The thirteen didn't fit. The fourteen did. Here I am fifty-seven and my feet keep growing and growing. There were times out here where my shoes were falling apart, and I would tape them over and over and over again with electrical tape. And then there were times the only shoes I could get didn't fit me, and I would have to cut them and tape them around. My size is hard to come by. People give me loads of shoes, but not too many people have big feet like me.

So whatever I have for shoes, I just leave by my wagon there and let the street people help themselves. A couple of weeks ago somebody left me a beautiful pair of Nike sneakers, brand-new. Unfortunately they were size six. I'm two hundred and forty pounds. Do I look like I have a size six? So I keep this stuff in my wagon, and whoever needed it, they were most welcome to it.

I'm outside all day. The only time I go inside is to get myself a cup of coffee or go to the bathroom. That's the only time. For the most part, I'm out there. You know, it's my environment. It's where I feel the healthiest during the wintertime. Summertime I'm miserable. I like the wintertime best.

It's dangerous during the summertime. Even though you have the police vans patrolling, they can't be here all night. Over by the Ravenwood Projects, that's the spot for Astoria. You got the drugs. You got the gangbangers. You got the wannabe gangbangers. You got the queers that come down here. You got the boyfriends and girlfriends coming down here. It's like a carnival down here during the summer, and when it really gets warm, oh, boy. Tempers start flaring. That's what I hate about the summer. People change. During the wintertime they stay indoors, right? During the summertime they come out here, hey, let's get high; it's beautiful. Where there's drugs or alcohol, then before you know it tempers will flare up and the shit will hit the fan.

I had one incident where I was pushing the wagon right around the corner from my viaduct and about six wannabes came over and they're looking at my wagon, picking up the cans and tossing them around. "Hey, what are you doing around here?" What does it look like I'm doing? Making some money. Well, you shouldn't be around here, it's dangerous. I said come on, guys; all I want to do is make a few dollars. So they looked me over and then they decided, oh, he's all right; let's let him go. But somebody else, perhaps it would have been a different story.

People beat on the homeless because they can get away with it. We got mental problems, right, so they say. People are malicious. That's their mental problem. To let their frustrations out they're going to pick on somebody like me. One time back in '03 I had the shit beaten out of me. I was by my wagon sleeping, underneath the viaduct, and the next thing I know there were three guys, and they were stomping on me. They were kicking me, over and over, just like my first Christmas out here. They were young. They really stomped on me before I could react. I was pissed off but I couldn't get to my bayonet in time. Oh, my gosh, they stomped my face in. I was a mess.

One guy kept saying, "Fucking bum." Another guy was saying something in Spanish. I don't know exactly what it was, but they were taking great joy in stomping on me. It seemed like it's an eternity, but in actuality it was less than a minute. When they left, I went back to sleep. There was nothing else to do. I went back to sleep.

There were other times. For me and my friends too. My friend Shaky in Astoria got beaten so bad a couple of Halloweens ago that he had cracked ribs, knocked some of his teeth out. Then again they did him a favor to knock those teeth out. You just have to deal with it sometimes. We had another guy, Eddie Egan, up in the Bronx, some kids came over and put some gasoline on his feet while he was sleeping and torched them up. Now you see Eddie going around in a wheelchair. You hear it all the time, all the time. Everyone says, you shouldn't have been out there to begin with. That's the bottom line.

So I've learned to fight. Or fight better, I mean. All my life I fought. I grew up in a tough neighborhood. Everybody fought. It toughened me up for the streets.

Out here, most fights are over within a matter of seconds. On TV you'll see people fighting for fifteen or twenty minutes, but that's bullshit. Most fights are over in seconds, maybe a minute tops, especially if you know how to use your fists. Most people fight like little girls out there.

You look at boxing. How long does a round last? They're three-minute rounds, and that's a lot of punishment, right? You have to have some stamina to last three minutes in a fight. Personally I like to have a fight done in fifteen seconds or less. That's why I'll go for certain spots of the body to take you down. I used to love doing two punches to the chest and then one to the face, or two to the face and one to the chest. That always works. Now I can't do it with my legs the way they are, but a nice kick to the stomach takes a person down.

Here's the strategy: You let the opponent have the first shot. People have a way of telegraphing themselves. You punch me, right, the first punch you always want to make your best shot. And once they come, for example, with their left, I say, ah, they're left-handed. Then the way they swing: Do they swing out, do they go in? That says a lot. When you do an outside swing, you're wide-open. Start the punch with your hand close to the body and go out, there's more power that way. Jab out, get the power behind it, and that tells me you know how to fight a little bit. I had some people go into martial arts stances and I had to laugh about that.

One guy came after me with a baseball bat. As terrifying as that may sound, with a baseball bat it's so easy to sidestep a person. Don't forget, you got to position yourself with that bat to swing it. By the time you position yourself, I've got you down on the ground. Any type of weapon, a bat, pipe, whatever, you've got to stop and position yourself. I'm not going to just stand there while you get set up to hit me. Another key thing: Once you get them down, keep them down. Don't give them a chance to get up. Most people think, oh, yeah, I got them down, that's it, the end of the fight. I can be on my way. No. When they're getting up, they're angry. I'll give you a kick in the balls, I'll stomp you in the stomach, I'll stomp your face in, break your nose, knock your teeth out. I don't care.

A lot of people use their knuckles to hit the chin. That's the worst thing in the world you could do, because your knuckles are going to go. So hit right above the chin instead. Sometimes your fingers will get cut with the lower teeth, but that's no big deal. Or you want to go for the nose, depending on the situation. If I was in a good mood, I would just give you those three shots and that's it. If I was in a bad mood, then I'm going to work on you until I got all the anger and frustration out.

I'm a lot more reserved now. Don't get me wrong, if somebody confronts me, I'll stand my ground. But now, you can call me a coward, pussy, whatever, it just rolls off. I don't know how many times I've seen people get killed over words. It's crazy. Now you touch me and I feel threatened, then we're going to lock horns.

Now I always have a weapon nearby. Always. My favorite was a bayonet or an ice pick. I had an ice pick in the very beginning. Then I went into an army-navy store and bought a bayonet. Easy to get and looks pretty scary. When I sleep, it's always by my left side, my power side. I'm happy to say I never had to use it. I would put it to somebody's throat, but just showing it would alleviate the situation at hand. Then other times if I felt giddy, I said the hell with the bayonet and ice pick, I use my fists or whatever I had available at the time. But when you're lying down, you're a target. So many crazy people out there and yet they think that we're crazy.

The other thing I hear al the time from people is, why don't you get a job? They're resentful that they're busting their ass making a living, and here I am with no problems. I don't care about a job. I got a few dollars in my pocket from canning, so why should I work? I don't want any part of that world.

I saw several things on that thing YouTube at the Internet café. I just happened to type in *homeless*. They had several films where people are interviewed about the homeless, and they all basically said the same thing. Why don't they get a job? It's not easy. It really isn't easy, especially now with the economy the way it is. With my background, what kind of a job could I get? All right, if I could get a job as a bouncer, I could make a few bucks there, but there aren't any real jobs I could do now. So I'd have to work in a Burger King or McDonald's getting seven dollars an hour.

Now if you offered me a job that paid like thirty-five, okay, I'd be willing to give it a try. But even so, a lot of people struggle with that. So for somebody to tell me to get a job, not possible. Who'll take me with my health problems, at my age?

I could have got with the public housing, but some of the areas where they want to put me I don't want to go. Maybe I'm being stubborn. Yeah, I'm being stubborn. This is what I want right here. I want to be with my family. I want to be around the people I love, not someplace else that I would feel uncomfortable.

Right now I stay nights in a garage not far from here. I've been doing that a couple of years now. The people that own the garage know that I'm in there. They caught me in there a couple of times. But fortunately they've been most kind. I take care of their building and do their garbage and everything and keep the place clean on the outside, and they give me a few bucks from time to time. It's funny, I keep winding up in garages, first

Harold, then Irish, now this. It's perfect for me. It gets somewhat chilly but I keep high and dry.

My one complaint: During the summertime, it gets too hot in there. Even at night forget it, I have to sleep outdoors. But during the wintertime I got a couple of couch pillows in there that I just put behind this one car. I sleep good.

That's my comfort zone, that garage. If that didn't work out, my other option was the cemetery, but that's out now. Some kids took some stained glass from the mausoleum at Saint Mike's, and they locked them all up. If worse comes to worst, I would even ride the trains. A common option, even if it's dangerous. One particular night years ago I decided to ride the rails. I got to the last stop on the N train, and as I woke up, I noticed these two guys. One was acting as a lookout. The other, very slowly and carefully was taking the jewelry off this guy that was sleeping. Not my problem, I went back to sleep. I had just a little carrying bag and the thing was loaded with Marlboro Milds. I was collecting them for this guy in the Port Authority who would pay me cash. I was using the bag for a pillow. When I woke up at Times Square, my bag was cut open on the side. My pants were cut open on the side. They took off with my Marlboro Milds. I can laugh about that now, but, oh gosh, at the time I was so pissed.

Still, I would do it again if I had to. I'm a very light sleeper. I could even just sleep right behind the dumpster around the corner if I have to. I think there's somebody there right now. There are lots of places. There are so many places you can plop down, or even inside the lot by the bank across the way from the viaduct, good spot. My friend Chris has been there for years, behind the bank, in the back of the lot right below Peter Vallone Jr.'s window. He's never been bothered. Ricky and his junkie girlfriend sleep under some boxes in a lot around the way. Some people sleep in the ATM holes in the bank, but I don't like that. That's too much exposure for me. I could see going in there to warm up for a few minutes, but to bed down, never.

The garage is perfect for me. It's ideal, one way in and one way out. You know no one is going to jump you in there. Some people would kill for a location like that. I found the place because I was checking the garbage for cans for quite a while and I became friends with one of the maintenance men. He said, you know what you should do, you should go in there once in a while. He told me what time they left and everything, so why not? The door has an access code to get in, and I know it.

The people in the residence next door, they know that I'm in there. But they're very kind. They won't say anything to them. If I time it just right, I don't run into them. They leave nine, ten o'clock, at the latest. The one guy, he has I believe a card game at least once a week, and he doesn't come pick up his car until after twelve. But other than that, smooth sailing. I'm usually out of there by six o'clock at the latest.

I've been sleeping there over two years. It keeps you out of the rain. The only thing I had to deal with, which was a minor annoyance, was the diesel fumes from the Mercedes once in a while. Other than that, and the bugs in the summertime, oh, it's perfect.

Everything's different now from my life before. You know, my thoughts are crystal clear. I'm more responsible now. I'm more responsible to myself as I am to others. There are some people that look up to me, and I've got a wonderful woman in my life too. In thirteen years I'd say I've had about six relationships, besides Penny. Two of them weren't homeless. That doesn't mean that I went into their place of residence, you know. We made it on the outside. People never think about homeless people being in love with one another. I had an interview with a psychiatrist through the VA once, and when I told him that I was in a relationship, he said, "And she knows that you're homeless?" I said yes. And he says, "I never heard of such a thing."

It happens all the time. Jimmy and a bag lady down the way—they were both homeless and it was a combustible thing and it fell apart after a while. There are quite a few lonely people out there, right? Some people just need someone to be with whether that someone is homeless or not. How long does a relationship last on the streets? With some it could just be day-to-day. But Dominican Tony, his girlfriend Mercedes had a place to live and their relationship lasted for years. Just like regular relationships, the things you fight about the most, the biggest issues, are money, sex, children. It's no different when you're homeless.

The woman I'm with now, things will take time with me, with the both of us. I know our relationship is growing. I truly love her with all my heart and soul. Now my thoughts are crystal clear, and that's why I get so many people that come over and talk to me. I try to tell them to be more open with themselves and not to be ashamed like they're doing something wrong. You know, get it out of your system. Talk it out. Part of the problem back then, I really didn't have anybody to talk to, besides my wife. If I had maybe one other person come over to me and say, hey, you need to snap out of this shit, to give me one word of encouragement, maybe things would be different. A wife has all good intentions, of course, but still can put you under some pressure. Kathy would tell me, well, do whatever it takes. That made me revert back to my hood mentality—do whatever it takes, but bring in some money. She was a good woman, though. She was. She wanted the American dream, family and everything, and I couldn't give it to her. I blew it. I really blew it. Jessica and Kathy deserved a good life. Sadly, I didn't give it to them. I should have tried harder. But I suspect they're doing really good now.

Health care is my biggest concern now. The VA treats me with respect, though. They keep me patched up. I've had six hiatal hernias, two mild heart attacks, infections galore. There's a big scar over where my belly button used to be. I had all but two teeth replaced—seven thousand dollars of dental work, done by Dr. Cambitsis in Astoria for free. Said it was "a gift from the community." Now the doctors at the VA tell me I got carpal tunnel, of all things.

Still, I've been here five years. I'm amazed. There are only a few other people around that have been here longer than me. Chris has been here about twenty years. Demetrius, who's in Wards Island now, God help him. Nick and Tony, Jose, Cockeyed, that's it. Everybody else is gone. Shaky, the last time we saw him was in May. I spoke to his junkie girlfriend, Debbie. He used to use her address to get his disability checks, and she told me that she had at least a half a dozen of them. Something happened. Of course, the street story is that he went back with his mother, even though he hated his stepfather. The other story was he went down to Florida, or he died out in Staten Island. Who knows?

Every year I lose more people, every year. When I first came over here in '02, we had thirty-five or forty street people around here. How many are there now five years later? What happened to them? Everybody thinks, well, they probably got a job or maybe their parents or family members came over and swept them away. No, no, no, no. Simply put, most of them went to other places. The remainder died.

But I'm still here. Still here.

The Old Man and the Shelters

Brooklyn, 1999

THE DAY I HEARD the Old Man had died, I guess I went a little berserk.

Bang, bang! Bang, bang! "You motherfucker!" I started slamming on the can machine while I was supposed to be redeeming. This was out in Bed-Stuy, near Ralph Avenue.

"What is the matter with the Cadillac Man?" Jo Jo asked.

"Why don't you go over and ask him?" Twinkies said.

"Who, me? No fucking way!"

"Somebody has got to stop him before the manager calls five-O, then the shit will really hit the fan."

"So what's up?" Jo Jo said.

"You know the Old Man?" Twinkies said.

"Sure, who doesn't. And by the way, he owes me fifty cent!"

"The Old Man did a Jack Frost at a construction site in lower Manhattan two days ago. Him and Cadillac were close friends and he just found out."

Apparently Twinkies had what he considered a foolproof idea to stop me from banging on the machine, the only way I know to take out my grief.

"Er, Cadillac, it's Twinkies."

"Take a fucking walk!"

"I have coffee, Cadillac Man."

"Coffee? Gimme that!" The coffee brought me back to my senses. "Why is everybody standing away and no one at the machines?" I asked Twinkies.

"Because of you," he said.

"Me?"

"Look at what you did to the can machine."

"Oh, boy. At least I didn't bend the can insert. See, it still works."

I waved to everybody to signal it was okay, and there was a mad dash to the machines.

"I'm sorry to hear what happened to the Old Man," Twinkies said.

"The stupid fuck, I warned him countless times to go someplace warm to drink his booze on the sly."

"I thought you guys were friends."

"We are. I mean, we were. And, damn, he didn't deserve to die that way!" Nobody does!

"Didn't he have any family?"

"Yeah, a sister. The bitch let him use her address to get his Social Security check. She would cash it, let him stay awhile. During that time she would spend it, and when there was no more, she would throw him out! When he told me this, I would get pissed and want to kick her crusty old ass, and he would say 'Aw, Cadillac Man, let it go, she is all that I have left in this world,' so I backed off. When he was shit-faced, you couldn't shut him up, but when he was sober, all he would do was grunt and nod his head."

Everybody around us was busy jamming the machines with bottles. I told Twinkies how sometimes I would take the Old Man canning to make extra money, and when he felt there was enough recycle, he would cash in and head to the liquor store. To get him to eat I'd threaten to shove the bottle up his ass.

"Twinkies, who spread the word about the Old Man?"

"Bones. He was canning in the area and found him."

"Was he sure?"

"Yeah, Jack Frosted with an empty fifth of Jack and his sneakers off."

"Fuck! Old Man couldn't afford Jack. He drank cheap rotgut whiskey or Mad Dog wine, and he didn't wear sneakers! I know because an out-sider gave me a brand-new pair of work boots that didn't fit, so I gave them to the Old Man. They fit perfectly if he wore heavy wool socks, and to play it safe I put his name in marker on the outside for all to see. I even told him to put his pictures inside them."

"Pictures?"

"Yeah, of his wife and son. He told me that his wife had died giving birth to their son, and he came back home from Vietnam a junkie."

"That is fucked up, man."

"I have a feeling he had company that night, either before or after he died. The missing boots and the fifth of Jack—something stinks here. Twinkies, spread the word around that I'm looking for Bones. And that I will pay for any info on the Old Man, no bullshit stories or theories. Here's a ten spot for you for starters. Now get going. I'll be hanging around the coffee shop if you find out anything."

I was really pissed off at myself for all the times the Old Man was with me and I never asked him his real name. But then, that's how it is on the streets. We don't ask about your past, and quite frankly we couldn't care less. But if you talk, we'll listen, and perhaps something you say we'll find useful in the future.

Take Bones, for example. A former five-O who could never keep his pants up and wanted to screw every woman on the planet. He got caught with two sisters-in-law in bed at the same time by his wife! She then di-vorced him, took their three kids, moved to a faraway state, and got his whole pension check. Now all he thinks about is pussy and gin.

But I needed Bones, I want to know what he saw.

Twinkies did his job and spread the word around. For the next few days I heard so many bullshit stories I was stuck knee-deep in it. Some of them were so outrageous it was hard to keep a straight face. I heard that the Old Man had been an ex CIA agent, astronaut, candy taster, a belly dancer!

Most informants I told to get lost, others I gave fifty cents or a dollar. One guy thought he was a tailor, and that made sense to me. Some time ago the Old Man and I were canning when I spotted a bag of cans behind a wired fence. No problem going over, but coming back, my pants leg got caught and ripped down to the cuff. I was pissed because my extra pants were on the spare wagon. The Old Man took one look and told me to take them off and he would sew it.

"You are fucking crazy, I have no underwear on," I said.

"Suit yourself. It's late and nobody is out and I'll fix them in a hurry."

So I gave in, handed them over, and hid behind my wagon. He went into his pocket, pulled out a spool of thread with a needle attached, then started sewing. I was amazed how fast he was. Then I heard a woman laughing.

There were two moons out that night. One up in the sky, the other was my ass facing an apartment building, and some broad who couldn't sleep was looking at me from a window.

"Hey, Old Man, hurry the fuck up, somebody is admiring my ass!"

"She is not admiring, Cadillac."

"How can you tell?"

"If she was admiring, she would be whistling, not laughing, and judging by the size of these pants, you have a fat ass!"

"Careful what you say, Old Man, I'll break you in two!"

"You want your pants done?"

"Yes, but—"

"Then shaddup."

The lady's laughter got worse and I was hoping she would have a stroke, then fall out the window before the whole building woke up.

"There. Finished."

I put them on quickly. He had done a great job!

So maybe he was a tailor, that made sense. But what kind? Did he work for someone or have his own business? Too many questions with no answers. Bones, where the fuck are you?!

More days passed. I kept myself busy canning, heard a few more bullshit stories about the Old Man. One guy came back twice wearing a different hat and coat but telling the same story!

I put my foot high and deep up his ass. Then one night as I was sleeping, someone was nudging me awake. "Psst! Cadillac Man, wake up."

I didn't recognize the voice, couldn't see him. My face was covered to block the wind. Under the blankets I reached for the bayonet.

"Who the fuck are you and what the fuck do you want?"

"It's me, Bones."

I flung the blankets over, looked up, and, yep, it was him.

"Man, put that pig-sticker away."

"If you help me up." He did.

"I heard you were looking for me."

"Yeah," I told him. "Let's get some coffee at the diner. Then we can talk."

"Is it that important to talk now? It can't wait till the morning?"

"It is."

After our second cup, he started talking. "There was this construction site, an office building going up where you could hide or get out of the weather. It was cold there yet bearable if you dressed right and didn't stay too long. I got halfway in and I could see him lying down with a blanket on. I yelled, 'Hey, Old Man, get your ass up, it's fucking freezing in here!' No movement, and then I knew. I moved the blanket, touched him—ice-cold. Cadillac Man, where did the Old Man leave his brains at?"

"What the hell do you mean by that?!"

"Calm down. What I mean is, looking at the Old Man, he had on a baseball jacket way too small and—"

"What? Fucking shit!" I said, banging my fist on the table.

"What happened?" Bones asked. Fortunately, the diner was nearly empty.

"I'm sorry. Go on, I'll tell you in a minute."

"He had no socks, his sneakers were off to the side, and . . . Cadillac Man, you're turning red!"

"Go on."

". . . no gloves, an empty fifth of Jack in his right hand resting on his chest, no hat, and he looked totally at peace." Bones studied me to see my reaction. Then he had a question: "Did the Old Man carry any ID?"

"No, nothing. You need an address to get ID. But he used his sister's address to receive the SS checks."

"What's her address?"

"How the fuck do I know? On check day he would disappear and then come back a week later, broke, and start canning or panhandling again.

She probably cashed it for him, and when the money was gone, he was gone.

"So after you found the body, what did you do?" I asked.

"I went outside and called five-O. When they arrived, asked the usual questions, then we waited for the detectives. They asked the same questions, treated it like any other homeless case under those conditions: cold weather, drinking, and passing out or falling asleep. An open-and-shut case."

"Don't close the door on the Old Man yet, Bones."

"Why?"

"I think the Old Man had company."

"Explain."

"What I am about to tell you I know for a fact. He never dressed right for the weather and I would get pissed and tell him so. I had to go to Brooklyn to take care of a problem for a friend, but before I left I gave the Old Man a woolen cap, gloves, heavy parka with hood, I wrote his name in big letters, used a marker on the back of it—pair of heavy-duty boots, marked them too, and two pairs of wool socks! What happened to them?"

"I see what you mean."

"Plus, the Old Man couldn't afford to buy Jack! He would buy the cheapest wine and liquor that was on sale. That is why I think he had company."

I must have looked upset, maybe murderous, because Bones said, "Take it easy, I'll get us some more coffee." When he came back, he continued, "Okay, here's what I think happened. The Old Man goes inside for whatever reason and the other guy is with him. Other guy wearing the baseball jacket is freezing, and he eyeballs all the warm clothing Old Man has on. Then he gets an idea: 'I got this fifth of Jack and I'm going to be real friendly-like to him.' So they play pass the bottle, and after a while he comments on the Old Man's coat. 'Would you like to try it on?' Old Man says, juiced up and not feeling the cold, and the other guy says okay. Part of his plan was to take little sips while the Old Man took bigger swallows. His gloves were already off because you can't grip the bottle properly and somehow find their way into the coat pocket. After a few minutes he says, 'Gotta piss, be right back,' and disappears not to be seen again, at least for a while. Now the Old Man is alone and smashed. He picks up, puts on, the other guy's jacket, not realizing his coat and gloves are gone for good. Perhaps he is sleepy and goes to the shopping cart, pulls out blankets, and spreads them on the floor. One last taste, all done, then lays down. It's beddy-bye time."

Bones and I both know people who went out this way.

"Then the other guy reappears," Bones went on, "sees him under the blankets. 'Hey! I'm back!' he says, and gets no answer. Walks over, shakes him, and still nothing. Then quickly he goes to work and takes off the Old Man's boots and socks. He has no time to put his sneakers on the Old Man so they are left by his feet. Pulls the woolen cap off, then splits."

"That fucking piece of shit!" I roared.

The diner owner yelled, "Hey! Pipe down over there!"

Now I was very angry and started to get up. I wanted a piece of this guy.

"Cadillac Man! Sit down, we don't want any trouble here," Bones said.

Still trying to control my temper, I sat. "So you think that's what happened to the Old Man," I said.

"It's possible, but we'll never know unless we find the other guy and he admits to it. Basically it is his word. And say he traded the bottle for everything and we don't have any proof or witness to say otherwise."

"Bag, tag, and off to the Land of Lost Souls."

"Not exactly."

"What do you mean?" I asked.

"As soon as Old Man thaws out, they have to do an autopsy to see if something else caused his death. For now it appears that he Jack Frosted. They'll also fingerprint him, and if he's ever been arrested or applied for a passport, it will show an address and somebody to contact in emergencies."

"Can they force his sister to pick up his body?"

"No, and they will keep him for only so long before they ship him out with the rest for burial."

"Damn, that is fucked up!"

"We both know the deceased's relatives couldn't care less," Bones said.

"I care and I'm going to do something about it, with your help."

"What can I do?"

"A lot, so listen up, then give me a price," I said. "First, do you know anybody down at the fridge who will give you info?"

"Sure, a clerk. Why?" Bones asked.

"I want his sister's address."

"Why?"

"I want to try to reason with her to do the right thing."

"And if she doesn't?"

"Then I'll walk away knowing at least I tried."

"Word," said Bones.

"Word is bond, Bones. Next, you know more street people than me. Do you have a few that can be trusted to keep their mouths shut and not ask questions?" I asked.

"Yes, a few. Why?"

"Good, I want you to send them into the shelters for a look-see."

"Now I know for sure, you are fucking nuts, Cadillac Man."

"Come on, Bones, they are not going to live there, I just need their eyes."

"It is too fucking dangerous. You know as well as I do what kind of scumbags hang out there."

"How much?"

"A hundred and a carton of smokes, and they will check each one at least once—but no sleepovers."

"A hundred and two cartons of rollies," roll your owns. "We don't want to spoil them."

"Deal. What do you want them to look for?"

"Just look at the boots and coat. They've got his name marked on them."

"And if they do spot them?"

"Then tell me, Bones. The chances are good that this guy will be there for a while, then I'll check myself in for the night. That is all you need to know, my friend."

"I don't like the way you're smiling," Bones said.

"Relax, I might be crazy but not insane. Now, how much for your services?" Out here, in there, wherever, everybody has their price.

"I don't come cheap. A hundred, smokes, and three quarts of gin. These are my terms."

"Done deal, Bones." We shook hands.

"Cadillac Man, one more thing. Now, you are going to buy me breakfast?"

"What for?"

"I'm hungry."

The night was gone and I was tired, needed some sack time, so I headed back to my spot.

Bones was right, I was a creature of habit. I got all comfy and was asleep in seconds. Slept good, into late afternoon, then I headed for the bullshit corner, off DeKalb near the subway station. The name speaks for itself, where all the street people met to bullshit.

Petey was the biggest bullshitter around. He was harmless. He told far-out stories, made you laugh. Loved the attention, and nobody had the heart to say, "Petey, you're full of shit!" Oh, and by the way, he was the rightful heir to the British throne, not Prince Charles, who had Petey locked up in a dungeon for thirty years, until he was rescued by aliens, who brought him to America.

"Hey, Petey! Come here!" I said.

"What's up, Cadillac Man?"

"Have you seen Twinkies or Pepper?"

"Sure did. Twinkies left a few minutes ago heading for the redeemer, and Pepper is taking a shit at Burger Plaza."

"Petey, here is a dollar. Go over and tell Pepper to meet me at the redeemer's, pronto."

"Huh?"

"*Pronto* means 'right now.' And don't talk about anything else, just the message, okay?"

"Consider it done, Cadillac Man," he said and saluted me.

"What are you waiting for, get the fuck out of here!"

He took off like a jackrabbit in heat. Now let's hope Twinkies was still at the redeemer, I thought.

He was, and yelling at a woman using a ziggy stick. A ziggy is a popular scam out here, a ruler or flagpole stick with a UPC attached that you insert into the glass machine and move back and forth past the scanner's eye. It is a slow process but it pays off. So if you don't want to go canning, carry several of these. Just don't let me see you do it.

"Come on, bitch," Twinkies was saying, "cut the shit and do it later. I'm fucking freezing."

She was totally ignoring him.

"We all know you understand English."

"Hey, Twinkies," I said.

"Hey, Cadillac Man. Do you believe this shit? She has no cans and she's playing with that fucking stick."

"I'm surprised at you, Twinkies, all you had to do is this." I reached over her shoulder and snapped the stick in two. She went fucking ballistic, cursing at me in a foreign language.

"Yeah, yeah, I did the same thing to your mother last night and she didn't complain."

Her anger turned to rage. She reached in her pocket and not for bubble gum.

As a rule I don't hit a woman, but she did a no-no.

Bang! One punch between those enormous tits and the box cutter flew out of her hand and she landed on her ass. She wailed and must have said the name of every holy saint.

"Get the fuck out of here before I hit you again." She did, leaving the box cutter behind.

"There is going to be trouble now, Cadillac Man."

"Why?"

"After what you did, she is going to come back with company."

"Nah, these people keep a low profile and only do something when they feel it is safe not to attract five-O. We can't let them shit on us, Twinkies. Here, take this. She didn't bother to pick it up." A nasty-looking thing, the razor was still sharp but rusted. Have a slice with a side order of infection.

"Cadillac Man, you got to control your temper."

"Fuck her. Listen," I said, "I need you and Pepper to do me a favor."

"What?"

"I'll tell the both of you when Pepper gets here."

"It looks like we won't have to wait, here he comes running like five-O is chasing him." Stupid bastard, his lungs will freeze up and he'll have a heart attack.

"Yo, Pepper! Slow down, you dumb fuck!"

He arrived, breathless.

"Pepper, I need you and Twinkies for a job that pays well, and I trust you guys to clam up about it."

"Why do I have this feeling that it has something to do with the Old Man?" Twinkies said.

"It does," I said.

"Old Man?" Pepper asked. "The dude that did a Jack Frost?"

"The same—and he was my friend, so watch your mouth."

"Sorry, man, I didn't know."

"I want you guys to check out the shelters for me."

By the look on their faces you would think I handed them a death sentence.

"Forget it, no fucking way," they said in unison.

I saw in their eyes that they'd had bad experiences. Who hadn't?

"Did you forget what happened to Moon a few weeks ago?" Twinkies said.

Moon was a new kid, early twenties but looked younger, with severe acne. That was how he got the street name, his face resembled the moon's surface. One night it got too cold for him. A shelter was nearby, so he decided to go in where it was warm and there was a bed to sleep on. Big mistake. He didn't know how bad shelters are, he didn't ask and everybody thought he knew. The word on the street spread that he was raped during lights out. The source, Tony C, was a close friend of Moon's. A blade to the throat, a sock in the mouth, he got his ass reamed all night. He couldn't report it to the square badges, knowing how they are, meaning useless. It was embarrassing too, not the sort of thing you would tell someone.

Moon was a different person now, quieter. Then one day he disappeared. Maybe he bought it somewhere or moved to a different area where nobody knew him or hopefully he found a way to go home.

Then there was Willie, who was confronted by two dudes, one with a blade, while he was taking a dump and had to give them blow jobs. During this time dudes came in and out of the bathroom and didn't see nothing! Yeah, right!

Gramps got beaten for cigarettes and change.

Stevie ditto for his sneakers and change.

George, for snoring and farting loudly, was in the hospital for three days, must have fell out of bed.

Pony for being in the wrong bed, the one he was assigned to.

Even I, but I was lucky.

I had been with a group of guys just hanging out one night. They were loud and everyone had been drinking wine except me, who was drinking coffee. A five-O van came out of nowhere and two officers jumped out and a sergeant said, "Okay, gentlemen, your choice: jail or shelter." They made the others empty their juice down a sewer grating and cans and bottles in a wastebasket. Next they searched us, nobody had any weapons.

They treated us with respect and all of us agreed to go to the shelter. We all knew the dangers, but there are five of us and there is strength in numbers. We were together so what could go wrong?

They dropped us off in Bed-Stuy, at a place that looked like an old army fortress. One of the guys said, "Oh, man, I've been here before. Watch your backs!" There were others outside eyeballing us, predators.

We went in and were greeted by square badges. "Okay, empty all the pockets, give your name to the social worker."

I gave my name but didn't empty my pockets.

A square badge yelled over at me. "Hey, didn't I tell you to empty your pockets?"

"Don't yell, and, yes, you did, I don't have anything."

"Let me see for myself, turn them inside out."

"No."

"No?"

"Before we got here we were thoroughly searched by five-O and they didn't find anything dangerous," I said.

"Do it or leave right now!"

I was all set to curse him out, then go, but I looked at my guys and they were shaking their heads no.

"This fucking sucks," I said, and pulled out cigarettes, lighter, pictures of my kids, twenty-eight dollars in mostly singles, and loose change. "There, are you happy now?"

"Thank you. Now go through those double doors and find a bunk. Lights out in an hour."

We went through the doors into a huge gym with over a hundred bunks neatly lined up, most of them occupied. Some people were sleeping, others were standing by or sitting on their bunks. The empties were scattered, so there went the thought of being together. I saw the bathroom and figured I'd better go now, there was no way I would get up in the middle of the night to go, I would rather piss or shit myself. It was crowded, the air was filled with cigarette and reefer smoke, nobody paid attention to the No Smoking signs posted everywhere.

I took my piss, made eye contact with some no-doubt predators, then left as the talking resumed behind me.

I found a bunk next to an old-timer already asleep. He was in a bad way, with a real nasty cough that sounded like a death rattle. It may sound cruel to say, but we out here know when your time is nearly up before you do. I had two army blankets, only needed one with all the heavy clothes I wore, so I put the other one on him.

"Heyyy! What are you doing with my blanket?"

I turn and there was this dude, a little shorter than me and about eighty pounds lighter, wearing double layers of clothing, street-style. A fucking crackhead with two of his cohorts behind him grinning. A game of intimidation.

"Your blanket?"

"Yeah, mine, and that is my bed you are standing next to."

"Really?"

"Tell you what, I'm feeling generous today. I'll rent you my bed for the night for two dollars and six smokes, pillow and blankets one smoke each."

"Okay," I said, "I don't want any trouble. And I'll give an extra ten dollars if you do something for me."

"Yeah? What?" He and his friends were smiling.

"Go over to the women's shelter, get your mother out, and bring her here to suck on my balls tonight."

The smile was gone. He had a stunned look now.

Someone said, "Oh, shit!" Then everybody started laughing. He came to his senses and lunged at me.

Two shots to the face and he lost his balance and went down. Everybody was hollering, and then came the square badges.

"What happened here?"

"He was walking past my bed and must have tripped on something, I was about to help him up," I said.

"Did anyone see him fall?"

Getting no answer, he and another square badge picked up the dude.

"He is going to need medical attention, the nose looks broken."

"Okay, everybody in your bunks, lights out in five minutes!"

Not exactly the Ritz. You can see why nobody's all that eager to pass a night in the shelters.

Pepper spoke first. "Look at the shelters for what or who?"

"You will be looking at coats and boots. The who I don't know, but if you see the right coat and boots, remember the dude who's wearing them and tell me."

"Coat and boots?"

"Twinkies, I think you know what I'm talking about," I said.

"Yeah, the Old Man's," said Twinkies.

"Right, you will be looking for a coat and boots with his name, Old Man, on them. I used a heavy marker so that they can't be washed off."

"Damn, I would rather go to jail, shelters are bad news."

"Come on, guys, we all got burnt one way or another, and some of our people too. Just in and out is all I'm asking, and you won't be doing it for nothing. You both know my word is bond. A half a yard and three cartons of rollies each whether you find them or not." (A half a yard is fifty dollars.)

They looked at each other and Pepper said, "Done deal. When do we start?"

"Tonight, if you find out anything, I'll be at the coffee shop or leave the word with Nickie. Gonna split now, there is somebody else I have to see."

We shook hands. "Be safe, guys."

Politicians claim they will make the shelters safer by adding more security.

What good would that do when the lights go out? Security is no good to us, staying in their warm, cozy office while someone is being robbed, beaten, or worse in front of the place. Why do you think some of us go into hiding and take our chances with Jack Frost?

The hardest thing for me then was the waiting, hoping that somebody had heard or seen something. Payback and a decent burial for the Old Man was all I wanted. Street justice is different. Punishment is swift. We clean our own house and save the taxpayers a lot of money and time.

I waited a few more hours at the redeemer on Ralph Avenue.

When I got back to Nickie's Diner, I could see Bones sitting in my spot, and judging by his looks, it wasn't good news. He must have smoked at least a pack, looking at the cup he used for an ashtray. He did not say a word. He lit a stick, which I snatched, then he lit another. He took a deep drag, then blasted the smoke through his nose and said, "I wish I had good news to tell you, Cadillac Man."

"Just talk," I said.

"The Old Man is going to be classified as a John Doe and shipped for burial unless his sister comes to claim the body soon."

"Shit! His check is two weeks away, and when he doesn't show up, the sister will probably think he is drunk. Wait a minute, you said that they fingerprinted him, didn't anything come back?"

"My friend at the fridge said there was no record of him anywhere."

"How is that possible?"

"Easy, I have seen it many times before. A person who has never been arrested, served in the military, applied for a passport, or worked in the security field, the list is endless! Old Man led a clean life to the very end."

"Damn! So it is off to the Land of Lost Souls we go." I couldn't bear this.

"He really meant a lot to you." Bones said.

"Yeah, he reminded me of someone I once knew. Any luck with your people at the shelter?" I asked.

"No, they are still looking, there are so many shelters it would take a small army to check them all out."

"I'm just guessing but I think the dude stayed local, not wanting to go to another borough where he doesn't know anybody," I said.

"You may be right."

"Let's hope so, I'm waiting to hear from my guys too. It's colder than a witch's tit. Maybe the dude will stay put."

"Or maybe the dude found somewhere else to crash."

"Bones, I don't think about that."

"We got to cover all bases, we all have crashed at one place sometimes in weather like this."

"Yeah, you are right. I did in the past but not anymore. Too many problems and I'll take my chances out there. In the meantime I'll buy you one more coffee, then get the fuck out of here and earn your salary."

"Aye, aye, skipper!"

"And, Bones?"

"Yes?"

"The next time we meet, have some good news for me. Okay?"

"I'll do my best."

I got another coffee and sat back down again at the table. I couldn't ask Twinkies or Pepper for more help, they were busy, so that left Petey. Even though he was a bullshit artist, he knew a lot of people. He could hold you spellbound or make you piss in your pants from laughing. The guy never shut up. Should have been a politician!

Old Man, I thought, wherever you are right now, I need your help. Help me find your identity, help me find where your sister lives, and help me find the scumbag who shortened your life. Please.

Enough of sitting on my ass, there was work to be done.

"Hey, Nickie, I'll be back in a few hours."

"Cadillac Man on a quest!"

"You better believe it!"

And there was Petey, as always, with a crowd on the same bullshit corner day and night. The only thing missing was a milk crate for him to stand on.

"Yo, Petey!"

I watched him run across the street, dodging oncoming traffic.

"Yes, Cadillac Man?" He saluted me.

"Do I look like a fucking general to you?"

"No, I—"

"Then knock it off with the salutes, okay?"

Like a little boy being punished, he stared down at the ground.

"Aw, forget it, I need you to do something important for me."

His head shot up and he had a big smile. Damn! A dentist could take early retirement with the amount of tooth work he needed.

"Now listen to me very carefully. I want you to spread the word that I'll pay a half yard to anyone who knew the Old Man's real name and address. If it checks out, they will get paid."

"I know where he lived."

"You do, where?"

"Buckingham Palace."

"What?"

"He once told me he had to go to the Palace to pick up his check."

"Petey, you of all people know where Buckingham Palace is."

"In England."

"Right, and do you think that the Old Man flew to England every month to pick up his check?"

"It's possible, but he wouldn't have much money left from the check after buying the plane tickets."

"Petey!"

"What?"

"Just do me a favor and repeat what I said earlier about what I need and how much I'm offering."

He repeated everything, practically word for word. I was impressed.

"Very good. Here is a ten spot, get busy!"

"Wow! Thanks, Cadillac Man."

"One more thing, wait for the traffic light to change. You can't spread the word for me if you're a hood ornament."

"I'll be careful, Cadillac Man."

So what did he do? He waited, the light changed, but to the wrong color, and he crossed anyway! Brakes were screeching and he was ignoring them and kept walking. Finally on the other side, he waved, then saluted.

I gave up, enough for one day.

By the time I reached Nickie my balls were touching the ground.

"Anything, Nickie?"

"Nobody showed up, Cadillac Man, want anything to eat?"

"Nah, too tired, let me get my nighttime usual, then it is off to la-la land."

"I don't know how you do it."

"Do what?"

"Drink four coffees before bedtime. I would be crapping in my sleep."

"Not me, it acts like a sedative and I sleep like a baby. See you in the A.M., Nickie."

"Don't let the bedbugs bite, Cadillac Man."

"What bedbugs? They all did a Jack Frost."

The thing I hate about the winter is that it gets dark earlier. I saved all my coffee cups and pitched them in one wastebasket. Tomorrow I would find a new location to bed down.

It was so cold even the river rats were probably with their cousins in the nice warm sewers.

Me, I was comfy all balled up in blankets with my weapons and piss bottle nearby. Amen.

Slept good, no interruptions. Only a nut would be out on this bitter cold morning.

Got up and did my exercises. I reached in my backpack, pulled out a portable camper stove, Sterno, and my trusty coffeepot. Hot coffee in minutes!

My backpack was a bag of tricks, and you will never know all the contents. Like a lady's handbag—many secrets within.

Repacked everything, tied up my bedding, and away I went.

"Hi, Alice, where is Nickie?"

"Hi, Cadillac Man, he's home, couldn't get out of bed, so I opened up."

"Your man puts in too many hours here."

"That'll end soon. His brother is coming to visit us for a few months and he knows the business, so Nickie's hours will be cut in half. So what'll you have?"

"Breakfast number two and number three with two big boys."

"Boy! Are you hungry?"

"Yeah, I forgot to eat yesterday—too busy running around."

I had just barely sat down with my breakfast and guess who came barging in?

"Hey, Cadillac Man!"

"Petey, next time come in quietly, and how the hell did you know I was here?"

"This place makes the best coffee around, I figured you would be here, and, boy, that breakfast looks good."

"It is. What's up?"

"Right after you left I bumped into Sammy and—are you really going to eat all that?" Sammy's another homeless in the neighborhood.

"Petey! My food is getting cold and my patience is running out!"

"Oh, sorry. Sammy says the Old Man lived in the Plaza Hotel."

"What?"

"He also said they had dinner, suite 888 was his room, and they stayed up to midnight watching a solar eclipse."

"And you believe him?"

"Sure, why not?"

"Petey, a solar eclipse occurs during light hours of the day."

"Oh!"

"Sammy told me last night he saw the president come out of a peep show on the Deuce then go into a massage parlor." (The Deuce is 42nd Street.)

"Wow! I wish I was there to see him."

"Petey, do me a favor, rather than coming over here every time you get some information, make a list, let's say at least five people, then bring it here for me to look at, okay?"

"Okay, want me to say anything to Sammy?"

"Yeah, tell him the Old Man moved out a month ago, then give him this dollar. Here, take the rest of my food."

"Are you sure?"

"Might as well, you've been drooling over it for the past fifteen minutes."

"Gee, thanks."

I got up for another big boy, came back to see that he ate everything and even licked the plates clean!

"Damn, Petey, when was the last time you ate?"

"An hour ago."

"If ever you and I were stranded on a remote island, I would have to kill you."

"Why?"

"Oh, never mind, here is a dollar. Now leave, I'm expecting someone."

"Okeydokey." Then he saluted me again! Sheesh! I give up!

Reader, surely you have noticed by now that Sammy and Petey have some sort of mental disorder. We all have it to some degree, and that includes you, dear reader. But I like these guys, they are happy in their own special way.

"Cadillac Man!"

"Huh, what?" I was on a bench, drinking my coffee.

"I didn't want to disturb you with that pissed-off look on your face."

"I'm okay, what's up, Pepper? Where's Twinkies?"

"He's in Brooklyn. A friend of his said that there is a dude wearing a heavy coat with a name, something MAN on the back, so he is checking it out. Keep your fingers crossed, Cadillac Man."

"I will, and you look frozen. Here, buy us two big boys."

"Mind if I get a hot chocolate instead?"

"Whatever warms you, my friend."

"Thanks, it is fucking freezing outside. Ain't nobody walking about except Petey standing around bullshit corner. He came running over to me carrying a notebook and pencil, saying you gave him a special assignment."

"That guy is going to drive me to drink again. Anyway fill me in on what you guys did so far."

"We checked out two shelters, the one at Bedford and Atlantic and the one on Fulton. Nothing there."

"I want this fucking guy, Pepper!"

"I know, we're trying. Maybe Twinkies will have some news. I just don't understand it. We got the word spreading, offering a reward, and some of our people in the shelters! Am I missing something?"

"Any idea what time you are going to hook up with Twinkies?"

"Tonight at his place, from there we're going to check out one of the Brooklyn shelters."

"If he has any news on the dude he went to see that I need to know, come here right away. Remember, in and out. Okay?"

"Man, I'm glad Twinkies will be with me. I heard the Brooklyn shelters are the worst of the worst! Whenever five-O has a call to go there, they bring along plenty of backup!"

"Go by your gut, Pepper. Twinkies' too."

"Later, Cadillac Man."

Well, it was time to stretch my legs.

"Alice, I'll be back in a few hours."

"Wait, here, take this for the road."

"Alice! Giving me a coffee on the house? What would Nickie say about that?"

"Pepper paid for it as he was leaving." We both started laughing.

"Later, Alice."

"Bye-bye, Cadillac Man."

It was getting late and I guess the dude that Twinkies went to check out didn't pan out. He would have been here by now. I was really worried about them, although they were quite capable in street fighting. Still, there was no defense for a knife in the back or worse. Walk softly, my friends, and do unto others before they do it to you! Bones, wherever the fuck you are, give me some news soon!

I grabbed my bedding from the stash point and headed to my new camping site. I knew about this place earlier, when I first scoped the area, an abandoned four-story walk-up, the tenants long gone due to a fire on the top floor, the whole front boarded up. But in the back the owner had done very little and it was easy access. Some of the windows were busted. I just climbed the ladder onto the fire escape and I was in.

The smell of piss and shit permeated the air, even though it was cold, and I had to watch my every step. Condoms, needles, bottles, and broken glass were everywhere. There were other people there too. No, I couldn't see them, but I could hear them, the whispers and muffled sounds. They wouldn't bother me and I wouldn't bother them. No doors. In every apartment a fridge and stove. I dared not open them for they might have had booby traps. I chose to stay on one of the upper floors for my safety. If anyone tried to come after me, I would hear them. The steps were old and creaked no matter how softly someone stepped on them. As an extra precaution I set up a half dozen large rat traps leading into the apartment. Get past these and I would greet you personally with my bayonet or ice pick or both.

With these kind of places five-Ó wouldn't enter unless they saw something or had a complaint. Do somebody in and who knew when the body would be discovered.

Damn you, Old Man, I thought, help me. I don't know what else to do!

A ray of light woke me up and at first I thought it was five-O that somehow got up the stairs, then bypassed my booby traps. I turned my head away and said, "What do you want?" and got no response or movement.

It was not five-O, they would have said something by now. I grabbed my bayonet and sat up fast, swinging it across, nothing! Slowly opening my eyes, squinting, nobody, but I do see where the light is coming from. The windows are boarded up, but the sun rays seeped through the cracks, then onto my face! Stupid bastard! Got to remember to change to a darker spot.

If you were to ask every homeless person in this country to make a list of the places they slept, you would have volumes filled with safe havens and a few places of sheer desperation. As an example of desperation, consider the building in which I was bedding down. Or a bridge trestle, sewer, or a subway tunnel, to name a few. I've tried them all.

I stashed my stuff away and went into Nickie's.

"Hi, Cadillac Man."

"What do you say, Nickie! And why the grim face? I hope you didn't run out of coffee. Ha ha ha."

"Here. Have a few gulps. I have some really bad news for you."

"What now?"

Then I saw the tears in his eyes.

"Nickie! What is it?"

"Cadillac Man, Petey's dead. I'm sorry."

"What! Dead? How?"

"Right after you left, one of your friends came running in here looking for you, and I asked what happened. Poor guy, he was shaking like a leaf, and I gave him some coffee. Finally he said that Petey was running across the street against the light when a moving van hit him."

"That stupid fuck! I told him to wait until the light changes."

"When Alice came in, I decided to go over to the spot. The cops were still there. In fact, one of them is a customer of mine so I went and talked with him. He said the moving van had the light, the driver saw Petey, but it was too late to do anything. There were a lot of witnesses to back up the driver's story. They found some ID on Petey and they were able to contact a member of his family."

"Damn! And I thought he didn't have anyone."

I ordered breakfast anyway, but it didn't taste right, not even the coffee. Nickie had the best food, yet my body was saying, now is not the time to eat. My brain was saying, you have to go and look.

"Nickie, I'll be back in a little while."

I arrived at bullshit corner and saw some of the guys who usually hung around there. Near them a makeshift shrine with lit candles in a cardboard box with a handwritten note that said *Petey RIP* within. I could feel their eyes but nobody dared to approach me.

"Hey, Felipe, come here," I said.

"Yeah?"

"Here, take this, I want you to go over to the bodega and buy me a candle and keep the change."

"What color do you want?"

"Color? I don't give a fuck what color, just make sure it is religious!"

He started for the bodega. I realized I was losing it. "Felipe, wait, come back!"

"What?"

"Sorry, man, that I yelled at you. Pick out a good candle for Petey."

"Okay, Cadillac Man."

A new guy came up to me, a young black guy with a face like a mouse. "Cadillac Man?"

"Who are you?"

"I'm Joey. Petey was my best friend. It was me who went looking for you."

"How did you know where to look?"

"Petey told me he worked for you and was on his way to see you with some important information."

"What information?"

"I don't know. He was very excited, talking about a reward."

"Damn! Damn! Damn! Joey, don't ask why, just walk away, and don't worry, you didn't do anything wrong."

I guess my tone of voice scared him into walking backwards away from me.

Right then I was feeling angry, not directed at anybody. I needed to be left alone to grieve, one more death to cope with. It wasn't fair, everywhere I went death followed me. It didn't pay to make friends. Like in combat, if you lose someone close, the pain is great.

I walked about and saw dried droplets of blood, then I stepped on something. I couldn't tell what it was, I had boots on, but I was curious. I lifted my foot up and, my God, I didn't believe it. Petey's pencil! And how did I know it was his? It was covered with dried blood!

All sorts of thoughts entered my mind as to why the pencil was at this very spot. Then I lost it. Screaming my fucking head off, saying "Why?" over and over. For some reason, I walked over to the corner, picked up a wastebasket, and flung it, causing everybody to scatter.

"Get the fuck outta here, all of you," I screamed. I was in no mood to talk or see anyone.

Then a voice came from down the street: "Cadillac Man!"

It was Felipe. He put the candle on the ground and ran off. I was suddenly a lot calmer then, and, good, he had bought a white religious one. There was a prayer written in Spanish on it but that didn't matter to me for God understands all languages. I walked over to the shrine and placed the pencil and candle within.

Then I prayed for Petey's soul.

Had the Old Man died on the outside, we would have set up one for him. I would do something later, a remembrance. We don't lavish our shrines like you do, we keep them plain and simple, a few tokens of remembrance. Perhaps you have seen one and just gave it a passing glance with no thought in mind. They are our funeral, mass, and burial in that cardboard box. The street priests know its meaning and would drop by and say a few prayers in remembrance.

I have seen so many and not necessarily for the homeless. Victims of crime, gangbangers, wannabes, auto accidents, I would stop and say a little prayer. Good or bad I will not pass judgment on them.

I prayed, "Petey, you did your job well. Say hello to everyone I know up there. Be at peace, my friend. Amen." What helped ease the pain was knowing that Petey had the sense to carry ID and maybe a family member would give him a decent burial. I hoped.

As I was leaving, everybody was slowly drifting back. Bullshit corner wouldn't be the same without Petey, but his memory would live on.

Enough of this shit, I'm hungry.

"Hey, Nickie, I know it's late but could you make me a number three breakfast?" I asked.

"No problem, Cadillac Man. You went over to see . . . ?"

"Yeah, I had to go and pay my respects."

"Bones is here, and, yes, he knows about Petey."

"For how long?"

"A couple of hours. Had breakfast."

"Give me one more big boy, he looks like he could use another one."

Indeed, getting closer, I could see that he was exhausted, and I bet he hadn't shaved or changed his clothes in days.

Without my asking, he switched seats.

I sat down and passed over the big boy and a stick, which he grabbed greedily.

"You look like shit, Bones."

"Thanks, the way I feel right now, I'll take it as a compliment. The last couple of days have been rough, really rough!"

"Talk to me, Bones."

"Do you have any idea how many shelters there are?"

"No, no idea. At least one for each borough?"

"Some have at least two, then take into account the private and church shelters and drop-in centers."

"Shit! I forgot about them!"

"Yeah, so did I until one of my guys mentioned it. We went to the ones we knew of and the others run by street people and homeless organizations. Unbelievable! So fucking many, the dude we're looking for could be anywhere! Oh, by the way, I seen one of your guys."

"Who?"

"Twinkies, at a soup kitchen. It was his idea. You know how many meals are served on a daily basis citywide?"

"Thousands?"

"Right, and it also means seeing new faces every day at each location, and that presents us with a big problem. We can't be everywhere and the chances are good that the dude will slip by us. What do you want us to do, Cadillac Man?"

He was tired and surely everybody else was, including me. The odds were against us, but we had to try for the Old Man's sake.

"Give it one more day, Bones, then call it quits."

"Are you sure?"

"Yes."

I reached in my pocket for some cash, then stacked it into two piles.

"Here, take this for your guys, have them or you come here the day after tomorrow to pick up the smokes. My word is bond."

After counting his money, Bones asked, "What is the extra twenty for?"

"A favor."

"I thought so."

"Petey is down at the fridge. Find out from your contact if anyone is going to claim him."

"I'm sorry about Petey."

"Yeah, me too."

"Let me see if my friend is working now." He got up and went to the pay phone. He was on the phone a long time, I thought it must be good news. He got off smiling, went to Nickie, and ordered two big boys. Now I knew for sure it was good news. Petey? Old Man? Both? Wishful thinking!

He lit a stick and I snatched it off his lips.

"Talk, dammit!"

He was smiling. "One down and one to go shortly," he said, lighting another stick.

"What the hell are you talking about?"

"The Old Man is gone, they released his body yesterday."

"Damn! Fucking shit!"

"Calm down, he was picked up and went to a funeral home."

"What?"

"My friend said a niece and the police came down to ID him."

"That's great! The Old Man is going to have a decent burial after all! High five, man! Yes! And Petey?"

"Going to be picked up tomorrow."

"Two for two! Great news!"

"So should we forget about the dude?"

"No way! Give it one more day."

"Why?"

"Besides the Old Man, I owe it to Petey too."

"I don't understand."

"The dude we're looking for caused two deaths! We know what he did to the Old Man and indirectly to Petey. You look puzzled my friend. Let me explain. You didn't know this, but Petey was coming to see me with info about the dude, so said his friend Joey, who saw the accident."

"What info?"

"Don't know, I wasn't here, but Joey told me Petey was very excited and had to tell me right away. It is a crazy hunch, I truly believe that he had good info this time, but the Big Man upstairs had other plans for Petey. Whether it was written down or not, he took it to his grave! The dude caused Petey's death!"

"I agree."

"Thanks for helping me, Bones, and thank your guys."

"Anytime, Cadillac Man. It may be over tomorrow for us, but I think my guys, me included, will look around from time to time."

"I appreciate that. Now, I gotta go and get some sleep, I'm piss-eyed tired."

"Be careful and stay out of trouble, Cadillac Man."

"I'll try. But if the fates are kind and we find the dude, I don't have to tell you what will happen to him. Let me ask you this. A loved one or a friend gets hurt or worse, wouldn't you want payback? Sure you would!"

Bones agreed.

Everyone kept their eyes open, but we never found the guy. So the Old Man is gone, then Petey after him. Gone but not forgotten. We looked, and that is a memorial too.

Dear Reader:

It's wintertime. My brethren are out there.
Some by choice, others by circumstance.
In their makeshift shelters, hiding amongst the shadows of night.
"Please come for me," they say.
My tears flow freely. Theirs don't, the frost prevents it.
And you know them, maybe a friend or family member.
"Please forgive me," they say.
Time is short, a new place beckons their arrival:
The Land of the Lost Souls.

—Cadillac Man, 2009

Acknowledgments

To my friends in Astoria, Queens, a heartfelt thank-you: Honorable Peter Vallone Sr. and Honorable Councilman Peter F. Vallone Jr.; Firefighters Engine #312, 49th Battalion; Police Officers, Auxiliary Police, 114th Precinct; Steve Beuttenmuller and Catherine Beuttenmuller (in memory); Anthony Spina; John Drobenko; Charles Steinhilber; Luis, Gladys, Peter, and Julia Baez; Nicole Toritts; George Psillides; Billy Douvas; Bobby "Spike" Micheli; Denise Carrillo; Janet and Jennifer Daly; Dega Omar; Mimi Sullivan; Neini Cipolla; Eliana Yarian; Dr. George Fisher, MD, and Mrs. Georgia Fisher; George Alexiou of Century 21 Alexiou Realty and John Alexiou of Alexiou Insurance; John Zias and Ourania Vokolos-Zias; Victoria and Morganne Regoj; Mark and Bridget Dunn; Jenifer and Margo Maple; Patrick, Sarah, Celia, and Kira Drury; Sarah Quinter; Dina M. Talotta; Tom and Elaine Sanidas, Kostas Kostoglou and Tina Koukounas of Astoria Internet; Joe Morales; Rose Marie Piacentile; Max Gordian; Mike (CTA); Mark Jacobson of KGB Bar; Michael Regan and Luan Bexheti of Hell's Kitchen Films; Coleman and Angie Cowan; Dr. John Cambitsis, DDS, and Dr. Andrew Cambitsis, MD, PC; Matthew and Abigail Monks; Janet Oldenbroek; Lorna Rainey; Eugene Richards; Jonathan Hulland; Ranger Phil and Spaceman and Carole; Eric and Martha Kunz; Phillip Markakis; Kristen Bloom; Matthew, Emma, and Baby Symons; Scott Ewald; Jason Moreland; Monica Casais; Joanne Galanos; Alexander and Mary Gay; Joseph Fahy; Thomas Wagner; Rip Gough; Kathy Nevins; Vicka Anagnostos; Jamie and Priscilla Romero; Nonny Ortega and Melina (Ocean) T. Yañez Ortega; Clare Lynch and the Gang; Anthony, Laurie, and Penelope; Greg Vanzo; Emmanuel and Emily

Kozadinos; Juan Rivera, Robert McCoy, and Caroline Lawson of VOA; Barbara Ashton; Evan and Demetra Ioannou; John Fotopoulos and Family; Nhu-Mai Simon; Michael, Molly, Anna, and Christina Rusich; Irene Kalimeris and Family; Rob Smith; E. Marista; Rita Coleman; Zofia Stefanowicz; Adriana Georgiou; Erin, Jill, Edison, and Bean Gould; Karina, Wilfried, and Sebastien Tenaillon; Rachel Mason; Teri Conti; Dave of 866BEFUNNY; Scott Dershowitz; Kostas and Katerina Mouzakitis; Matthew Rey of the NYPD; Jim, Elaine, Ryan, and Julia Long of the NYFD; Dyana Chan; Gail Gavin; Rafael Marquez; Cesar and Emily; Lucille Kalandranis; Malikka Phillips; Pam Feicht; Effie Fradelos; Oren Yaniv of the *New York Daily News*; Jeff Van Dam of the *New York Times*; 23rd Avenue Deli (Sally); Dunkin Donuts; Last Stop Restaurant; Mike's Diner; Sal, Kris, and Charlie Deli; Twin Donut (RIP).

To Nick Trautwein of Bloomsbury USA: A special thanks for spending countless hours, days deciphering the street language into something the reader will follow and learn to understand my people's world.

To David Granger and Mark Warren of *Esquire*: Because of the *Esquire* article, I received several hundred e-mails from around the world. People changing their opinions on homelessness. Asking how they can help my people. Your magazine started it all, so many lives now have a happy ending. Thank you.

To Sloan Harris: You believed in me, honest and straightforward with your advice. I learned so much as to what is fair in my new career. A true professional in the literary field.

To Will Blythe: My brother, friend, and mentor. You were the first to read about my world, your opinion sincere and trustworthy. Felt that others should read my experiences to let them know I'm human, too. I was given a second chance in life thanks to you. A man I hold with high regard. Word is bond.

To Mrs. Gloria Blythe: Thank you for sharing Will, a truly caring man. I see his smile, I think of you. When I express my feelings I sense your presence by his side. Waiting for the day, till we meet again. I love you.

A Note on the Author

Born in the Hell's Kitchen area of Manhattan, Cadillac Man has lived on the streets in four of New York's five boroughs. His journals have been excerpted in *Esquire* magazine. He can be reached at thestreetwalker33@ yahoo.com.